GIVE PEACE A DEADLINE

WHAT ORDINARY PEOPLE CAN DO TO CAUSE
WORLD PEACE IN FIVE YEARS

Nathan Otto and Amber Lupton

GREENLEAF
BOOK GROUP PRESS

Published by Greenleaf Book Group Press
Austin, TX
www.greenleafbookgroup.com

Distributed by Greenleaf Book Group LLC

For ordering information or special discounts for bulk purchases, please contact Greenleaf Book Group LLC at PO Box 91869, Austin, TX 78709, (512) 891-6100.

Design and composition by Greenleaf Book Group LLC
Cover design by Greenleaf Book Group LLC

Cataloging-In-Publication Data
(Prepared by The Donohue Group, Inc.)

Otto, Nathan.
     Give peace a deadline : what ordinary people can do to cause world peace in five years / Nathan Otto and Amber Lupton. -- 1st ed.

     p. ; cm.

Includes bibliographical references.
ISBN-13: 978-1-929774-86-9   ISBN-10: 1-929774-86-9

1. Peace movements. 2. Peace-building. 3. Pacifism. I. Lupton, Amber. II. Title.

JZ5538 .O88 2009
303.6/6   2008938562

Part of the Tree Neutral™ program, which offsets the number of trees consumed in the production and printing of this book by taking proactive steps, such as planting trees in direct proportion to the number of trees used: www. treeneutral.com.

Printed in the United States of America on acid-free paper

09 10 11 12 13 14   10 9 8 7 6 5 4 3 2 1

First Edition

This book is dedicated to every human
who has ever prayed for peace.

CONTENTS

INTRO

WE HAVE A DEADLINE FOR WORLD PEACE—DO YOU?

It is about spirit, it is about energy, it is about a contact with the divine, and when people shift in negotiations or shift in their thinking of conflict, this is when the worlds above and the worlds below touch.

—Aaron Wolf, professor of geosciences at Oregon State University, speaking at the Forum 2000 11th Annual Conference

OUR PROMISE

When we talk about world peace, we mean business. We are not talking about tie-dye, free love, peace marches, or "everyone just be nice." We are talking about world peace as a project with milestones, a deadline, and effective action.

By February 14, 2014, we promise to create world peace. Giving a specific deadline to world peace is audacious, inspiring, foolhardy, or motivating, depending on your point of view. People have different reactions to our promise, but all of them agree: World peace would be good for everyone. Are *you* willing to have peace by 2014?

WHO WE ARE AND WHY WE HONESTLY BELIEVE WE CAN CREATE PEACE IN FIVE YEARS

Nathan Otto is the grandson of Bill and Vieve Gore, the visionary founders of W. L. Gore and Associates, a three-billion-dollar family-owned company that has been on the Fortune 100 List of 100 Best Companies to Work For since the inception of the list. The unique culture of Gore, which empowers individuals and small teams to innovate for value creation, has been studied at all major business schools. It was recently featured, along with Whole Foods and Google, in *The Future of Management*, written by London School of Economics professor and business consultant Gary Hamel and Bill Breen.

Nathan built two Internet-based companies from scratch and sold them in a fifteen-year career as an entrepreneur, then he founded a consultancy called Plenable Solutions to apply principles of user-friendly business processes to other companies. Nathan also teaches a seminar for people who inherit large estates about how to align their contributions with their core values.

Amber Lupton is an expert on personal development and transformation, having studied at a young age with teachers as diverse as Tony Robbins, Deepak Chopra, and Ken Wilber. She has taught workshops all over the world, incorporating cognitive and motivational approaches, breathwork, yoga, and personal inquiry. Amber also cofounded the Holistic Alliance, a successful specialized website-hosting company serving psychotherapists, massage therapists, and sustainable construction contractors. Nathan and Amber together are cofounders of DharmaMix, an Internet-based social venture media company that produces inspirational and personal development messages over music.

In seeking a deeper mission, Nathan and Amber traveled around the world to speak with global leaders such as F. W. de Klerk and Václav Havel and with groups of philanthropists about the best contribution they could make to the world. The result is this guide and workbook for a global movement from war to peace.

MOMENT OF INCEPTION

Our strategic discussion had been revolving around the use of cognitive dissonance in images to create urgency: show a picture of where we are, and show a picture of where we want to go, and then the dissonance between the two images creates a natural motivation to progress. We wondered what images would create motivation toward achieving world peace.

A lot of people who are a lot smarter than we are have tried to create world peace and have not yet succeeded. Why? In business, most underlying issues cannot be addressed by applying the management idea du jour to a specific problem. The whole culture of the company must shift in order for real positive change to manifest. Likewise, it seemed to us that most peace efforts were aimed toward one conflict at a time, rather than addressing the global culture of war in a businesslike way.

Amber said, "Yes, treat peace like a business; give it milestones."

Nathan said, "Peace in five years!"

We looked at each other, and Amber said, "Give peace a deadline."

We both laughed, then got very thoughtful. What would a deadline actually look like? Has anyone ever given a deadline to world peace? Is the time right for world peace to have a deadline? It seems like we need a deadline to build a project around it—so that "peace someday" becomes "peace in five years."

What is the measurement that lets us know if we have reached it? After a few minutes, we wrote a pledge for peace on our whiteboard, and without hesitation we each signed it. The original pledge looks like this:

BY FEB 14TH, 2014 I will have created World Peace as measured by The Economist Newspaper.

The text reads, "By Feb 14th, 2014 I will have created world peace as measured by *The Economist* newspaper." We gave ourselves a year to organize the project before launch in 2009.

We looked at each other for a long moment. We realized we had just made a huge promise. We take our promises seriously—and here in front of us was our signed, specific promise to the world; our signed contract, without a lot of wiggle room.

Up until then, our activities had reflected a deep inquiry into the fundamental questions of life: What is all this *for*? What is all this business *for*? What is all this philanthropy *for*? What is all this personal transformation *for*? What are peace conferences *for*? We had all the practicalities of life: enough money, friends, skills, stuff, love, opportunity, and so on. It was obvious that more of any of this kind of stuff was not going to provide any answers. Our crisis was internal: We noticed that, even though our lives had love, challenge, abundance, and fun, we intuited a greater purpose as yet unrevealed.

In the midst of this questioning, we noticed that a fairly consistent theme in our lives is to go straight to the top: If we meet someone in a company, it tends to be the CEO. If we go somewhere, we end up meeting the owner, the boss, the president, the celebrity. If we study with a teacher, he or she is the best in the field. We wondered, what good is it to know a network of leaders? What is it for? Fundamentally, we asked ourselves, what is our time on this planet *for*? What is the culmination of the deep practice and teachings we have received, the privilege we enjoy, the understandings that arise? This inquiry burned in us for more than two years, consuming our attention, resources, and time.

Finally, having read dozens of books, filled journals, gone on retreats, traveled the globe, and engaged in many marathon conversations, we felt it was time to create an outward focus. We started a media company, and the answer finally arose as to the "why" of our skills, our resources. That answer is inspiring, necessary, large, and practical: Give peace a deadline.

Full disclosure: We enjoy and profit from our media company, and we enjoy helping other people succeed in doing what they love while contributing to the world. We are businesspeople. Many people on the left think that doing good and making money cannot go together, and many people on the right feel that making money is the highest good. While both of these views can be true at one time or another, we think people can make money and make a difference at the same time. We chose to publish this book through mainstream methods and profit

from it. In addition to the other contributions we make to world peace, we will donate a portion of the proceeds to our peace movement.

We are leaders. Our background, practical perspective, experience, skills, resources, and passion make us uniquely qualified to lead the world, in this moment, toward world peace in five years. We know other leaders are willing to step forward. Are you one of them? Let's collaborate!

There is a myth that change occurs only when one has a position of power and then uses that position to create change. The myth says that one must be a CEO, political leader, elder, spiritual leader, celebrity, or wealthy in order to create change. Consider people like Erin Brockovich, Karen Silkwood, and Mahatma Gandhi, individuals who met none of these criteria but took responsibility, declared themselves accountable for important issues, and worked toward change. No matter your position or financial status, you have the power to create change.

Our lives are focused on peace in five years. We are committed to this campaign, and we look forward to the dawn of a new era of constructive conflict resolution. We cannot create world peace by ourselves, however. Many people and businesses have already joined us in our work, and we hope that this book will inspire millions more people to give peace a deadline.

We defined our goal as "a worldwide end to politically organized, deadly armed conflict." Once we signed the pledge, we launched a global campaign. We gave the movement a title, P5Y, for peace in five years. We set our launch date as February 14, 2009.

One reason we don't have world peace today is because it has not been defined. One of our practices is businesslike specificity. The mainstream view of peace has been vague, and it can benefit from clarity. For instance, P5Y is a movement, but we are specific about what we are moving away *from*—a world with war—and what we are moving *toward*—a world in which the specific safety practices of peace prevent war. We are moving there within five years.

We created P5Y to run the campaign, established P5Y.org, and launched an extensive research project. We wrote this book, and we began to travel to meet with people and talk with them about the campaign. Thus far we have been to England, Morocco, Italy, France, Monaco, and the Czech Republic. We have representatives in Uganda, Rwanda, Jordan, and India. We have met with philanthropists, diplomats, heads of state, and artists. We have consulted business strategists and marketers, received branding from ideaocore of Santa Barbara, California, held brainstorming sessions, and met with media moguls and public relations experts. The leading law firm Sheppard-Mullin represents P5Y pro bono. We have received an invitation to launch P5Y at the Forum 2000 peace conference. Please visit P5Y.org for up-to-date information and to discover what contribution you can make to create peace in five years.

WHY NOW?

By many broad measures, the world is better off now than it ever has been. Officials at the Stockholm International Peace Research Institute (SIPRI) claim that they expect the next few years to see an increase in high-level talks on disarmament and arms control. In 2007, the Cato Institute published Indur M. Goklany's book *The Improving State of the World: Why We're Living Longer, Healthier, More Comfortable Lives on a Cleaner Planet*, which argues that thanks to free trade, economic growth, and technology, the world is in much better shape than we think. Fareed Zakaria, author and journalist, quotes Steven Pinker of Harvard University's Department of Psychology as saying that "though it may seem illogical and even obscene, given Iraq and Darfur, we are living in the most peaceful time in our species' existence." According to Zakaria, if you set aside the deaths in Iraq, world deaths from terrorism have gone down more than 40 percent since 2001. The purpose of this book and of this movement is to accelerate this trend toward peace.

Despite the positive trends, despite the vast majority of people desiring peace, war is still with us. According to SIPRI, there are seventeen major armed conflicts active in the world as of this writing. That is, right now there are seventeen areas of the world with two or more sides shooting, bombing, raping, killing, and inflicting the horrible damages of war on each other on a large scale. Unfortunately, war technology has grown to such a point that it can cause our extinction. The race to develop new, more destructive war technologies continues around the globe. Nations continue to create new types of nuclear weapons, as well as to experiment with chemical and biological weapons that can hurt or kill you without even being aimed at you. Cyberweapons and nanoweapons are under development. With every day that passes, the threat of destruction from war increases. If we continue on our current path, nuclear war is inevitable.

Three hundred years ago, we were separate tribes without radio, TV, or any electronic media. The enemy was not necessarily contributing to our lives, well-being, or nation's economy. However, as you can see from the global nature of the current economic crisis, today we are all connected, and the global system is sensitive in unpredictable ways. Economically we can only make war on ourselves. Now killing is only within the family. The stakes for giving peace a deadline could not be higher for all of us. The human world hangs in the balance. Procrastination could mean not only death for you and me but also of our global civilization; at the very least it could be the end of hope for our children.

Whatever cause is most important to you—family values, environmental sustainability, religious freedom, poverty alleviation, disease control, education, human rights—your cause is hurt by war. Even where there is not open war, the miasma of suspicion and noncooperation among nations as a result of an international culture that still permits war causes extensive human suffering. For example, as this is being written, the government of Myanmar is preventing aid from reaching its typhoon-stricken population because of deep suspicion of military motives. Here is an excerpt from a story by Agence France-Presse:

> Nearly a month after the storm tore through swathes of Myanmar, about 60 percent of the 2.4 million survivors remain without foreign aid, despite some opening-up by the military rulers after an intense UN-led diplomatic push.
>
> The junta blocked entry to overseas aid workers in the critical days after Cyclone Nargis pummeled the impoverished nation on May 2–3, leaving 133,000 people dead or missing.

"Unless the regime changes its approach, its policy, more people will die," U.S. Secretary of Defense Robert Gates said. "I would describe it as criminal neglect."[1]

This is just one example of how even a cloud of war hanging over the planet causes us suffering. Imagine a different scenario, in which the ruling junta of Myanmar knew that all of the donor nations were pledged to peace through an international treaty. Imagine that those donor nations understood that the criminal neglect of the Burmese population by its government was a clear violation of global peace safety, requiring urgent action. Then the likelihood of donors getting into Myanmar to aid the storm victims becomes much higher.

Today, war is still acceptable. World leaders can threaten war and "rattle sabers." They can solemnly proclaim patriotic code phrases for war. They may declare that

---

1. "More to die if Myanmar doesn't changes approach," Agence France-Presse, June 2, 2008.

they will ensure your safety, carry out justice, or defend sovereignty. We, their constituents, and the family of nations nod soberly and prepare for the inevitable. We ignore human rights violations if they take place in the context of war. We accept restrictions of our freedoms in the service of war. We use the term "collateral damage" as a euphemism for the killing of innocent people, and we find this result regrettable, but not criminal. As novelist and soldier Ernest Hemingway said, "Never think that war, no matter how necessary, nor how justified, is not a crime." When we consider war to be an illegitimate criminal activity, like slavery is considered today, it will end.

In today's world, we do not have a viable and consistent system for resolving conflicts in a dignified and timely way, so leaders still use war as a legitimate means of conflict resolution. Although our own nation, the United States of America, has often led the way in helping to resolve international conflicts constructively, lately this has not been true. We tolerate genocide in the name of sovereignty while the needs of whole populations go unmet, breeding "terrorists" along with unrest and violence of all kinds.

While some politicians still rely on war, we have powerful forces working for peace. Many of the wealthiest 20 percent of the world's population (if you have more than $2,000 in the bank, you are in this group) recognize that they have a responsibility beyond comfortable survival, and they are looking to make a difference in many ways. There is more private wealth today than at any time previously in human history. Many of the individuals who control this wealth are directing it toward solving humanity's problems like war recovery, conflict resolution, poverty abatement, education, disease prevention, women's rights, and environmental conservation. The Council on Foundations expects charitable foundation giving for all manner of causes to top $300 billion a year by the middle of the century. New initiatives like Women for Women International connect smaller donors directly to individual recipients. Large, innovative institutions like the Bill and Melinda Gates Foundation are transforming how we approach problems such as HIV/AIDS in Africa and global poverty.

Governments are recognizing that foreign aid in the service of narrow policy interests is ineffective, both from a humanitarian and a policy standpoint. Today we understand how collaboration can yield better results, and things are slowly improving. For instance, tied aid, as a proportion of foreign aid, has decreased in the past decade from two-thirds to one-half. Tied aid is an ineffiecent policy whereby donor nations require funds to be spent in the originating country. Projecting these trends, it seems we might eventually have world peace. However, *might* and *eventually* are not worthy or reasonable goals when faced with the costs of war.

BARRIERS AND ARMIES NO LONGER KEEP YOU SAFE

Sitting in our front-row seats at the Forum 2000, we heard Paul Wolfowitz, former deputy secretary of defense under U.S. President George W. Bush, say, "I am very sympathetic to the idea that we need to reform the whole issue of nuclear weapons in this era: their framework of deterrence was something that grew up during the Cold War, and we are still kind of stuck with it. It needs to change, and it needs to take much more account of the fact that we are all potentially vulnerable to disasters and terrorist use of nuclear weapons."

The danger to us and the world lies in the fact that the rate at which we are bringing about change may surpass our wisdom in managing that change. Wolfowitz and others have noted the threat of nuclear arms. Futurist and author Bill Joy stated in his *Wired* magazine essay, "Why the world doesn't need us," that advances in bioengineering and nanotechnology have the potential to devastate our lives and planet if not properly managed. It is hard enough to contain these threats without using them as weapons.[2]

It used to be clear who had the power to kill mass numbers of people. Now people can kill and maim you from greater distances for less money. Soon, not only heads of state will control weapons of mass destruction; small groups and individuals will be able to kill millions anywhere. Unless we act, the planet will continue to suffer the costs of "conventional" war and terrorism, and the technology of war will continue to develop. Nanotechnology and cyberwarfare are just beginning to make an impact. Like nuclear, biological, and chemical warfare, these new technologies disregard borders.

The strategic news service Stratfor sent an email alert on July 30, 2008, titled "Geopolitical Diary: Cyberwarfare Beginning to Take Center Stage." The alert said in part:

> For example, some experts claim that the massive 2004 blackout in the American northeast was precipitated by a Chinese hacker tinkering with systems relevant to the power grid. In 2007, in what has become one of the few true case studies in cyberwarfare, a massive cyberattack brought Estonia to a standstill in the wake of the controversial relocation of a Soviet World War II memorial.

2. Bill Joy, "Why the future doesn't need us: Our most powerful 21st-century technologies—robotics, genetic engineering, and nanotech—are threatening to make humans endangered species," *Wired*, April, 2000.

The alert goes on to note that cyberwarfare disregards borders, is invisible before it happens, and can bring a country to a standstill: no email, no websites, no bank transactions, no air traffic control, and potentially no electricity.

Nanotechnology, which is developing quickly, has even more disruptive potential. The following is a quote from the Web page of the Center for Responsible Nanotechnology (CRN) (www.crnano.org/dangers.htm), an independent nonprofit think tank:

> Admiral David E. Jeremiah, Vice-Chairman (ret.), U.S. Joint Chiefs of Staff, in an address at the 1995 Foresight Conference on Molecular Nanotechnology said: "Military applications of molecular manufacturing have even greater potential than nuclear weapons to radically change the balance of power."
>
> An excellent essay by Tom McCarthy (unaffiliated with CRN) explores these points in more detail. Molecular manufacturing will reduce economic influence and interdependence, encourage targeting of people as opposed to factories and weapons, and reduce the ability of a nation to monitor its potential enemies.

These new types of potential warfare are coming; the threat of nuclear annihilation will remain, and weapons of mass destruction will continue to threaten us with toxins and diseases too terrible to contemplate. Now war makes things worse. If we do not create world peace soon, we risk destroying our world.

Author Robert Heinlein wrote "an armed society is a polite society." He meant that when individuals possess increased destructive power, they must treat each other with respect or destroy one other. As we move toward a world in which individuals and small groups can wield enormous destructive power, we must become fundamentally more polite.

The only thing that can protect us from annihilation is a systematic practice of constructive conflict. Peace is our only worldwide "safety." Just as safety precautions like seat belts and earthquake-resistant buildings protect us from car accidents and temblors, so the active practice of peace as safety protects us from the ravages of war. According to corporate safety consultants, the practice of safety is instilled into a corporate culture. Until we instill the practice of peace into our worldwide culture, the risks increase each day.

The United Nations has been promoting a "culture of peace" for some time. This is laudable, but in our view, not effective enough. The UN has not defined what the practice of peace is beyond principles; they have not given peace a deadline, nor verified that the principles they are promoting are related to the prevention of war. However, we are pleased that the phrase "culture of peace" has become more widely known because of the UN's initiatives.

In all of these points, examples, and statistics, we might forget that war and peace are just about people, and what people choose to do. We chose to give peace a deadline.

WHAT IS POSSIBLE FOR YOU IN A PEACEFUL WORLD?

Imagine what will be possible for you in a world without war. What new resources and opportunities will open up for you? In a world at peace, travel, tourism, trade, and cooperation of all kinds will be greatly increased. Advances in science, mathematics, aerospace, energy, water, and healthcare could occur with freed resources. Without war, we will be free to work on the remaining major human challenges: poverty, education, public health, economic development, communication, etc., without threat of destroying what we have worked on. We are not suggesting that world peace will bring an immediate utopia, but we are suggesting that many positive trends will emerge or accelerate once we reach this crucial milestone. World peace is the ticket to the future, not just for everyone, but for you personally. One thing is certain: *We* want to find out what our world looks like when we've agreed to constructive conflict. Don't you?

HOW WE CAN CREATE WORLD PEACE IN FIVE YEARS

Proven solutions have already been designed by experts for all aspects of preventing war: meeting peoples' needs, conflict resolution, mediation, policing, state-building, witnessing, technology for communication and e-government, trauma healing, economic development, and more. What is missing are the tools and resources that coordinate and implement those solutions. Along with the deadline, P5Y provides planning, collaboration, and infrastructure to ensure that the well-known solutions are applied effectively.

Although trauma healing, conflict resolution, education, etc., have been going on for years, these efforts are hampered by a number of challenges. Fundamentally, all of these efforts have been taking place within a context which permits war. Many more resources are put toward reaction than toward prevention. Problems are not addressed holistically but piecemeal, on a project basis: Aid supplies, safety, education, micro-finance, etc., are not applied together and are often counterproductive. Funding challenges restrict the scope of the solutions and distract from the mission. Some solutions face policy restrictions from donors or recipients that prevent them from being applied or being effective. Many nongovernmental organizations (NGOs) do not coordinate their efforts with each other. Until now, all of these reasons have made world peace difficult to contribute to. By providing collaboration and tools, P5Y makes peace accessible.

The good news is that we have adequate and growing resources to create world peace. It was recently noted that private funding of NGOs reached $27 billion in 2005, or nearly one-third of the total ($84 billion) spent by governments.[3] All we need is effective leadership and collaboration.

Our invitation to you, businesses, NGOs, foreign aid programs, politicians, and foundations is to help end war through coordinated application of known solutions.

In addition to the existing solutions, our P5Y organization will use social networking and communications to develop new ways for individuals and groups to make commitments of time and money to create world peace. Taking into account needs, talents, resources, and inclinations, we aim to answer the question for you and organizations: What is the most effective thing I can do for world peace? Once you know what you can do that will be effective, you can use the P5Y.org website to make a specific commitment to a person who will hold you accountable. You can also contribute by accepting commitments. The system is voluntary—you make only a commitment you wish to be held to.

P5Y is also initiating a global marketing campaign to reposition world peace, taking it back from the hippies and showing that it is urgent, mainstream, purposeful, and doable. This campaign will piggyback on advertising for corporations that make commitments to help create peace in five years. DharmaMix and Media One, for-profit partner companies, are already poised to promote P5Y.

P5Y is powerful because we inform ourselves and the world about the most effective things anyone can do for world peace. Armed with that knowledge, we invite everyone to participate—regardless of politics, religion, race, profession, or background. Thus "world peace" is freed of political constraints; corporations, the military, governments, monarchies, and all manner of people can contribute to and benefit from peace.

---

3. "The future of aid: A scramble in Africa," *The Economist,* September 6, 2008, 69.

P5Y measures and tracks commitments, deadlines, and results. You can know exactly what you are participating in, and how effective the entire effort has been. Through the P5Y.org website, you or anyone can make a commitment of time, money, or skill, have your commitment valued through a process of accountability, and see your commitment measured along with others' similar commitments.

Also, we have a program of discreet communication and coordination among global leaders. P5Y communicates and consults with a wide array of leaders, diplomats, and heads of state to help make our efforts effective, to minimize suspicion and surprise, and to maximize cooperation and understanding among all parties.

In addition, P5Y is coordinating an international team to create a Global Peace Treaty (GPT) for ratification by all nations. Like the Geneva Convention and other international standards, the GPT will set forth the standards for participating nations to effectively engage in the practice of preventing war.

The following are some of the tactics we see as probable:

- The United States must set an example—a principle-based U.S. foreign policy is essential in creating world peace; and U.S. citizens are specially invited to help by registering on the P5Y.org website.

- Peace in the Middle East is essential—every leading thinker agrees that the Middle East is a source of many ongoing conflicts elsewhere in the world, and that settling the Israel-Palestine conflict in particular is a high priority.

- Effective, coordinated action by individuals is essential—we are in a new era of information and power in the hands of individuals, and many of us must assume the roles of diplomats, peacemakers, and activists in order to create world peace. The role of P5Y is to make peace user-friendly—to make it easy for you and any other person, group, government, or corporation to know what to do, how to do it, and what the result will be, without compromising values, purpose, or mission.

A PURPOSE BEYOND YOURSELF BRINGS JOY

World peace is a necessary goal, and we intend to reach it. However, world peace in five years is also a proxy for that which is inspiring, motivating, worthy, and fun. Having a purpose beyond yourself aligns your life and brings joy. If you don't have such a purpose orienting your life already, world peace in five years might be a good choice.

You already have unique skills and talents to bring to world peace. You have the power to communicate with hundreds of people in person, or maybe millions of other people online. You don't have to do or become anything new in order to contribute to world peace—just bring yourself, find what is interesting, necessary, and well suited to your passions, and commit to doing it!

This book will teach you about the problems of war and peace, and the possibilities for a solution. As you read on, you will learn a great deal more about our campaign, our overall strategy, our six-step process for realizing peace, and the activities that are going on right now to give peace a deadline. By working the exercises in the book, you will learn how to align your life with peace, how you can personalize the peacemaking process, and how you can save lives. We invite you to read this book. We invite you to make yourself accountable for world peace. We promise it will change your life, as well as the world.

WORLD PEACE IS THE BEGINNING

When organized political violence is over, there will be more opportunity for individual contribution and collaboration. Five years is not very long. Once we have world peace, we will have plenty of other interesting problems to tackle. One thing is for sure: Whatever problem we choose to face will be better and easier to solve in a peaceful world.

The most effective thing you can do for world peace is to read this book, complete the exercises, and make your measurable commitment with a deadline.

PART I

OUR PROBLEM

WAR IS PERSONAL

We are confronted by a mode of thinking that divides all the world into us and them, and by a mode of acting that prescribes killing all of "them" before they kill all of "us." In this view, the dividing line between good and evil is starkly etched, and efforts at compromise are equated with heresy.

—Madeleine Albright

LET'S BE CLEAR: War is about killing. It's not about glory and duty and saving small children and acts of heroism. It's about killing another living human being before he can do the same to you—in order to achieve some goal established by a political entity. If you are directly attacked you will defend yourself in a moment of desperation. On the other hand, premeditated murder is considered to be the most heinous crime and carries the heaviest punishment. Yet war is politically organized premeditated mass murder. Condoned killing is what separates war from all other human social activities. Although individuals are punished and taken out of society for murder, political entities are usually not delegitimized for waging war.

This chapter describes the realities of war, the way our society trains for war, the cost of killing to society, and the impacts on the individuals we finance to kill. This is a tough subject, but if we were writing a book about slavery in 1852, for example, we would not just give our strategic plan for ending slavery; we would describe the actual human pain and cost of slavery in every detail. Just as abolitionists took personal responsibility for slavery, so too must we take personal responsibility for war. When our country kills in the name of war, we kill and you kill as well. We don't mean you are picking up a gun and shooting someone, but the reality is that our pervasive tolerance and tax dollars pay for war. Nothing we can write on this page can actually capture the horrible reality of one human being killing another human being. Although we can't bring the reality of killing and war to these pages, we can demonstrate that both killing and war are about you and us.

THE REALITIES OF WAR

Merriam-Webster's dictionary defines *war* as "a state of usually open and declared armed hostile conflict between states or nations." But we prefer this more evocative definition: War is a violent conflict carried out by at least one political group against another group or population. War is political violence.

Under our definition all of the following would be considered war: planning attacks, shootings, bombings, terrorism, violence by mercenaries, extraordinary rendition by the CIA, political kidnappings, and genocide. And these are all happening *right now*, at this very moment. Out of your sight and hearing, people are dying in pools of their own blood. Mothers are burying their children. Infants are starving. Innocent people are being imprisoned and tortured.

The amazing, maddening fact is that modern history tells us that war doesn't work! War doesn't achieve its long-term political ends. If it does achieve its short-term aim, it's with massive death and destruction, which render any gains pointless. War is the most blunt instrument for change anyone can imagine. So why do we keep going back to it again and again? At some point, we must learn that war no longer works.

Whether war works or not, we still have it on our planet. While a hundred years ago war in a distant land could be said not to involve you or me, today it does. War is personal. In this chapter we are going to look at how personal it is. There are no longer any unknown distant lands, and all of us are involved and affected by war. Let's start with the most personal part of war: killing.

War is about killing. In a book about world peace it is natural to ask: Are human beings natural born killers? The answer is no.

WE ARE NOT KILLERS

You may have heard people argue that humans are violent by nature and that war is inevitable. Respected anthropologist Raymond Dart's "killer ape theory," based on his analysis of bone piles in African caves, suggests that early humans were violent cannibals. The theory states that ancestors of humans were distinguished from other primate species by their aggressive tendencies, and humans have retained these tendencies throughout evolution. Dart's theory, however, was later refuted decisively by anthropologist Bob Brain, who showed that the bone piles were produced by predatory cats, not humans. Dart graciously retracted his theory, and although it is largely discredited, it nevertheless remains popular.

William Ury, also an anthropologist and founder of the Harvard Negotiation Project, wrote in his book *The Third Side*, "There turns out to be little conclusive evidence in the archaeological record for the story of pandemic human violence during the first 99 percent of human evolution."[4] We humans, by and large, are not designed to kill other humans. Ury refers to humans as "Homo Negotiator" for our inherent ability to negotiate conflict.

Douglas Fry, a research scientist in the Bureau of Applied Research in Anthropology at the University of Arizona, argues that even though aggression is a part of human nature, how it plays out is based more on culture, and generally, people have an immense capacity for peacefulness. He supports this theory in his book, *The Human Potential for Peace: An Anthropological Challenge to Assumptions about War and Violence* (Oxford University Press, 2005), in a discussion about the very low levels of aggression and the absence of warfare he was able to find in more than eight present-day hunter-gatherer societies. He also argues that Western researchers usually study male chimps, who tend to be more aggressive, to the exclusion of female chimps and the more affectionate primate species bonobo. Frans De Waal, a leading primatologist, in his book *Our Inner Ape* (Riverhead, 2006) describes how human nature falls between chimp and bonobo behaviors. You and we are not doomed to violent behavior. As humans we are culturally capable of educating ourselves not to kill. In fact, we have natural tendencies toward negotiation.

4. William L. Ury, *The Third Side* (New York: Penguin Books, 2000), 33.

Lt. Col. David Grossman, in his book *On Killing* (Back Bay Books, 1996), notes the startling fact that if faced with a stark choice of killing a stranger face to face in war or possibly being killed, 98 percent of men would rather die than kill. He gives many examples of men violating direct orders to kill, even in combat situations.

Ury, De Waal, and Grossman all point out how the human capacity for war is based on culture and conditioning. Ury suggests that the advent of war was a cultural phenomenon based on the transition from hunter-gatherer societies to agrarian societies. We have now made the transition from an agrarian society to a technological society, which makes war far too risky for you and us. If war is a cultural phenomenon, not an inborn human trait, then we can end war the same way that we began it a few thousand years ago: through a cultural phenomenon. We ended slavery in this way.

Even those of us who are culturally exposed to violence can renounce killing. Badshah Khan, for example, was born into the fierce mountain tribe of the Pathans, but he was also a follower of the peace leader Mahatma Gandhi. Khan created a nonviolent army of 100,000 Muslim tribesmen who had previously believed in killing as a matter of honor. In *Nonviolent Soldier of Islam*, author Eknath Easwaran tells courageous and moving stories of Badshah Khan's inner struggle to fight nonviolently for the dignity of his proud people under British rule:

> Throughout the thirties and early forties Pathans had to endure mass shootings, torture, the destruction of their fields and homes, jail, flogging, and humiliations. Khan himself spent fifteen years in British prisons, often in solitary confinement . . . But the Pathans remained nonviolent and stood unmoved— suffering and dying in large numbers to win their freedom.[5]

The Pathans suffered enormously at the hands and guns of the British but did not waver in their commitment to love, forgiveness, and nonviolence. In their day, these people were reviled in the Western press. It was considered impossible that they could choose the path of peace.

Today, the descendants of these same Muslim tribesmen are known for their belief in violence. They are called the Taliban. Does it seem possible to you that the Taliban could take the path of constructive conflict today, like some of their ancestors did? If enough of the world's people, including the Taliban, give peace a deadline, we can build on our strengths as negotiators and agreement makers to

---

5. Eknath Easwaran, *Nonviolent Soldier of Islam: Badshah Khan, A Man to Match His Mountains*, 2nd ed. (Tomales, CA: Nilgiri Press, 1999), 20.

settle conflicts, meet basic human needs, and work for the good of ourselves and all humanity. However, if peace is not given a deadline and we allow war to continue, we will continue as a species to waste huge resources in training individuals to overcome their natural reluctance to kill.

TRAINING TO KILL

The more up close and personal killing is, the more difficult it is for us to overcome our natural revulsion toward the act. For most people, killing a stranger in hand-to-hand combat is nearly impossible without special conditions: protecting our family or our close combat buddies, being enraged, or "going over" to an extreme psychology of dehumanizing the enemy. Likewise, stabbing, eye gouging, and other close-up methods of force are extremely difficult to tolerate psychologically. The more clearly we can see a potential enemy's eyes and face, the more personal the killing becomes. We see the enemy as human.

For this reason, organizations that wish to train men to kill do their best to increase what is known as the killing distance, the psychological and physical distance from another human that objectifies the event in order to overcome the natural resistance to killing. Soldiers are never told, "Shoot that person in the head so that his brains and blood are spattered all over you and the ground." Civilians are not told that in news stories or advertisements either. Rather, so that they can overcome their natural aversion to killing, our soldiers are trained to hate the enemy, to "eliminate the target," to kill from behind, to kill in pairs or close-knit squads, and to use weapons with maximum distance.

In modern warfare, literal distance is increased as much as possible by the development of weapons that can kill from far away so that soldiers never have to come into personal contact with the individuals under attack. With long-range missiles, modern tanks, intercontinental bombers, drones, and remote-controlled weapons, the act of killing is increasingly becoming a sanitized process directed from a quietly glowing control room. When you hear about glory and honor in military advertisements or political arguments for war, does that create a killing distance for you? Knowing the truth about killing distance and the cost to military personnel and society of creating it gives you the power to choose.

Some people are able to kill without damaging their psyches. These people are not generally criminals and monsters, although some are. According to Grossman, about 2 percent of men are able to kill a human enemy at close range without conditioning, and without suffering damaging psychological effects. After military training that includes extensive behavioral conditioning, the percentage of men able to kill a human enemy at close range rises from 2 percent to 40 percent. For those who are not natural killers, the cost is very high.

An old high school friend, a solid good guy from the Midwest, called Amber the other day and started talking about what he had been up to the past fifteen years.

> I decided to go into the military, and you know I was really cocky riding in the rodeo, and I used to be prejudiced. I'm ashamed now after what I've seen about how I used to be. I signed up for this special part called recon where we went out first. We were in Africa. It was terrible, these fifteen-year-old boys with guns. A little boy died in my arms after I tried to save him. I swore an oath to die for my country and I love it, so don't get me wrong. The power to decide when another person is going to die should never be taken from God and given to a person. It's just not right. I took fourteen lives in total, and anybody who tells you they don't know the number of lives they took is lying. I sometimes cry when I'm alone and think that I am a monster for what I have done. Nobody else knows the details, not even my wife. I am afraid that the man that left is not the man that came back, and I have fears she would think bad thoughts of me. When a good man knows that he is capable of ending a life, he always fears that he is really nothing more than a killer. I am haunted by what my final judgment might be. I don't think God cares about stars and stripes and doing one for my country. I'm counting on Mercy.

This story is not unique. The majority of people are emotionally damaged by killing. This is part of the system in which you and I are participating.

Modern military conditioning comes at a financial and moral cost to you and to us and at a psychological cost to the individual. Depending on your personal morals, there is a cost to consistently violating your integrity. Grossman describes the case of Duane, a CIA veteran who was assigned to guard a Communist defector in a safe house in West Germany during the mid-1950s. Locked together in a small apartment, the defector repeatedly started to attack Duane, only breaking off the attack at the last minute. Duane was told by his superiors to draw an imaginary line on the floor and kill the defector if he crossed the line.

Duane felt certain that this line was going to be crossed and mustered up all of his conditioning. "He was a dead man. I knew I would kill him. Mentally I had killed him, and the physical part was going to be easy." But the defector (apparently not quite as crazy as he appeared to be) never crossed that line. Still some aspect of the trauma of the kill was there. "In my mind," Duane said, "I have always felt that I had killed that man." Duane is an example of how even preparing to kill another human is psychologically stressful.

Although Duane himself may seem distant, and you may not know someone who has participated in war, imagine this: Multiply Duane's example by all of the people you encounter in your daily life. Chances are that you have interacted with someone today whose life is touched by the damage of killing and military conditioning to kill. Think about people at your job, at the grocery store, your mail-delivery person, the person who sells you coffee. The people who are directly affected by war are all around you.

What are the costs of being a killer? For the dead, the suffering is over. For the one who kills, the suffering can continue. A soldier can take pride in destroying the enemy, but as soon as the soldier realizes the enemy was somebody's father, mother, sibling, or child, the killing distance is closed and the killing becomes psychologically traumatic. Dennis Reeves, a retired Navy psychologist, testifies to the psychological trauma military personnel endure after killing:

> When our guys felt or thought that they had maimed or wounded or killed some of the innocent Iraqi civilians . . . that was quite devastating to them because it was very psychologically traumatic for them to believe that they had killed somebody's father or mother or child.[6]

Post-traumatic stress disorder (PTSD) is not uncommon. Figures provided by the Rand Corporation in 2008 showed that more than 300,000 soldiers sent to Iraq and Afghanistan suffer from depression or post-traumatic stress syndrome. Some soldiers lose the ability to feel emotions at all. Others are consumed by guilt or self-doubt. Still others experience uncontrollable fits of rage or suicidal thoughts and actions.

Physicians for Social Responsibility estimates that the total healthcare cost for mentally wounded veterans of the war on terrorism in Iraq and Afghanistan will top $650 billion. The societal cost in broken families and ruined lives will be incalculable. Many of these men and women will develop PTSD for one simple reason: They were ordered to kill another human being, an act that challenges their human nature no matter how much training they have undergone.

---

6. Dennis Reeves, interview by *Frontline*, November 3, 2004, http://www.psb.org/wgbh/pages/front-line/shows/heart/interviews/reeves.html.

We are quoting statistics for U.S. soldiers because these statistics are reliable and readily available, but these same costs apply to the soldiers and civilians of any war.

Even criminal organizations must train their members to overcome their natural aversion to killing by using distancing language: *off the guy, take him out, make a hit, snuff him,* and so on. Gangs hold hazing initiations in which the new member must commit some violently criminal act in order to join. They use the same psychology as the military: join a small group of dedicated "brothers" who protect each other, avenge each other, and reassure each other that killing and maiming is okay.

We are not saying the military is wrong, bad, or evil. We are all participants in this conditioning. The army is our army, the country is our country. We are all participating in this system with our taxes, conversation, and tolerant indifference. If this system of conditioned killing does not represent your values and morals, it is up to you to change it, even if you didn't create it.

In the majority of cases, only with the establishment of a killing distance can individuals overcome their natural aversion to killing. Even when such a distance has been established, the results of killing can be devastating to the individual. In the same way, societies must be trained to distance themselves from the violence of war. The results of this distancing can be even more devastating for the world as a whole.

TRAINING YOU AND SOCIETY TO DISASSOCIATE

Just as trainers depersonalize killing for individuals by creating a killing distance, political leaders and the media depersonalize killing for society as a whole by packaging war in neutralizing language to create a killing distance. According to this technique, government spokespeople, along with the media, use a vocabulary that is clinical or demonizing. This has been true for centuries. During World War II, we were not killing Japanese people; we were killing "Japs." In the Vietnam War we were not killing Vietnamese people; we were killing "gooks." In the Iraq War that started in 2002, the news was full of the "shock and awe" that was going to result in a swift

Peace Action

What you can do today to further peace by 2014

Organize a group to honor the war dead in your community peace efforts and post your activities on www.P5Y.org.

U.S. victory. Americans could feel pride in the power of their military that was going to beat the Iraqis. The buildup to the war was reported in the media as if it were a mismatched football game. However, *shock and awe* really meant "kill or maim tens of thousands of men": men who were there at gunpoint under a brutal dictator; men who had no idea they were about to be killed; men who had been lied to by their own government, just as the U.S. government was lying to its own people and military. *Shock and awe* was a propaganda phrase that was used to distance and conceal the reality of mass premeditated killing.

This type of vocabulary is used for a reason. Military advocates will argue that such cold language is necessary, in part, to keep soldiers from feeling empathy for their human targets and thereby becoming unfit to do their jobs.

Similarly, the media refers to human beings as enemy assets, targets, threats, something to be neutralized. People are insurgents, yellow bastards, white demons, commies, imperialists, rebels, collateral damage, casualties, and so on. Killing distance works not only on soldiers but also on the home population of a country at war.

Distancing speech is pervasive, and it can be found in many areas of our lives. For example, rather than say someone has been fired, we now say he's been downsized, laid off, furloughed, or given early retirement. Even in social situations we tend to use squeamish or circumspect language to avoid facing the reality of certain situations. While at times social delicacy is called for, if it is used to obscure truth, we all suffer.

Peace Action

What you can do today to further peace by 2014

Watch an hour of news programming and write down the number of times that violence is depersonalized.

Unfortunately, today's wars have become so sanitized in their presentation, few, if any of us, have the slightest idea of the terror, violence, cruelty, humiliation, and death that are the true face of war. While it is beyond the scope of this book to delve deeply into the relationship of mass media to war reporting, we encourage you to look into it for yourself. For instance, there was a furor a few years ago about the U.S. media not "being allowed" to show coffins containing dead soldiers as they arrived at Dover Air Force Base in Delaware, or even graphic images from the Iraq War.

Today, politicians and the media have to work harder to maintain a killing distance. Though we would like to believe war is fought strictly between trained soldiers, today's wars pull in people who never signed up for the national army.

War is fought with fathers, mothers, children, college students, clergy, shop owners, and pets. More civilians than soldiers are being killed in current wars. Unicef and the Global Movement for Children report that an estimated 2 million children have been killed in armed conflict, and more than 6 million have been injured or disabled in armed conflicts in the decade since the adoption of the Convention on the Rights of the Child. More than 12 million children have been left homeless because of war. And at this very moment, an estimated three hundred thousand children are being used as soldiers.

When so many children and civilians are killed due to combat, war violates the very family systems we value and want to protect. It would be much more difficult for both the military and the general public to support the war in Iraq if we had information and photos of the Iraqi mothers, fathers, and children who have been swept up in the violent storm of war.

We experience the sanitization of the killing process when states execute individuals. Lethal injection has replaced electrocution, hanging, and the firing squad as the preferred method of execution in most U.S. states; it seems as if the individual being executed is just going to sleep. No neck is broken, no hair catches on fire. Even so, no state allows photographs or recordings of the executions themselves. Why not? It's all part of the way our society depersonalizes killing to minimize the effects it will have on the general population. And we participate in this killing by passively flipping through television channels in the comfort of our own homes.

These techniques work. They work extremely well. Demonizing our enemies, clinicalizing and repackaging the act of killing into less messy, less personal terms makes us less likely to react or have much empathy. But no matter the apparent distance, killing a human is killing, and the act affects you. Imagine the person being killed is you or your family member—it is pretty hard to place any fig leaf of language to conceal that.

We assert that if you allowed yourself just a moment to actually and deeply reflect in order to feel the full emotional impact of brutally taking a life in war, you would become violently ill. Any normal human, when directly confronted with the reality of war, would do the same. If we can feel this impact as a global people, we would most likely fall to our knees to pray for forgiveness, and end war instantly and forever.

There is good news: Killing distance does not work forever. Nearly any soldier who has seen combat will be touched by the stark reality of killing and what it is, and what it actually looks like. Andrew Pomerantz, chief of mental health services for the Veteran's Administration in Vermont, said of one of his patients, "To the day he died he could still describe the face of the man he was about to kill."[7] The dead man's face haunted this veteran for his entire life, seared into his conscience.

WAR IS PERSONAL

War is personal, not only for the soldiers who are conditioned to kill but also for all of us whom these soldiers represent. If our soldiers are killing, then we are killing. This is difficult for us to accept. No one wants to believe that he or she is a killer, but ultimately, we must take responsibility for wars carried out by our nation, and the killing that goes with them.

If we could accept the fact that we are personally responsible for war, we would refuse to participate in it any longer. The pain would be too great. If someone close to you has died, then you know the cost of death to the living. Not only do the living lose the physical presence of the deceased, they also lose all possibility of that loved one's presence in the future. We lose every contribution that that person could have made to the world.

What if enough soldiers, leaders, and concerned citizens on all sides took killing personally and began to recoil from the horror of war? What if enough people on all sides refused to support war any longer? This isn't about peace marches and wearing T-shirts with the peace symbol. You and we support war through making no effective effort *to bring ourselves into integrity with the system that we live within.* However, we can roll up our sleeves, make a plan, and make the change in five years so our children don't have to. This isn't something we can tell you, and then you can just nod your head in agreement. In order to get this— to create world peace—you have to "do the math." Make it your responsibility to know and be an active part of the solution.

When the cycle of life is complete, death can be an occasion for mourning or a celebration of a natural passage. When Nathan's grandmother died at the age of ninety-one, peacefully in her bed at home, surrounded by loving family, her contribution felt complete, her death natural. When a friend or relative dies young, the misery of loss is compounded. When Nathan and Amber's friend Justin died at the age of twenty-seven in a car accident, the loss was agonizing. The pain was compounded by the fact that Justin was an extraordinary person, a staff member

---

7. Andrew Pomerantz, interview by *Frontline*, October 5, 2004, http://www.pbs.org/wgbh/pages. frontline/shows/heart/interviews/pomerantz.html.

and adviser to President Clinton at such a young age; a person with enormous potential for contribution to the world. People like Justin die in war all the time. The experience of losing someone close to us is personal. It is so painful that most of the time we do not wish to think about it. What would happen if each one of us experienced the killing of a stranger in war in the same way that we experience the loss of someone close to us, as a personal loss? The pain would be unbearable, and war would be unthinkable.

Take a moment to consider how someone dies in a war. Most of the time, such a death is preceded by agony, terror, and loneliness, punctuated by the most horrible violence imaginable. Imagine a bullet tearing through a human body in slow motion, rupturing organs, smashing bones, and tearing apart the delicate tissues that comprise the living wonder we know as the human body. Pain and shock spread throughout. Bleeding causes blood pressure to drop. Vital functions begin to fail. Breathing and the heartbeat stop forever. If the cause of death is exposure, disease, starvation, or infection, the process may take more time, but the end result is the same: a human life is lost forever.

The dead individual had a mother, a father, relatives, and friends, just like you have. Survivors grieve the loss of their loved one, their mourning made all the more bitter because of the shocking violence of the death. Many of those left behind do not have the opportunity to grieve. Caught up in war, they have to struggle with the horrific violence, dislocation, abuse, attack, torture, disease, exposure, or malnutrition that claimed the life of their loved one. The living lose the income, support, and love of the war dead. They are left with nothing but the image of death and the pain of loss.

The cost of untimely death to the living is very high. The ripples of this cost spread outward for years after the event. Children grow up without mothers and fathers. Family systems break down. Economies are devastated. Communities and businesses are destroyed; depression and suicide increase. For more than a generation after a war has "ended," the effects continue to damage life and happiness.

The living struggle to make meaning out of their loss. As Jeff Hubbard, a retired California police officer who lost two sons in Iraq, said on ABC News, "I just hope they're right, and I hope we get something accomplished out of all this after all the sacrifice we've made and the rest of the country has sacrificed."[8] Reading between the lines seems to reveal what Officer Hubbard believes but

8. "California Family That Lost Two Sons in Iraq Speak Out," ABC News, http://media.abcnews.com/US/Story?id=3543348&page=2.

does not want to believe: namely, that his sons' deaths were a waste. "I just hope they are right" suggests that he was told by the authorities that his sons made a valuable sacrifice. Did they?

What is the real price we pay for killing in war? Václav Havel, playwright and first president of the Czech Republic, who led the peaceful separation of Czechoslovakia from Russia, talks about the hypnotic charm of an ideology:

> It offers a ready answer to any question whatsoever; it can scarcely be accepted only in part, and accepting it has profound implications for human life . . . One pays dearly for this low-rent home: the price is abdication of one's own reason, conscience, and responsibility, for an essential aspect of this ideology is the consignment of reason and conscience to a higher authority.[9]

Similarly, Shirin Ebadi, the first Iranian and Muslim woman to win the Nobel Peace Prize, spoke these words:

> Faith, ideology, democracy, human rights. All these are sacred concepts, sacred words, which we must liberate from the prisons of the government and give to the people. And we must not allow these concepts, these words, to be abused by political powers. Let us extinguish the flames of war, let us disseminate the seeds of friendship. This war has no victor.[10]

If we accept and are honest about our own inevitable connections to the globe, then we are personally involved in war and every death that occurs in war. Although this may be a painful realization, it is also a heartening one. If we are personally involved, then we have the power to do something about it. We can rely on our own nature to end war, and we will show you a way to end it within five years.

---

9. Václav Havel, *The Power of the Powerless*, ed. John Keane (New York: M.E. Sharpe, 1985), 25.

10. Shirin Ebadi at Forum 2000, October 8, 2007, Prague, http://www.forum2000.cz/en/projects/forum-2000-conferences/2007/transcripts/panel-2-freedom-and-responsibility-in-international-law.

IS PEACE POSSIBLE?

Peace is possible.

—Mahatma Gandhi

WHEN WE SET OUT to achieve an objective, we want to know that it is at least possible to win and define the terms of success. What is *peace? Merriam-Webster's* defines it as "a state of tranquility or quiet, as a freedom from civil disturbance, a state of security or order within a community provided for by law or custom." We define *peace* as "constructive conflict." The outcome of peace is safety—dependable, physical safety. Peace is the material security to know that while you're reading this book, you will not have to worry about your door being kicked in by secret police, or a mortar shell destroying your home and killing you, or your son blowing himself up in a crowded marketplace. Peace is the safety that provides you with the time, the energy, and the security to address other crucial human needs such as hunger, healthcare, education, and social justice. Safety comes first.

Everyone wants to be safe. When we define peace as constructive conflict or the practice of peace-safety, we depoliticize the concept of peace. We free ourselves from peace as a social or ideological cause. Peace as safety practices is politically neutral. Everyone wants to walk their streets without worry, to let their children attend school without fear, to speak their minds without reprisal. Everyone who wants to be safe wants peace. According to this definition, world peace is the practice of constructive conflict among the family of nations, safety from war and from the threat of war. When we have achieved world peace, war will have no legitimacy in human society, just as today, legitimacy has been removed from the practice of slavery and human sacrifice. What relief will you feel knowing that the family of nations has sorted out this fundamental problem?

You are invited to refine and update your concept of peace. For this purpose, we have listed a few of the many things that peace is *not*. Peace is not

- the end of all conflict;
- the end of all violence;
- a global super-happy consciousness;
- worldwide friendship and understanding;
- humorless;
- an umbrella for every worthy cause fulfilled.

As humans we are at the point where we can, with sufficient will and focus, arrange for our family of nations and peoples to prefer the safety of peace to the growing danger of war, although some people may still argue that peace is not part of human nature.

YOU ARE HUMAN NATURE

What is your biggest fear or frustration about creating peace? What is the first thing that comes to mind? Are you afraid of being seen a certain way, of failing, or of taking on an obligation that may be a lot of work? Is that truly your biggest fear about peace, or is there something deeper? How could you take care of that concern? How could you answer for it when the world is organized around peace?

Peace Action

What you can do today to further peace by 2014

Have a conversation with your friends about the common definitions of peace. Discuss the areas of your life where you feel safe and where you would like to create more safety. Update your definition of peace when talking to people.

One argument against the possibility of world peace is that "human nature" forbids it. Let us look closely at this for a moment. You are human nature. If you are reading these words you have as much authority on the nature of being human as any other person. It is important for you to consider your intimate knowledge of being human. What do you have control over when you are conflicted? Are you doomed to violence? We all have specific points of view that come into conflict with others. When you have a conflict, do you feel compelled toward mass murder? Do you think that even if you were angry and felt compelled to physically hurt the other person that you could refrain?

Our loosely held view is this: Most of what we take to be "true" as humans is based on assumptions and long-held biases that we are loathe to change but that we must change. For thousands of years, slavery was held to be inevitable, justified by the accepted assumption that the nature of some peoples was less "civilized" and therefore not worthy of equal freedoms or respect. The ugliness of racial prejudice has been blamed on human nature, yet as this book was being written, the United States nominated and elected its first African American presidential candidate. Human nature is usually an excuse for being unwilling to tackle difficult change, but change we can. This is the good news. It is time to change and accept peace—not war—as the natural state of the world. Many people are already on this track of thinking. Peace, not war, is part of human nature.

Once we know that peace is a series of safety practices, and that peace is a natural part of human nature, together we will be able to overcome those who sell war. War advocates will lose their willing populations. They will become the outsiders. Their position supporting war will be seen as a position outside of human nature, and they will be ridiculed and ostracized.

In *The Tipping Point* (Little, Brown & Co., 2000), Malcolm Gladwell highlights the crime reduction in New York City in the 1990s brought about by the "broken windows" policy. According to this policy, New York City officials created an environment in which criminality was viewed as not permissible by taking small actions such as repairing broken windows, erasing graffiti, and preventing fare-jumping on the subway. Our goal is similar: to remove the context in which political war is a permissible option for resolving conflicts, so that warmongers no longer have a global environment that supports war. Peace actions such as addressing conflicts before they escalate, hearing peoples' voices in oppressive situations, and meeting desperate needs create an environment that is safer than war. Removing the context of war altogether and taking preventative steps creates the most safety for you and us.

Still, the question comes up, "What if 'they' attack us?" Can't we defend ourselves? Of course we can. Peace is not a suicide pact. However, the goal of P5Y is to reduce the possibility of any attack so it becomes implausible. Any threats or signs of war will be met by effective global safety measures. Evil only succeeds when good people fail to act. In our neighborhood, if someone commits a crime, the police handle the situation. Crime is the exception not the norm. Once we have accepted peace as human nature, we will understand that it is only natural to have peace. The only thing that stands in the way of taking constructive conflict actions instead of creating war is our attitude.

YOUR BELIEF DETERMINES YOUR PERCEPTION

Have you ever heard people say they would like world peace, but they feel powerless to cause it? Other people think we need to fight just one or two more wars to set things right before we can have peace. Still others believe we have implacable, unreasonable enemies who are determined to utterly destroy us, so we must defend ourselves. Some people believe they must fight a war for what they want because there is no other way. Or they believe it when leaders promise they are going to secure something, such as freedom or security, through fighting a war. Still other people hold the belief that peace will come someday when a spiritual event happens, so they try to live their lives in accordance with that belief. Others are out there—in their lives and in their communities—doing their utmost to create as much peace as they can.

None of these beliefs is wrong or right. Each comes with plenty of supporting evidence and abundant positive or negative social reinforcement. Most of us have not thoughtfully considered the question of peace and war and have lost our authentic power. We have buried our true expressions under layers of resignation and compromise. We have delegated the job of monitoring peace and war to political leaders, soldiers, saints, diplomats, and social workers, as though peace and war were somehow external to our lives.

The sum total of these beliefs represents the status quo, and it determines our reality. Neuroscientific research into how our beliefs filter our perceptions has shown this conditioning to be powerful. One example of this is the research conducted by Dr. Drew Weston at Emory University, published in *The Political*

Brain (Public Affairs, 2007). He studied the MRI brain scans of John Kerry and George W. Bush supporters who were viewing conflicting statements made by their candidates. Overwhelmingly, a person's brain went into overdrive to suppress cognitive dissonance and bolster preexisting biases rather than to use logic to assess whether their preferred candidate was right or not. Usually it feels good to have our beliefs affirmed, which is why our brains go into overdrive. But that temporary pleasure is at the price of a deep-seated *knowledge of living aligned with what is true for you.*

There are more than twenty-six well-researched and widely accepted cognitive biases. The evidence is conclusive: What we believe, we see, and what we don't want to believe, we don't see. Fortunately, we all have the capacity to see our beliefs, and thereby free our perceptions if we are willing to look.

War is a historical habit of thinking with a physical structure that has become acceptable, and most people need reminding that there are other ways to resolve conflict and deal with our differences. To illustrate, ask yourself what is socially normal and acceptable for you to say about peace and war. What common platitudes do you say and hear? The following are a few examples:

- We will have world peace someday.

- Human nature demands war.

- Big military business will never allow peace.

- Only wisdom is peace.

Now write what is socially normal to say and not say about peace and war among your friends and colleagues _____

_____

_____

Is it socially normal to say meaningless slogans, like "We need to win the war on terror"? Could someone say to you, "We should kill all the Taliban!" or "Nuke Iran"? Could they say, "Peace is inevitable when world consciousness reaches a certain high point" or "World peace would be great, but there is nothing I can do about it" without getting an argument from you? Do you have opinions that you do not express because you might offend your friends, or they might scoff at you? What do you think about the idea of peace? Consider all these questions as you fill out exercises later in the chapter.

The prevailing belief among people and nations that war is an acceptable option needs to be examined, challenged, and transformed in order for dignified constructive conflict to become the new norm. Every generation of humanity has its challenge to solve. This is our pressing problem. We see that *now* is a unique moment in history to create world peace in five years.

IT'S ALL IN THE TIMING

The Fourth Turning (Broadway Books, 1997), by William Strauss and Neil Howe, describes the rhythm of generational change in Anglo-American history since the fifteenth century. Based on observations and studies of historical patterns, they claim that a systemic societal change is possible once every four generations. The four stages they describe are a High, an Awakening, an Unraveling, and a Crisis. According to Strauss and Howe, we are presently in a Crisis and the time for change is upon us. The destruction of the World Trade Center tailed the downturn of the tech boom and marked the beginning of a Crisis. The last Crisis was the Great Depression and World War II. After a Crisis there is a crucial moment for a paradigm shift and a new order of values to emerge. The resolution of a Crisis is a new world order. According to Strauss and Howe's research, a better time will not come along for eighty years or more. What values as the whole of humanity do we want to carry into the future together? What are the rules of the game we want to play by in this new era? What would you like those rules to be?

The Chinese ideogram for crisis is the same as for opportunity. Supported by the assertions of Strauss and Howe, the change in administration that will begin in Washington, D.C., in January 2009 is an ideal time to launch P5Y. Because of the brutality and increasing war crimes and risks seen in recent years, we are ready for a major change. If we do not make it now, there may not be another chance for a century. If we have not achieved world peace by that time, it may already be too late.

Fortunately, peace under the new paradigm of removing the context and legitimacy of war is already happening here in the United States, as stated in the March 29–April 4, 2008, issue of *The Economist*:

America and the rest of mankind will benefit alike from tackling climate change, and from spreading democracy, free markets and a liberal trading system—and the peace upon which such a system depends. A new president needs to make this case anew.[11]

11. "All change: Whether it is Clinton, McCain or Obama, the world will still quarrel with America's foreign policy," *The Economist*, March 29, 2008.

PEACE IS NEARLY UPON US—IT IS INEVITABLE

Obviously, serving our American interests with a view primarily within our borders has still left us vulnerable to war. We could have a far greater impact with a worldwide application of our resources. For example, in the same issue of *The Economist*, a writer pointed out that even though the Bush administration stated earlier that the 82nd Airborne Division should not waste time escorting schoolchildren in Iraq, that same fighting unit was now spending a great deal of time building schools, refurbishing mosques, and doing what the magazine called "armed social work." Most Middle East commanders say they need more farmers, anthropologists, and veterinarians than soldiers. The *International Herald Tribune* reported on April 25, 2008, that even Pakistan's top Taliban leaders urged a ban on acts of "hostility": "The lull follows the election of a new government which has vowed to negotiate with militants who renounce violence . . ."[12] The Pakistani government is in talks with the elders of the Mahsud tribe in South Waziristan. And in May 2008 Lebanese people made handmade signs that read "Don't come back without an agreement!" demanding that their leaders come up with a solution other than civil war. The fact that military leaders understand that peaceful nation-building activities are more important than combat missions clearly indicates that the first stages of world peace in five years are happening already.

Peace is happening—reconciliation, forgiveness, dignified resolution of disputes, trade agreements, peaceful exchange, and economic development. The Truth and Reconciliation Commission created in South Africa to address the crimes of apartheid was a stroke of genius that showed us that "an eye for an eye" isn't the only way. There is actually much more peaceful, dignified conflict resolution than war. Peace is already winning. World peace is actually a tide rising all around us, and we can begin to spread its legitimacy as an alternative to armed conflict if we can just clear our outmoded ideas of war out of the way. The mission of this book is to enlist you to become part of the peace trend. Complete the following exercise, recording your own moments of truth and reconciliation.

12. "Taliban leader urges halt to violence and Pakistan government talks peace with key tribe," *International Herald Tribune*, April 25, 2008, http://www.iht.com/articles/ap/2008/04/25/asia/AS-GEN-Pakistan-Peace-Talks.php.

MY TRUTH AND RECONCILIATION

Write down a time when you forgave someone for something and how it made you feel. Then write down a time when someone forgave you for something and how that made you feel.

I FORGAVE: _____

IT FELT: _____

WHO FORGAVE ME? _____

IT FELT: _____

War and peace happen inside all of us, all the time. Let's look from the inside angle. By feeling the difference between war as a residue of anger and resentment that creates distance between people, and peace as an experience of neutralizing that anger and distance through forgiveness, we can feel the possibility of peace for the whole planet. As you complete the following exercise, contemplate your own feelings of anger, and how you can overcome them with feelings of forgiveness.

FORGIVENESS, THE SEQUEL

Write the name of someone who did something to you that you are still angry about. Can you forgive this person? Why or why not? Either way, write down why.

WHO OFFENDED ME: _____

THE OFFENSE: _____

I: ❏ CAN FORGIVE   ❏ CANNOT FORGIVE

WHY? _____

WE HAVE THE RESOURCES NOW

One common misperception of peace is that while we have put huge resources toward war, we have put very little toward peace. Although peace budget numbers are dwarfed by military budgets, it is worth noting that some portion of military spending is directed toward peacekeeping, such as "armed social work." In

2005, governments spent about $84 billion on foreign aid, and NGOs chipped in a hefty $27 billion. And these aid amounts are growing, especially the NGO portion. Why, the Bill and Melinda Gates Foundation alone spent $3.3 billion in 2007. As we noted in the introduction, these resources, as a whole, are not spent efficiently. Given sufficient leadership and coordination, we can most likely have world peace without putting any additional money toward creating it.

YOUR VISION OF PEACE

You have most likely participated in conversations about and determined your own beliefs about war and peace. By this point in your reading, you should understand society's attitudes toward war and peace, and if you completed the exercises, you should have a better concept of your own attitudes about reconciliation and forgiveness.

Let's use that cleared space to consider the possibility of world peace in five years. Look at some of the times when change has occurred even though change was thought impossible: the rule of law under the Magna Carta, the Reformation, the American Revolution, the founding of a Turkish state amid the chaos of the Ottoman Empire's collapse, the creation of personal computers, the elimination of smallpox, Indian independence from the British, landing on the Moon. What is never attempted is impossible, and impossible frequently translates to "It has never been attempted!"

The people responsible for those tectonic shifts in human events—Martin Luther, Thomas Jefferson, Mustafa Kemal Atatürk, and Mahatma Gandhi, among others—held on to their visions of what was possible before it was real. These people are the public faces of our vision for world peace. In order to create world peace in five years, we need millions of people to act on that vision.

Try the next exercise. Even if you are not committed to world peace in five years, close your eyes and imagine the world as peaceful. What does it look like? What is possible for you? For your family or community? For the organization you work for? For causes that you believe in? For your country? Here is an example from Nathan:

> In a world without organized armed conflict, I am now free to travel to areas that were once closed to me. My four children can enjoy a new political environment in a world that is safer, more joyful, and more prosperous,

with greater resources for tackling many other pressing problems, such as environmental issues, disease, poverty, and education. My community can now enjoy greater prosperity, more open borders, freer exchange of ideas, and a more global outlook. My country, America, has fulfilled its promise to "create a politics that makes all previous politics of the earth insignificant" (in the words of Walt Whitman). The world enjoys an international culture and system of dignified conflict resolution, fewer resources devoted to the military, more universal human rights, and greater opportunity for every human being.

Now it's your turn. Write what is possible for you when the world is without political armed conflict.

YOUR PEACE VISION

Write out what a peaceful world will mean to you, your life, the people you care about, and your community.

_____

_____

_____

_____

Now that you have articulated your vision, write about what the world will need to do and stop doing to make your vision happen. Be as specific as possible about who and when and what. For example, do the countries of the West have to find a way to cooperate with Iran to help that nation build a civilian nuclear power program without contributing to the world's nuclear weapons arsenal? Does the United States need to create a civilian award, with the same prestige as medals awarded to military heroes, to be given to the greatest heroes for peace? Will the United Nations need to launch a program in which each member nation will donate just 1 percent of its military budget to a pool that will fund programs to build schools, promote sustainable farming, and teach nonviolent conflict resolution?

WORLD CHANGES FOR PEACE

THINGS THAT PEOPLE (WHETHER A LOT OF PEOPLE OR A FEW) MUST DO TO CREATE WORLD PEACE:

_____

_____

_____

THINGS PEOPLE THROUGHOUT THE WORLD NEED TO STOP DOING:

_____

_____

As we continue to refine our vision for world peace and what the world needs to do to realize that vision, it is comforting to know that many other people are joining with us in the movement.

WE'RE RICHER, MORE CONNECTED, AND MORE COMMITTED

The number of wealthy people in the world has increased hugely in the past twenty years. If you live in the United States and have more than $2,000 in your bank account, you are in the top percentage of wealthy people in the world. According to the World Wealth Report 2007, there are 9.5 million millionaires in the world controlling total assets of $37.2 trillion. These people are global, frequently progressive, and politically aware. Many of them want to move beyond simply enjoying their wealth; they want to improve the lot of humanity. These people represent smart, fast-moving, innovative resources that can jump-start peace in five years. Think of Bill Gates launching his assault on AIDS in Africa, or Bill Clinton's foundation and his MyCommitment.org organization. When Hurricane Katrina hit New Orleans, the highest amount of contributions did not come from the Red Cross or the government, but from ordinary citizens. More than ever, concerned and connected people are getting involved in the fate of our global civilization.

Cynics most often claim that corporations will never sign on to peace. But most corporations have every incentive to create constructive conflict. Business is better in peacetime. Resources and labor are cheaper. Sure, some companies make products that are needed for war, but there is no reason those same companies couldn't turn their efforts to peaceful ends, at a profit. Corporations have been rapidly developing ways to make their organizations more relevant to the higher ideals of humanity. Five years ago, when the documentary *Wal-Mart: The High Cost of Low Price* came out, the company's move to spend $500 million a year to go green looked impossible. Now, however, the world's largest retailer "has unveiled an environmental plan to boost energy efficiency, cut down on waste and reduce greenhouse gases tied to global warming as part of a wider effort to address issues where it has been pummeled by critics."[13]

We have every reason to believe that corporations will lend their marketing muscle, their expertise, their products, and their good will to our efforts to create peace in five years.

In addition to individuals and corporations, nations are ready to create peace in five years. As the economies of the world become more interconnected, nations increasingly find it is in their best interests to find constructive solutions to international problems.

To summarize, peace in five years is possible because of the following reasons:

- Peace is constructive conflict and offers safety, and everyone in the world wants safety.
- Peace is part of human nature, just as waging war is not necessarily part of human nature.
- Our attitude toward peace and war determines how we perceive reality.
- The timing is right for world peace.
- Peace is already happening all around us.
- Reconciliation and forgiveness feel wonderful, both personally and politically.
- We all have a vision for peace and how to achieve it.
- People around the world are ready to commit to new constructive conflict practices.

Can you and we create world peace in five years? In a word, yes.

13. MSNBC News Services, October 25, 2005.

WHAT DOES PEACE IN FIVE YEARS MEAN?

The more we sweat in peace the less we bleed in war.

—Vijaya Lakshmi Pandit

WHAT IS WORLD PEACE anyway? The clearer your understanding, the more powerful you can be. The phrase "world peace," as it has rung through centuries of political and religious speech, has several different meanings. The Romans considered it their destiny to bring peace to the world under the Pax Romana, and dozens of continent-spanning empires since then have created a kind of conquered peace within their borders. The ancient Egyptians had relative peace inside their empire for five thousand years. Hundreds of wars have been fought, ironically, with the idea of pacifying, or making peaceful, a region or people. A more accurate word would be "oppressing." Oppressive peace imposes upon a population a condition that is not their choice, and does nothing to teach conflict resolution or address any underlying feuds, hatreds, or rivalries. In such wars there are no winners, just victims and occupiers. As Jeannette Rankin, the first female member of the U.S. Congress said, "You can no more win a war than you can win an earthquake."

In contrast to the definition of oppressive peace, we define world peace as constructive conflict and the safety to improve the world and all of its wonders. The world is full of organizations working to create world safety: Doctors Without Borders, the Peace Corps, Christian missions; even U.S. military units in Afghanistan have worked for world peace by building schools and undertaking other socially beneficial projects. Now we are expanding the borders of world peace to include all nations and lands of the earth.

ASSUMPTIONS ABOUT PEACE

Write down your immediate thoughts about peace, especially all the clichés you hear or say.

1. _____

2. _____

3. _____

4. _____

5. _____

6. _____

HOW TO IMPROVE THE DISCUSSION OF WORLD PEACE

We all have ideas about peace, based on where we grew up, our education, our conversations, and our friends and acquaintances. Based on what you know after reading thus far, what do you think of the assumptions about peace you wrote? Do they seem simplistic to you? Now, ask yourself how you came by those ideas? Were they planted by your parents? Did you pick them up from the media? Are they the products of your own careful analysis and consideration? This step is essential because peace in five years requires independent thinkers who are willing to question how things have always been done.

One of our goals with P5Y is to make your discussions of peace and war (and the world's) more mature. We want to take the war conversation from its current toddler level, where the exchange is mostly about primitive emotion and who can be tougher than whom (the "my dad can beat up your dad" school of geopolitics), to a more adult level, where we can shed the emotional and the political baggage we associate with war and peace and see them for what they truly are: cultural agreements that can be changed. The reason we want the conversation to mature is that by staying at the toddler or even the adolescent level of conversation, so many people are hurt.

We have found in our symposia and conversations around the world that peace and war bring up deep personal issues for most people, including us. You may find, as we do, that as you honestly look at your own ideas and feelings, you become upset, fearful, emotional, or defensive. This is a good sign—although it may not feel good—that you are successfully reaching a point where you can honestly update your ideas of peace and war. What is available for you is a new sense of integration and power to affect peace and war in alignment with your values.

A friend witnessed an example of this mature type of approach at a rally held in a small California beach town to protest the Iraq war, which was then in the planning stages. As participants gathered, an older man in an Air Force cap approached and asked tentatively, "Can veterans help out?" He obviously assumed that the "peaceniks" would reject him as part of the war machine, but no such thing happened. The leader of the group smiled and said, "Of course. Peace is for everyone." That was an adult view.

Understand, world peace is not an end to conflict. We will still argue and disagree and sometimes threaten and fight on an individual level. People will still have needs. When those needs are not met, tempers can still get hot and worries can escalate. With war off the menu of options, however, we will choose negotiation, economic penalties, public opinion, appeal to common interests, adding resources from the rest of the world, or mutual understanding and cooperation to resolve the underlying issue. Wars have recently been prevented in Macedonia and Kenya through application of these peace safety measures.

In Kenya, all-out war was about to break out in 2008 over a disputed election. In this nation of 32 million, more than 1,000 people were killed and 300,000 made homeless in the civil unrest following the election. However, war did not happen, to the amazement of pessimistic international onlookers. *The Economist* reported on March 13, 2008: "Although outside pressure helped, it was Kenyans themselves who forced the deal. Television pictures of young men brandishing machetes should be set against the dovish work of many other Kenyans. Leaders in business, the media, law and religion all worked hard for reconciliation."[14] This is an example of peace safety at work: Although there was a severe violation of peace safety in the form of a blatantly unfair election, unrest did not turn into war because both outside forces and internal ones organized effectively to prevent it.

People have already begun a more mature dialogue about war and peace. Once more people join in, we will be able to address a variety of issues with increasing clarity and effect. Take the war on terror, for example. The accelerating pace of change and ever-more-powerful and far-reaching global technologies have provided individuals with tremendous creative and destructive power. Nuclear technology, biotech, nanotech, computers, and networks each hold the potential for marvelous benefits or appalling destruction. Today, a small team of determined people organized for violence can cause global mayhem—halting air travel, wrecking financial markets, and killing large numbers of people. Considering the immediate threats, we can see that the war on terror has not gone *nearly* far enough for safety. We have not yet begun to address the root causes of terrorism. Until we accept the new realities about what creates safety, and how that relates to war and peace, our efforts to combat terrorism will be inefficient and counterproductive, and the human race will be more vulnerable than ever to the terrorist threat.

If we cling to the old model, each nation will act in its own interest. Angry rhetoric and military posturing could lead to war between resource-rich and resource-poor countries. Imagine water wars in which powerful, growing countries like China and India attack their water-rich but impoverished neighbors. Clearly, new challenges demand a new philosophy toward resolving our differences, a philosophy based on constructive conflict. Things could get much worse between now and 2014. As a race, we need to declare war on war by peaceful means before circumstances overtake us.

YOU CAN BE EFFECTIVE IN A NEW KIND OF ORGANIZATION

To create a new approach to dealing with war and peace, we have developed a new kind of organization, one that generates the energy we need to grow as we

14. "A new dawn amid the golf carts," *The Economist,* March 13, 2008.

progress toward our goal. As we mentioned earlier, we started this organization when we made our pledge to give peace a deadline. We created a nonprofit, Peace in Five Years (P5Y), to develop this campaign. As we have been writing this book, people have joined our group, taking the pledge and devoting substantial amounts of time to achieving our goal. (We will describe our strategy and what P5Y offers in more detail in the next chapter.)

One new aspect of P5Y is how it depends almost entirely on collaboration. P5Y borrows from the model of open source software development and also from the W. L. Gore & Associates model of small, accountable teams to rapidly and effectively stitch together a global effort to create peace in five years. The overall strategy of the structure is clearly delineated and communicated, but the precise resources and means of accomplishment are left to teams and individuals who make themselves accountable to each other and other teams. Resources of commitment and money are allocated nimbly and fluidly to the most effective solutions, all coordinated inside effective strategies. All of this is accomplished through the development of peace software, which delivers the precise information to the people who need it, when they need it, and communicates what needs to be done.

As the effort gains momentum, the small teams and leaders are networked to maximize their efficiency and to attract resources from the rest of the network. Results, both successes and failures, are reported promptly and transparently through the system, giving anyone a view of the "peace dashboard" to see how we are doing overall, and how each area, both geographical and functional, is doing according to precise metrics.

P5Y is

- an invitation to the family of nations to solve our conflicts nonviolently;
- a plan for collaboration to solve the seventeen current armed conflicts worldwide;
- a system of interaction supported by software that makes peace user-friendly;
- a pivotal historical moment;
- an invitation to heads of state, businesses, nongovernmental organizations (NGOs), and individuals to collaborate and create peaceful solutions by 2014;
- an achievable and measurable goal with a deadline;

- the renaissance of dignified conflict resolution; and
- the ticket to the future for humanity.

P5Y is by no means the first organization to work for peace, but we believe that our effort will be substantially more successful than previous efforts to promote peace because we are adding two essential elements: collaboration and ease of use of peacemaking processes.

WHY OTHER EFFORTS HAVEN'T WORKED

Many other organizations and campaigns have worked tirelessly and passionately to bring about peace. If P5Y succeeds, it will only be because of these people and organizations. However, whatever such movements have achieved, they have all fallen short so far in the most critical mission of all: ending war itself worldwide. Why have so many smart, hardworking, passionate people spent so much time and money trying to end war only to find themselves frustrated? We think we know some answers.

Overseas, insular "technical advisers" and lack of respect for local conditions and leaders have been consistent features in the efforts of many governments and NGOs in creating peace, even when those efforts are well intentioned, which nearly all of them are. A staff member of Oxfam, a large British NGO, was quoted in the article "The Future of Aid: A Scramble in Africa" (*The Economist*, September 6, 2008) as saying that in Mozambique alone, donors are spending a staggering $350 million per year on 3,500 technical consultants, money enough to hire 400,000 local civil servants. That's how many people work in manufacturing in the entire state of Florida.

Adherence to failed policies, failed ideas, and murky budgets, combined with ignorance of local conditions, power structures, and cultural responses, have been very expensive in terms of lost opportunity and human suffering. Many foreign-aid programs are designed to benefit narrow national or corporate interests and fail to produce positive results on the ground. Often projects are either underfunded or overfunded, both of which result in inefficiency. Fortunately, these problems have been identified and are being addressed. In fact, incremental improvements have been seen already: The share of aid budgets worldwide that are recorded accurately has risen from 42 percent in 2005 to 48 percent in 2007—which means that 52 percent of aid budgets are still opaque. Additionally, the proportion of notoriously inefficient tied aid (that is, foreign aid that donor governments require to be spent in the originating country) decreased from 57 percent in 2002 to 47 percent in 2006.

Our approach includes systematically inviting collaboration inside national plans and a workable system of accountability to increase the effectiveness of organizations in creating peace. We also invite alignment with stated goals and objectives of foreign aid.

Here at home, most antiwar groups have focused on acts of protest to convince governments to stop actions related to war. Their tactics have included a huge range of actions, including marches, protests, boycotts, letter and email campaigns, concerts and festivals, making documentaries, and civil disobedience.

Don't get us wrong: Most every effort made on behalf of peace is laudable. P5Y is possible only because we can stand on the backs of those who have worked for peace before us, like the International Peace Bureau, the United Nations Peacekeeping Forces, the Fellowship of Reconciliation, PAX Christi, Peace Corps, Peace Now, Witness for Peace, International Crisis Group, Code Pink, Veterans For Peace, A.N.S.W.E.R., Nuclear Age Peace Foundation, the Gandhi Foundation, (RED), American Friends Service Committee, the Council for a Parliament of the World's Religions, and the Peace Alliance. Amnesty International has been reporting violations of peace safety since 1961.

Our approach is different because we are not protesting individual conflict areas; we are seeking a change in attitude toward war in general. This is why public protest had something to do with ending the Vietnam War, but it did nothing to prevent the United States from invading Iraq. If we can't take action that permanently brings an end to large-scale, government-backed conflict, where's the good in temporary victories?

P5Y takes a different approach. We believe that what was previously accepted as the legitimate basis of war is no longer so broadly accepted. As we have discussed previously, modern war has never been a successful way to create peace and security. We have lost our reasons for war, and we, as peacemakers, are now at a point where we can bring an end to all wars, not just one particular conflict. In our view it is *easier* to end all war by removing the legitimate context of war from the planet than it is to end or permanently solve any particular conflict.

We must undermine war at its source: the minds of individual men and women for whom war is acceptable. If enough people take the attitude that war is never an option, then only rogue or terrorist groups will go to war. Without the legitimacy of nations to shield them, these groups will be stamped out quickly, and peace practices applied on every level will ensure that they cannot gain traction again.

What is the political action you could take to delegitimize war? Although marches, protests, civil disobedience, and the like have been effective in the past, today we have the Internet, distributed media, and blogs. While past political actions have been aimed at ending particular wars, today our efforts must be aimed at ending all war. People working for the abolition of slavery did not consider that their job was done when slavery was outlawed in England, or in the northern states in America. Our work for peace is not done until we have abolished war worldwide.

Effective action means we support the adoption of the Global Peace Treaty (more about that in chapter 4), soon to be presented to the family of nations. On a national level, we must inform and support our representatives who take a global view and who can actually protect our safety through effectively preventing war. On a local level, we must encourage candidates for city councils, school boards, and judgeships in cities large and small to talk publicly about peace as safety and include peace as part of their platforms.

THE PEACE DIVIDEND

World peace brings with it enormous benefits. With the context of war removed from our planet, the most obvious benefit is that hundreds of billions of dollars and incredible amounts of human and industrial power will be freed to address the many other problems facing our world. Beyond the obvious, the freedom of thought that will result will open the door to quantum leaps in science, the humanities, and human rights. What will be possible in travel, art, and entertainment? In government, education, and the environment? What benefits would come to you and your community?

PERMISSION FOR PEACE

Once you understand the benefits of peace, you can begin to realize what we are missing in a world that permits war. The present world, including you and us, gives its permission for war, just as it once gave its permission for burning witches at the stake. Many factors that we have inherited contribute to the present context: underlying assumptions about the role of nations and foreign

---

THE BENEFITS OF PEACE

List five benefits that peace will bring to you and your community. Which benefit means the most to you?

1. _____

2. _____

3. _____

4. _____

5. _____

---

policy; resignation; international laziness about upholding concepts of war; outdated ideas of security and safety, national sovereignty, and human rights that developed in the eighteenth and nineteenth centuries.

The reason that deadly organized conflict will end is not because some people become more like others, or that an epidemic of niceness breaks out. It will end when the context for war is removed from the planet and replaced with the practice of peace as safety, so that would-be warmongers will have no arena in which to play out their wars.

By launching our P5Y campaign, we declare that the time has come for the world to give permission for peace instead of permission for war. To realize peace, we must act on a step-by-step global plan to consciously change our culture. This is no different from a corporation or a nation consciously changing its culture, which has happened many times—British Petroleum, and Turkey and China are some examples. The only differences are the scale and the stakes. Humans are acutely sensitive to their environment: Some environments allow us to relax, while others encourage us to work hard and stay focused. Remember the broken windows approach to crime prevention in New York City? We are encouraging everyone to treat war in a similar manner. Think of it as the broken nations approach.

It is up to all of us who naturally feel a personal responsibility for world peace to change our environment and create one in which deadly organized conflict is not legitimate for any reason. The predictable signs of war will be monitored and effective preventive action taken. When we do not give permission for war, we permit peace and allow for many positive alternatives and incentives for dignified conflict resolution.

World peace *is* understandable, achievable, manageable.

NOW IS THE TIME

Let us repeat that *now* is the time to create world peace in five years. Why? Because we are so much closer than we realize. There is more global understanding of the causes and solutions of conflict. There is more global cooperation and many more resources available to us than ever before. It only needs to be organized. P5Y is about collecting and focusing the resources we already have. Very little needs to be researched—but a great deal needs to be organized, directed, measured, and communicated.

The United States holds a special promise for world peace. Without this nation, it won't happen. The American people need to be squarely focused on creating world peace in five years, and the American government needs to be actively cooperating with the efforts of the American people. The United States is ready to make a huge contribution to the world. With the change of administration in 2009, the country is poised to ride a wave of hope and lead the world to peace. And P5Y is positioned to help America give peace a deadline. You can be a part of this contribution.

PART II

OUR SOLUTION

THE OVERALL STRATEGY

Strategy without tactics is the slowest route to victory.
Tactics without strategy is the noise before defeat.

—Sun Tzu

IN THIS CHAPTER, you will see the cutting-edge thinking that gives you the perspective of how to treat attaining world peace in a businesslike way. This is critically important because it is how you and we are going to save ourselves, our planet, and humanity's future. If you want to make this chapter ten times more interesting and relevant to your life, take the pledge in chapter 15 before reading it.

The heavy metal group Megadeth performs a song called "Peace Sells" from the album *Peace Sells . . . But Who's Buying?* Lead singer Dave Mustaine wails, "If there's a new way/I'll be the first in line/But it better work this time." P5Y is a new way. If you've been wondering "how?" this chapter will answer that for you.

You will also begin to see how you fit in. While you are reading, notice ways in which you can forward the plan. Then you will be able to help others—organizations, family, friends, and community groups—see how their contribution fits within the plan. The excitement of P5Y is something interesting to bring to your network.

WHY FIVE YEARS IS THE RIGHT AMOUNT OF TIME

Though five years may seem like a relatively short time in which to create peace, we are galvanizing peace efforts that have been going on for hundreds of years. George Fox, who founded the Quakers around 1647, believed that the teachings of Jesus Christ prohibited war. He declared that neither he nor any Quaker would take up arms for any reason. The abolitionist movement started in the 1700s and didn't succeed until a strong push from the Quakers in the 1800s. It was three years after Abraham Lincoln gave the first executive order of the Emancipation Proclamation that approximately 4 million African-Americans were freed.[15]

The New York Peace Society was first founded in 1815. Alfred Nobel established the Nobel Peace Prize upon his death in 1896. His will designated the prize should be awarded "to the person who shall have done the most or the best work for fraternity between nations, for the abolition or reduction of standing armies and for the holding and promotion of peace congresses."[16] The current trends toward political peace indicate it is going to happen one way or another. P5Y is the exciting result of years of work. We chose five years as the deadline for this great accomplishment because most people can plan realistically for five years, and they also tend to underestimate what they can achieve within that time. Five years is inspiring because we get to see it in our lifetime.

As we look at what is required for this final push to peace, our approach is straightforward: With the overall outcome firmly in mind, divide the goal into smaller milestones. For a goal to be practical, it must be defined in time and space and be measurable. The space is our little planet. The time is the five-year period from February 14, 2009, to February 14, 2014. Our measurable goal is world peace, which we define as world safety from war, or "a worldwide cessation of politically organized deadly conflict."

Long-term goals are achieved with a plan, strategy, tactics, and resources. By definition, a *goal* is not a present condition or circumstance but an intended future condition. A *plan* is a series of connected lesser goals and actions that are intended to produce a result by a specific time or deadline. *Strategy* is what we intend to do, and *tactics* are how we intend to do it using our resources. *Resources* are the people, money, ideas, means, and leverage we have to achieve our goals.

15. www.sonofthesouth.net/slavery/slave-maps/slave-census.htm.
16. http://en.wikipedia.org/wiki/Nobel_peace_prize. "Excerpt from the Will of Alfred Nobel," Nobel Foundation. Accessed March 31, 2008.

We derive the P5Y principles and strategy from our conclusions. Some of the conclusions are counter to the clichés of peace. Knowing these helps you speak powerfully about peace. Fortunately, we get to share the benefit of our knowing many people with intelligence and experience who have gathered information and spoken with us or written books about numerous topics related to creating world peace: nation-building, negotiation, peace making, neuroscience, social networking, international relations, business, marketing, media, personal development, activism, philanthropy, history, war, philosophy, human development, anthropology, and more. The result of our inventory is a set of assumptions—what we believe to be true—that we use to make our plan.

The following is a list of conclusions that drive our strategy (elsewhere in the book these conclusions are described in more detail):

- Technology enables new threats, which can be deployed anonymously by small groups across borders. Safety is no longer found in barriers, borders, or deterrence.

- Technology also enables whole new forms of efficient, enjoyable collaboration, cooperation, information, and interaction.

- Human behavior is highly contextual, learned, and flexible. We are capable of maintaining a planet without war. Humans are not "killer apes."

- Proven effective and reasonably efficient techniques, solutions, and models already exist to create world peace.

- We are in a crisis, an "open moment" in history, during which the rules can be updated.

- Trends are moving strongly toward global cooperation, constructive conflict, and prosperity.

- Present resources devoted toward peace and other humanitarian issues are numerous and increasing. If adequately coordinated, these resources are sufficient to create world peace. Present efforts are generally uncoordinated and sometimes wasteful and counterproductive.

- Failed states, defined as populated areas in which governments do not or cannot supply goods and services to meet basic needs of their citizens, are one of the key causes of war. Injustice, corruption, failed infrastructure, insecurity, dysfunctional markets, humiliation, discrimination, oppression, and incitement are violations of peace safety.

- "World peace" as a concept is presently positioned as vague, impossible, idealistic, leftist, hippieish, trite, and hopeless.

The strategy is not dependent on all of these conclusions, but it is designed to take advantage of them.

STRATEGIC OVERVIEW OF "THIS WAY TO PEACE"

Four strategic principles:

1. Make peace user-friendly
2. Reposition world peace
3. Invite and include everyone
4. Increase collaboration

Six tactical modules:

1. Global Peace Treaty
2. Standards for peace safety
3. National plans for peace
4. Implementation tools
5. Grassroots action
6. Media services

Six procedural steps for implementation:
Inspire➜ Discover➜ Commit➜ Collaborate➜ Measure➜ Communicate

Strategic diagram:

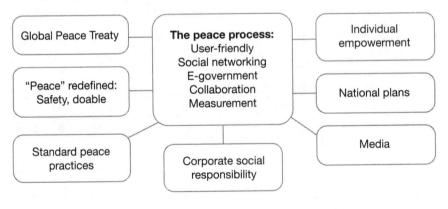

THIS WAY TO PEACE: FOUR PRINCIPLES

When you absorb these principles you will gain a compass for what creates world peace. Any plan related to P5Y will be inside of these four objectives. By understanding the principles, you can create a plan for peace that pulls in the same direction. If you are already working for peace, you can apply these in order to be more effective. The four principles are:

1. Make peace user-friendly: For any nation, organization, or individual, make peace easy to understand, use, and contribute to. Think about what you can do to create world peace for any individual or organization.

2. Reposition world peace: Make it mainstream, fun, participatory, understandable, and achievable. Invite every resource into creating world peace, including the military, corporations, politicians, and individuals. Rescue world peace from vagueness—define peace as an active practice of safety.

3. Invite and include everyone: Generate intense interest and participation in causing world peace from a broad array of people and organizations.

4. Increase collaboration: Provide coordination, planning, tools, incentives, and resources to make collaboration easy, effective, and inviting.

SIX TACTICAL MODULES IMPLEMENT THE PRINCIPLES

You need to know these tactical modules because they give form to the four strategic principles and represent areas of collaboration in which you can contribute. You can see how these components reinforce each other to implement the four strategic principles.

1. **Global Peace Treaty:** P5Y has begun a worldwide campaign for a Global Peace Treaty (GPT), which is the political anchor for creating peace in five years. Any activities you undertake that lead to support and adoption of the GPT move us all toward our goal.

   The GPT repositions peace among the family of nations; provides a practical and user-friendly mechanism for the global practice of world peace; provides an invitation, framework, and infrastructure for collaboration; and provides an exciting political focal point for P5Y as a rallying point for grassroots activism.

The GPT is similar to the World Trade Organization in that the treaty provides a set of ground rules for international practices of peace safety and agreements on what participating nations must do when violations occur in the world, such as incipient civil wars, incipient genocide, severe oppression, incitement, and so on. The GPT is a set of rules and processes, not a static declaration.

P5Y will be responsible for drafting the treaty and getting the campaign under way. A key resource we are seeking is partners, such as foundations, to lead the campaign, and experts and dignitaries to endorse it.

2. **Standards for peace safety:** These standards define peace as an effective action you can take. They move peace from "passive" to "active." This is about repositioning world peace and precisely defining and clarifying what the practices of peace are.

The standards are in the form of a manual developed by experts that describes in detail the practice of peace safety at various levels, from individuals through governments. The manual sets the standards, principles, and guidelines for the GPT, for the peace plans, and for NGOs and agencies operating within the peace plans. Standards for peace safety act as a guide for journalists to hold governments and corporations accountable for peace safety, and to highlight violations of peace safety. The manual also outlines principles of nonviolent conflict resolution and ways that peace safety can be introduced in education.

3. **National plans for peace:** The national plans address the need for coordinated collaboration. National plans are blueprints for building safety in each chaotic area. The plans let you plug into and contribute effectively to a particular area of conflict in measurable ways.

National plans for peace make peace user-friendly for you because the plans are dynamic tools of decision making, collaboration, information gathering, and reporting—not static documents. Peace plans increase collaboration by providing a framework to understand and prioritize projects in a national context, and to help the leadership of peace plan countries quickly make decisions and recommend collaborations.

P5Y will help develop specific prioritized plans with milestones for each war zone and potential conflict area. These plans will be published and integrated into the operation of the P5Y website that will invite collaboration from NGOs, agencies, local leaders and governments, as well as donations and volunteers.

Nascent governments or governing bodies of these areas can use the plans to make decisions about which aid projects to encourage and allow, and which to forbid or retool. The goal of the plans is to create functioning states in order to ensure the practice of peace safety in these areas.

4. **Implementation tools:** P5Y will create a series of user-friendly processes to implement the national plans for peace, taking into account each type of user: individual, NGO, agency, local municipality or department, foreign government, and so on. These tools are under development as of this writing and will continue to appear on P5Y.org. The system will provide ongoing tools for measuring progress, reporting problems, and requesting commitments, resources, collaboration, and best practices. Implementation tools integrate a peace plan globally, giving you and all interested parties access and opportunities to contribute and create world peace.

5. **Grassroots action:** This invites and provides a way for massive streamlined collaboration and helps you develop personally from your interaction with P5Y, through aligning your life with peace and other tools. It is the primary tool for recruiting people as a resource (see the resources section on pages 62–65) and making that resource effective through timely, appropriate, and effective information and interaction. Grassroots action is the way that NGOs operating within the peace plans connect to resources.

   Anyone can register for individual grassroots action on the P5Y website, which runs in multiple languages. Once registered, you can learn how to contribute: directly—by volunteering a commitment; monetarily—to NGOs or P5Y; and politically—to help with adoption of the GPT or policy changes that help world peace. Website members can also see a wide variety of reported measurements related to their commitments and to the overall progress of peace in five years.

   Grassroots action touches on all four principles from the point of view of an individual. The existence of the P5Y website and its functions reposition peace as specific and doable.

6. **Media services:** Media is the primary engine for generating mass participation through awareness. If you want to make a global announcement, you have got to do it through media. With regard to the strategic principles, media services is about repositioning peace and inviting participation through awareness and repetition of message.

The following are the main components of media services:

- Corporate sponsorship of P5Y safety principles; integration of P5Y into consumer-marketing campaigns—similar to the (RED) campaign created by Bono of the rock group U2
- P5Y website with member features and benefits
- Coordinated marketing and public relations campaign for P5Y, including ongoing press releases of progress and invitations to participate
- Consulting for corporations on creating a corporate social responsibility (CSR) program that integrates with P5Y to take advantage of the branding power and consumer recognition
- DharmaMix integration, with free DharmaMix peace exercises
- Creation of documentaries
- An ongoing TV show

Each tactical module is designed to attract and reinforce resources into the service of world peace by making participation simple, clear, and advantageous for all parties.

RESOURCES AT YOUR DISPOSAL

Let's look at what resources are available to you and what might align those resources with our effective global plan for peace. As you read this list, consider how you might apply these resources to create world peace.

People of the world: The people of the world are a resource for creative solutions, hard work, volunteers, money, and putting political pressure on their home governments. People in war zones are especially motivated to increase their prosperity and security, to make the transition from survival to something better for their children; while people in relatively peaceful zones want to maintain their safety. The following will align you and other people with P5Y: understanding that violations of peace safety are global, not local; knowing what is available on the other side of world peace; and knowing about a credible plan and a way to participate. Anyone who takes the pledge will be a valuable resource. People, including you, are the ones who will keep going, make adjustments, learn, adapt, and ultimately succeed.

Foreign aid agencies: These agencies provide an opportunity to effectively channel vast resources into world peace. Although there are some notable foreign aid successes, such as the Marshall Plan that helped Europeans rebuild after World War II, a more common story is one of lost opportunity. The present opportunity in foreign aid is for the countries of the world to unify and coordinate their efforts under the Global Peace Treaty, and for the NGOs that receive foreign aid grants to collaborate effectively.

NGOs: These organizations are numerous and important because they are on the ground in chaotic areas, they have expertise and experience, they are organized globally, and most of them have missions related to peace. Many NGOs make important contributions, but they are constrained by narrow missions, budget cycles, or project proliferation without coordination. Often, large NGOs receive block grants from donor governments and become subject to some of the same constraints that taint foreign aid. Most NGOs do not have a long-term planning process or budget transparency. The opportunity with P5Y is for NGOs to plug into national development plans and collaborate with other NGOs and agencies to be more effective and have a lasting impact relative to their missions. There is a two-way opportunity for P5Y supporters and NGOs to plug into national development plans and collaborate with still other NGOs and agencies to be more effective and have a lasting impact relative to their missions. For instance, according to "The Future of Aid: A Scramble in Africa" (*The Economist*, September 6, 2008), the number of aid projects has ballooned from 10,000 to 80,000 in the past ten years.

Corporations: These well-organized, results-oriented, efficient, and global organizations are a leverage point for exponential impact. Economic development is key to lasting peace, and this is most often provided by private enterprise, including multinational corporations. (See chapter 10 for additional material on corporations.) Corporations that align with P5Y not only will enjoy the generally improved business climate of a peaceful world but also will gain specific CSR benefits. Once an effective invitation is made to corporations, they become, like media, a fast way to get information out to large numbers of people.

Media: A key resource, media are more available to you than at any other time in history. Even a little media goes a long way. Your access includes news media, popular talk shows, bloggers, social networks, services like Twitter and mass texting, and, of course, the Internet. P5Y is a rich source of stories, content, commentary, and authentic news.

Experts: Peacemakers, academics, think tanks, business experts, logistical and infrastructure experts, political experts—we need many kinds of expertise to achieve world peace in five years. Experts love to contribute their expertise to relevant causes, and they can be your best friends in creating peace.

Civic organizations: You can inspire civic organizations like the Elks, YPO, Rotary, and many others that are an important force in the world. These groups already have international infrastructure and experience in implementing global projects. The mission of these organizations is to contribute to humanity in some way. Whatever their humanitarian mission, it is most likely aligned with creating world peace and can benefit from collaboration with P5Y.

Religious groups: You already know that peace is at the heart of every major religion. Religious groups of all kinds are already involved, and are often quite effective, at improving communities around the world through meeting needs and education. By being aware of and aligning themselves with P5Y-sponsored national development plans, these groups can improve the effectiveness and long-term impact of what they are already doing.

Foundations: You can collaborate with such foundations as Carnegie, Ford, Hewlett, Gates, Templeton—of which there are thousands. They can support P5Y in many ways: financially, intellectually, collaboratively, politically. Foundations can also benefit from P5Y because P5Y is aligned with their missions, and it supports their current initiatives.

Universities: Universities can provide key points of validation and legitimacy when they endorse programs related to P5Y. Universities represent a resource for communication, education, and research, as well as expertise. Universities have local connections and programs and physical infrastructure for meetings and communication. P5Y aligns with the interests and mission of the faculty and students. Often, universities have guest speaker programs that can give you a forum for speaking about P5Y in front of groups.

International conferences: The Forum 2000, Davos, TED, and other international conferences are important places for new ideas to take hold and become part of the conversation among global leaders. These gatherings are always looking for the cutting-edge—they want to be the most relevant and trend setting. P5Y is a bold new idea for thought leaders to tackle and for conferences to support if they are to maintain their relevance.

Keep these resources in mind as you work to develop your own unique contribution to world peace in five years.

APPLYING THE STRATEGY

Now that you have an understanding of the strategy, we are going to go into considerable detail about how to apply it. In reflecting on these examples and ideas, you will become familiar with the strategy and begin to make it serve your goals. Within the four principles and the six tactical modules, you—or any individual, organization, country, state, NGO, foundation, or corporation—can apply the following six-step action plan:

Inspire➔Discover➔Commit➔Collaborate➔Measure➔Communicate

1. **Inspire:** Everyone, including you, can give peace a deadline of February 14, 2014. You can help retrieve the concept of peace from its political and cultural stagnation, to promote clarity, collaboration, peace safety practices, and conflict resolution. We can piggyback on corporate marketing communications to make the new message of peace pervasive. We can use public relations, P5Y press conferences, progress reports, real-time website graphic reports, documentaries, and TV shows to promote P5Y. On the personal level, this step incorporates DharmaMixes, personal peace plans, and social networking to invite people into P5Y.

2. **Discover:** Help yourself, organizations, and nations make their unique and valuable contributions. Let everyone in the world know that they have something to contribute to P5Y. Help them discover what that contribution is, how it integrates into the overall effort, and how to make it effectively. Use the P5Y implementation tools online to continue to discover, for yourself or for your organization, how and what to contribute effectively.

3. **Commit:** With inspiration and discovery, you or anyone can make a commitment within the P5Y framework. For nations, the Global Peace Treaty (GPT) is the most actionable peace item to start with. Nations can then commit publicly to the practice of peace and coordinate their actions through the institutions that support the GPT. NGOs commit to lasting positive outcomes through collaboration and coordinated action in each area of chaos and conflict. You and other individuals commit with specific actions, outcomes, and deadlines to the overall effort. P5Y is responsible to make it fun, easy, and rewarding for you and everyone to make and keep commitments.

4. **Collaborate:** Once you have committed, amplify your results with collaboration. Encourage collaboration among agencies, NGOs, local leaders, and citizens by creating a practical, flexible, comprehensive peace safety plan for each area. Provide blueprints and tools for collaboration among nations through the Global Peace Treaty with clear standards and practices of peace safety. Invite individuals to cooperate and collaborate with their commitments through the P5Y website. Enable citizens to coordinate their national Global Peace Treaty campaigns and peace policy initiatives. The heart of collaboration is user-friendly online peace software that creates the Facebook for peace, only more task oriented.

5. **Measure:** As your commitment unfolds, create milestones and set clear metrics. Make field reporting of progress and results as easy and quantitative as possible. Create tools, reports, and web-based dashboards relevant to every kind of peacemaker—national leader, local leader, journalist, individual, project manager. Measure what matters to you, record and aggregate the measurements, and report to the people who are most interested and affected. Create a global report that is updated every week and sent to anyone who subscribes to it. Aggregate similar commitments to inspire collaboration. Highlight areas that are in need and focus resources.

6. **Communicate:** Let people know what you have done and are doing. Facilitate communication of all kinds: among nations, NGOs, local people, individual peacemakers. Make communication as efficient, complete, relevant, and truthful as possible. Use the media as a positive tool for peace

by reporting successes and failures, problems, needs, and overall progress. Communicate stories of peacemaking, principles of peace safety, and the benefits of peace. Enable communication among friends and small groups that results in commitments to peace projects. Provide blueprints, training, and talking points for people to be maximally effective in their communication. Aggregate messages to political leaders for policy change and GPT adoption.

With this action plan in place, we are ready to treat peace as the achievable goal that it is.

OUR ACTION PLAN: DETAILS

Each of the areas in our action plan is crucial to the success of our great adventure. The following discussion of the six steps will help you understand and absorb key elements of our program.

1. Inspire

Our inspiration is to make the distant, vague goal of peace definite and urgent. We all take action when we understand what we can contribute to meet a need we recognize, and we know that the need is urgent and relevant to us.

Inspiration must be tempered with reality and followed with effective action. Peace in five years is a sufficiently audacious goal; in order to stay focused, we ought to be aware of what our focus is *not* going to be. Just as the abolitionists made a wrenching choice in England to focus their finite resources on suppressing the slave trade rather than freeing slaves in pursuit of their ultimate goal, we have chosen in P5Y to focus on putting an end to political violence through repositioning peace and making it easy to apply through collaboration. Although the following objectives are related to world peace, we are not focused on them:

- Eliminate poverty and hunger
- Cure most diseases
- Create global social justice
- Empower all women

- Spread democracy and the rule of law to all corners of the earth
- End violence and crime
- Save the global ecosystem and stave off climate change

Along with an understanding of our focus as an organization, you and the people we inspire benefit from focus as individuals. If we want to be effective, we have to realize what *we do not have time for*. When we personally asked ourselves what we would not have time to do if we focused on fulfilling our pledge to create world peace by February 14, 2014, we came up with the following list:

- Solving all of the world's problems
- Getting permission
- Doing everything perfectly
- Hesitating
- Developing political positions or a platform
- Returning all phone calls (we delegate this when possible)
- Reforming general legislation and institutional processes

We are not giving up on these items, just putting them aside personally while we focus on peace. This is a very personal list. Our focus as individuals and our choice of activities will not be the same as yours. Take a moment to make your own list. What would you not have time for in order to create world peace by 2014?

NONPRIORITIES

List what you do not have time to do or to wait for when you are working to create world peace by 2014. What must you de-prioritize?

1. _____

2. _____

3. _____

4. _____

5. _____

2. Discover Your Greatest Contribution

We are discovering what the world will look like as a peaceful place. Although our plan is solid, there are many details to work out, and no one can know exactly how to create peace in five years. We *do* know that the average person is an untapped resource—and that includes you. Our job is to encourage individuals to ask the question of themselves over and over: How can I create world peace in five years or less? We hope answering this question will help people discover what unique contributions they can bring. People have resources and solutions. Together we can come up with the answers we need.

One important peacekeeping function, articulated by William Ury, is the Provider. The Provider meets people's needs so they don't fight a war out of desperation. One of our friends, Paula Perlis, attended a brainstorming session we held in La Jolla, California, in which we were asking the key question, How do we create world peace in five years or less? Paula, a born Provider, is a genius with food—her business card says "Food Alchemist." She came up with an innovative twist on providing basic nutrition. She has known for years that balanced nutrition reduces violent tendencies, and she collaborates with leading neuroscientists on research in the area of well-being based on nutrition and neurotransmitter balance. Paula has developed food products that are extremely inexpensive, portable, storable, lightweight, and delicious. Eating these products generates optimum well-being and energy. Paula's solution to world peace in five years is the widespread manufacture and distribution of these foods to undernourished populations. She believes that the resulting well-being will increase cooperation and intelligence and reduce aggression and desperation. She is particularly excited about the possibilities for children.

Her assertions are backed up by a study on prisoners in Britain, where significant reductions in aggressive actions were correlated with taking simple nutritional supplements. The following is from the *Psychology Today* article reporting on the study:

> They studied the behavior of 231 inmates . . . Half of the group received daily capsules containing vitamins, minerals and essential fatty acids, while the other half took dummy pills. . . . The supplement group broke prison rules 25 percent less than those on the placebo . . . Instances of fighting, assaulting guards or taking hostages dropped 37 percent.[17]

17. Willow Lawson, "Fighting Crime with Nutrition," *Psychology Today*, Mar/Apr 2003. Article ID: 2759http://psychologytoday.com/articles/pto-20030514-000001.html. Last accessed on August 30, 2004.

In another example of an ordinary citizen discovering an essential approach to world peace, Nathan's nine-year-old son, when asked how to create world peace, said, "Truth. Definitely more truth."

Anyone can make a creative contribution to the P5Y movement toward world peace. Paula is one great example, but we need to discover every kind of peacemaker: teacher, social worker, truck driver, bookie, politician, nurse, lawyer, banker, office drone, military general, road maker, engineer, student, critical people, loud people, people of every religion and every culture. We need individuals, not just governments, stepping up to take responsibility in their specific areas. Every human has the capacity to contribute to our movement. As we write this we are most in need of strategists, peace experts, peace organizations, accountants, lawyers, journalists, tacticians, business leaders, technologists, and philanthropists. Very soon we need heads of state, activists, global communications and marketing experts, etc. Soon after that we need the combined efforts of about one hundred million people willing to commit to measurable actions for peace. Different people will be in a better position to contribute at different points in our process.

3. Commit—and Enjoy

Peace is a goal that benefits you and everyone on the planet, so making it happen should be enlightening, joyous, and exciting. Committing to a goal and making yourself accountable to your fellow peacemakers can be an enriching and fun experience. Our P5Y.org website makes getting involved and making a commitment to peace fun, rewarding, and easy to do.

The following are some of the types of commitments we need:

- A team to write and legitimize the Global Peace Treaty. We need a crack team of international lawyers and UN policy wonks to craft a simple, clear treaty that invites every nation to commit to world peace.
- Governments to ratify the Global Peace Treaty and align their policies with the interests of their people and the world.
- NGOs to create and collaborate on effective national and regional peace plans.
- Individuals to make their unique contributions, add volunteer and financial power to the agencies and NGOs, and to actively support adoption of the Global Peace Treaty.

- A software team to develop the software that will create world peace.
- A standards of peace safety team to write the manual that will guide the GPT and the national plans. Expert peacemakers, UN staff, NGO personnel, and academicians are all needed to generate a high-quality, clear, understandable, well-structured manual.
- Teams for each area to create the national plans. The Israeli-Palestinian plan is of particular urgency.
- Media partners to help reposition peace, market P5Y to the world, and invite and inspire you, us, and everyone.

Connecting with the P5Y community can be an enriching experience for everyone who chooses to. To get an idea of how exciting it is to involve different people in the peace process, complete the following exercise. You will see how powerful the peace network can be.

INFLUENTIAL PEACEMAKERS

Write the names of four influential people you know or know of who would make a huge impact if they were working for world peace in five years.

1. _____

2. _____

3. _____

4. _____

Now, imagine that each person agreed to get involved, and you were assigned to give them one task to do or change to help reach our goal. What would you assign each of them? Make each task very specific and assign a DEADLINE. Be as effective as you can with this resource.

PERSON #1: _____

ASSIGNMENT: _____

PERSON #2: _____

ASSIGNMENT: _____

PERSON #3: _____

ASSIGNMENT: _____

PERSON #4: _____

ASSIGNMENT: _____

How might you invite or inspire your chosen people to commit to your assignments? Would they be inspired by your leadership and creativity?

Now, let's try a similar exercise with a twist.

UNUSUAL PEACEMAKERS

Write the names of four influential people (media stars, politicians) who you believe would NOT work for peace in five years.

1. _____

2. _____

3. _____

4. _____

Imagine each person DID agree to get involved, and you were assigned to give them one thing to do or change to help reach our goal. What would you assign each of them? Make each one very specific and assign a DEADLINE. Use your sense of humor, but don't abuse your power. Be as effective as you can with this resource.

PERSON #1: _____

ASSIGNMENT: _____

PERSON #2: _____

ASSIGNMENT: _____

PERSON #3: _____

ASSIGNMENT: _____

PERSON #4: _____

ASSIGNMENT: _____

Unlikely contributions can be some of the most valuable. From this exercise, we hope you see that everyone, including those whom you do not believe have a contribution to make, can make one if they choose. It is up to all of us to make the invitation.

4. Collaborate

By working to increase collaboration, you push world peace forward, and you are on the cutting edge of the next human leap in evolution. Giving peace a deadline implies that we must work with what we have now. We do not have much time to wait for the completion of laws or treaties (even the Global Peace Treaty) in order to begin accomplishing our milestones. Fortunately, the world has ample resources—technology, know-how, expertise, communication, and money—to apply to this critical problem. Our job is to collaborate with organizations and individuals so that we can focus all of these resources to create peace.

P5Y is responsible for generating the national and global plans for the effective practice of peace safety, both to create peace and to sustain it. Using modern business and technology tools, P5Y will facilitate the integration and coordination that is essential to collaboration. Different organizations believe in various "theories of conflict" that attempt to define the root causes of war. Each of these theories yields a different approach to peacemaking. Our goal is not to find the perfect theory. Academics will still be debating theories long after we have peace in 2014. We will use what business types call an empirical process to measure and identify the approaches that work best without concerning ourselves too much about the underlying theories. However, we do have a few assumptions about the causes of war.

- Each conflict is unique in its particulars.
- Each conflict has key leaders who are important as individuals to the outcome.
- Desperation fuels war.
- Failed states, defined earlier, are fertile ground for wars.
- Objectification of the "other" incites people to fight war.
- War takes place in a global context that permits it.
- Past wrongs, whether real or imagined, fuel war. "Wrongs" are violations of peace safety.
- War is foreseeable, if we keep our eyes open.
- War is preventable, if we implement the practices of peace.

Since we must begin immediately, we don't have time to find the perfect, most effective approach to creating peace. Fortunately a great deal has already been done.

As a starting point, we will use the peacemaking model proposed by William Ury in his book *The Third Side* and website (www.thirdside.org). We describe the model in more detail in chapter 12.

As a basis for our national plans for peace, we use the model proposed in *Fixing Failed States* by Ashraf Ghani and Clare Lockhart. To summarize very briefly, the authors propose that effective state-building is key to world peace, and that the current methods of dealing with failed states—namely, military and humanitarian interventions—"cost billions but do not leave capable states in their wake." They propose a program to establish states capable of entering and benefiting from the global economy and providing a system of government to their citizens to ensure adequate liberty and security. A key component of their program is to create a national plan to build the state and monitor that the various stakeholders, agencies, NGOs, local government units, etc., follow the plan. They propose a collarborative process, not an externally imposed "technical assistance" program. They write about national programs in a way that is highly congruent with P5Y's proposals.

National programs are a glue—of flows of information, rules, money, and decisions—that can combine the spontaneous ingenuity of networks with the hierarchical form of priority setting and resource mobilization to harness and balance energies in relationships of mutual accountability. In national programs, citizens are not inert objects to be acted upon or delivered to but are active agents with capabilities and ideas for collective action.[18]

The model we are using for making peace user-friendly is derived from Nathan's work with his business partner Paul Tarnoff, called Plenable Solutions. In a nutshell, all business processes are viewed as tasks with triggers, information, action, and confirmation. The P5Y website and tactical implementation aims to identify and streamline tasks for all participants. These tasks will be streamlined for national plans, for political action, for individual participation, and anywhere else necessary. Participants would include, among others, developing government leaders, NGOs, individual volunteers, and P5Y management. Examples of tasks include making a commitment, creating a report, or integrating an NGO specialty into a national plan.

The aim of making peace user-friendly and collaborative is to allow maximum ease, flexibility, and communication while streamlining action. Including local leaders and citizens in developmental zones is vital. Making P5Y tools indispensable to national leaders, government agencies, NGOs, and journalists is also important, as well as encouraging use by funneling resources to participating parties.

5. Measure—to Build Trust for Collaboration

You get to see the impact you are making on world peace when you measure your contribution. Certainly if we are businesslike in our approach, we need measurements to mark our progress. But as far as we know, no one has used measurements in a campaign for peace. Currently, the United Nation's millennium goals, which include some measurable targets, don't include an end to politically organized deadly conflict.

One of the most valuable effects you get from measurement is building trust with other peacemakers. When facts are known and agreed upon, your scope for disagreement is narrowed, and your opportunity for collaboration is increased. When countries, NGOs, corporations, and other peacemakers report on their measurable results, trust is built.

18. Ashraf Ghani and Clare Lockhart, *Fixing Failed States: A Framework for Rebuilding a Fractured World* (New York: Oxford University Press, 2008), 202.

As an application of measurement, we have to set milestones. Here are some of our preliminary milestones, which we're always refining and developing.

Resolution of the Israeli/Palestinian Conflict

If you want to have the greatest effect on world peace right now, focus your efforts on resolving this conflict. The conflict between Israel and Palestine is not just between those two countries, nor does it affect just those two countries. This conflict violates the safety of *all* of us, as we witnessed at the collapse of the Twin Towers in New York City and in numerous bombings around the world. Although there have been many peace attempts reported in the news over the years, it appears that a comprehensive approach such as we propose with P5Y has not yet been tried.

A Return to Principled U.S. Foreign Policy

Through the Global Peace Treaty and P5Y collaboration tools, the United States can be guided back to a principled foreign policy that uses principles of peace safety to create real safety and prosperity for Americans and populations in the rest of the world. The United States is special, and it has a special responsibility for world peace. As mentioned elsewhere, the United States' violations of human rights, including secret prisons, waterboarding torture (simulated drowning), the Abu Ghraib prison scandal, Guantánamo, extraordinary rendition (snatching suspects off the street in foreign countries), and domestic spying are all violations of peace safety. These violations create and encourage enemies, and they undermine peaceful processes everywhere.

At present, U.S. foreign policy is all tactics and no strategy, with the result as predicted by Sun Tzu in the quotation at the beginning of this chapter: It is the noise before defeat.

The United States must return to an understandable, principled foreign policy based on the highest ideals of the nation. Ratifying the Global Peace Treaty would be a good start, but policy can change before that. Once the United States understands that the long-term interest of the country is served only by promoting peace, then policy will shift. The administration that will be sworn in January 2009 provides an excellent opportunity to make that shift.

6. Communicate

Your commitment to clear communication is what will create peace in five years. Communication may be considered so fundamental, that when it fails, we have war, and when it succeeds, we do not. Like actor Strother Martin said in the movie *Cool Hand Luke*, it may be said of war, "What we have here is a failure to communicate."

Communication is your tool for generating clarity, commitment, and concrete results. You may feel you have accomplished something for world peace, but until you communicate it to the people who need to know what you have accomplished, and who can use and build on your accomplishment, your task is incomplete.

Communication is the glue that holds the whole plan together. Responsibility of communication lies with the person communicating. If you are communicating something important, then it is your responsibility to verify that your communication was received.

Chapter 10 is devoted entirely to communication and to media.

Now you have a familiarity with the four principles, the six tactical modules, and the six procedural steps to apply the strategic plan. Armed with this understanding, you can initiate potent and inspiring conversations and other actions to create world peace in five years.

INSPIRE: HOW TO MOTIVATE YOURSELF AND OTHERS TO GET INVOLVED

Inspirations never go in for long engagements; they demand immediate marriage to action.

—Brendan Francis

WE TALK ABOUT inspiration because we all need it. Inspiration is the very stuff of life, but while it may seem random, it is not. You can learn how to cultivate your own regular sources of inspiration, and then overflow with optimism in what you say and do. We all know people who inspire us. Are you aware, however, that you inspire people in your life? You can get in consistent touch with your own aligned, inspired energy to offer even more. "A combination of high challenge coupled with high skill" is how author Mihaly Csikszentmihalyi defines a state of flow in his book *Finding Flow*.[19] When we are in these flow moments, we are inspired. Life is delightful and satisfying. Finding your inspiration and flow is key to making your most effective contribution to world peace in five years. What is available to you through connecting to your inspiration is an ongoing sense of happiness and contribution.

19. Mihaly Csikszentmihalyi, *Finding Flow: The Psychology of Engagement with Everyday Life* (New York: Basic Books, 1997).

Every human is born with the internal desire to contribute his or her unique gift. As children, we have a wish for all people; usually, it's a simple wish. We might want all people to be happy or to have enough to eat or to enjoy beauty or to speak the truth. At some point in our childhood, however, something happens and our desire may be stifled. We are told to be realistic, or our idealistic expression is quashed with ridicule or even just a moment of impatience from an older child or adult. Or perhaps we just quietly set our desire aside—the world does not seem to want it, or we feel we can't express it well enough.

This simple, idealistic wish is so much a part of us that it is hard to see that our life is influenced by both the wish and the stifling. Giving up our positive desire is giving up on a part of ourselves in order to "grow up" or "be realistic." At the same time, whatever we decide about the world in order to give up our wish—whether the world is unfair or unfeeling or dangerous or rude—also becomes part of how we view it. It is just "how things are." Although things may be dangerous or rude at the moment we set aside our wish as a child, it is a pretty good bet that the world is not that way for all time, for all experience. Yet your life is arranged on the basis that your belief about the world is true. From then on, many of our actions try to make up for our missing idealistic wish, while we struggle in a world we have decided will not accept it.

Later in life, with adult powers of action, discrimination, education, and willpower, it is possible to resurrect our idealistic wish for all humanity in a new way. We can reconnect to our deepest expression of joy and contribution and give up our rigid filters about "the way things are." Our wish for all humanity is now no longer simplistic in its expression but endowed with the full skill and power of a human adult. Without being connected and aligned with this wish we lose the juice, power, and flow of it. At any point in life we can connect and align. That's what we call inspiration. When something inspires us, a spring of emotional possibility or a deep knowing emerges. Inspiration can be evoked by anything. We can connect through art, dancing, beauty, conversation, friendships, family, a transformational experience, or even hardship, challenge, and setbacks that force us to reflect.

Knowing your wish for humanity can consistently connect you to your inspiration. You may already be connected to your wish for humanity; you may already enjoy the purpose and connection that is possible with that discovery; and you may have already passed through the sometimes wrenching adjustment of noticing that some of what you thought was true about the world is not true at all. We suggest you take a few minutes right now to pull out your journal or a piece of paper and write out your wish for humanity. It might help to think of the one thing you could whisper in every person's ear and know they would grasp. Or consider what feeling you would want everyone to have, and describe it. What need would you like to see met for everyone? If now is not the time to consider your wish for humanity, create a reminder now on your to-do list or in your schedule to do it later.

CONNECTING TO WHAT INSPIRES YOU

When we are seeking to connect to our inspiration, one of the first places to look is our surroundings. In chapter 10, during our discussion on media, we describe how we are all deeply affected by the media that enter our field of experience, whether we notice it consciously or not. Although you may think of "media" as Internet, radio, and TV, our brains accept all forms of experience equally, including conversations, random noise, nature, and our own thoughts. Although internal and external experiences may seem very different, research on mirror neurons and neuroplasticity, or brain rewiring, shows that brains do not differentiate between the two. For instance, neuroscientists tell us that basketball players who practice free throws mentally and those who practice physically, on the court, improve at about the same rate. When consuming "media"—be it live-action real life all around us or on a screen—our brains actively create our experience *as though we were directly engaged in it.* The more focused attention we bring to the media, the more our brains adapt as a result of it.

Media that hold our focused attention, like movies, are especially powerful because alert attention is the key to rewiring our brains.

What forms of environments and media inspire you? What kind of music and images? What do you consider beautiful? Some people find an intense experience of beauty in mathematics. Others find it in a touch or a vision. The philosopher Franklin Merrell-Wolff defines the experience of beauty as "finding the subject in the object." We find ourselves in what we are experiencing and "lose ourselves" in the experience. In inspired moments we lose ourselves, lose track of time, feel unlimited energy, and focus. We are in the zone.

WHAT INSPIRES YOU?

Recall one or more moments of inspiration from your past. Allow your mind and feelings to drift freely into such a moment. Who inspired you most when you were a child? What environment inspires you to relax? How has your best friend inspired you? What inspires you to work hard and deliver your best? What inspired you to buy this book? What inspires you and leaves you feeling full and satisfied with the experience of life?

WRITE HERE WHAT INSPIRES YOU: _____

_____

_____

_____

DESCRIBE THE PART OF YOURSELF THAT GETS INSPIRED. WHAT IS TOUCHED IN YOU? COMPLETE THIS SENTENCE (OR MAKE YOUR OWN):

WHAT WAS INSPIRED AND TOUCHED IN ME WAS MY…

_____

_____

_____

WRITE ONE ACTION YOU COULD TAKE IN THE NEAR FUTURE TO INSPIRE YOURSELF:

_____

_____

_____

We should also look at what drains or stops our inspiration, so we can avoid it. What is the opposite of inspiration? What stops us, confounds us, slows us down? It is not difficulty or challenge—in fact, challenge is often essential to inspiration. The opposite of inspiration is resignation. Resignation is a state of giving up, of knowing that we cannot find what we most want—what we intuit is best for us and for the world. In resignation, we feel hopelessly cut off from our source of inspiration. We experience a loss of power or freedom. We feel stifled and limited. Resignation is so painful that we may bury it deeply. We may fear examining the basis of resignation because we may experience the moment of dashed hopes again, or discover again that we are "right" to be resigned and hopeless because that is just the "way things are."

List in your journal or on a piece of paper situations in which you feel resigned. Look for those instances when you feel powerless or frustrated, or consider the things you consistently complain about that you don't try to change. These all point to places where you have resigned your truth. Now, complete this sentence: "I am resigned about . . ."—notice what is underneath the resignation, what is true for you, and continue the sentence—". . . because what is true that I can't change is that . . ."—and write the true thing. For instance, Nathan used to complain about the government, high taxes, and wasteful bureaucracy. He would write, "*I am resigned about* bad government *because what is true that I can't change is that* I have to pay taxes that are used without any say on my part." If you don't have time to make this resignation list now, then make a note on your to-do list to complete it later. There are more exercises like this in chapter 13, "Aligning Your Life with Peace."

Simply knowing and noticing what impedes your inspiration can help you enormously. You can stop generating and consuming "media" or experiences, such as complaining and feeling powerless, and use your extremely valuable focused attention for media that generate inspiration and happiness for yourself and others.

Sometimes the way things are becomes intolerable. Inspiration often comes from the force of necessity, when we see a need or injustice in our environment that we are called to correct. What is that thing that clicks in? What is that thing that makes the difference between mere outrage and actually deciding to do something about it? The difference comes when the necessity feels greater than the apparent obstacles. We make a shift from being daunted to taking a stand. Previous resignation becomes fuel for the fire of what needs to happen. Resignation transmutes into resolve.

People who have made a large positive impact have had to overcome their resignation. They do not give up. This is not because of some grit-your-teeth-and-suffer attitude; it is because they have deeply connected to their source of inspiration, beyond what anyone could tell them. Amelia Earhart, Ernest Shackleton, the nonviolent Afghani hero Badshah Khan, Nelson Mandela, George Washington,

Galileo, and the team that sent a person to the Moon for the first time: they all acted in the face of what appeared to be impossible. Not all of them succeeded, but they were all inspired. The connection these people made to their inspiration is possible for anyone, not just someone in a history book.

OVERCOMING RESIGNATION

When have you wanted something and decided it was not possible? What is the hope that you gave up on? What did you or someone else say about how the world is or, more important, how the world is going to remain for all time? If you could say one truth about it at this moment, what would that be?

WRITE HERE WHAT YOU GAVE UP ON:

_____

_____

NOW WRITE WHAT YOU DECIDED IS BOTH TRUE AND UNCHANGING FOR THE FUTURE THAT MADE YOU GIVE UP:

_____

_____

EVERYTHING CHANGES, AND YOU HAVE INFLUENCE OVER YOUR LIFE. WRITE ONE CHANGE THAT, IF IT OCCURRED, WOULD MOVE YOU TOWARD WHAT YOU MOST WANTED BUT GAVE UP ON:

_____

_____

IS THERE ONE ACTION YOU COULD TAKE TOWARD MAKING THAT CHANGE HAPPEN? WRITE THAT ACTION HERE. IF YOU CAN'T THINK OF AN ACTION, TALK THIS EXERCISE THROUGH WITH A FRIEND TO COME UP WITH AN ACTION, AND WRITE IT HERE:

_____

_____

Inspiration can come from a new view, from increased alignment with our internal compass of what is true. Or it can come when we are faced with a challenge, and we suddenly realize we have the power to shift what previously seemed insurmountable.

YOUR PRACTICE OF INSPIRATION GENERATES IT

The inspiration to give peace a deadline was a perfect storm of sounds, images, media consumed, years of conversation, inquiry, physical practice, business habits, and spiritual practice. Our inspiration is the product of our whole lives. We stepped into a stream of inspiration that started long before us. Like all great inspiration, giving peace a deadline was clearly obvious and unavoidable.

As we work to give peace a deadline, we continue to be inspired by the words of many different people, past and present. Our conversations with Václav Havel, Alex Gray, John McLaughlin, Madeleine Albright, and the present Dalai Lama have refined and extended our understandings and planted the seed of peace with a deadline globally. The Fourteenth Dalai Lama spoke at a peace conference in Prague in 2006, contributing a key understanding of inflexible belief as the basis of conflict. Talking to controversial figures like Paul Wolfowitz added a dimension of breaking stereotypes about who a peacemaker can be.

Sitting down in London with Nobel Peace laureate F. W. de Klerk influenced and inspired us. One idea that particularly interested us was principle-centered foreign policy, played out in his example of peaceful transition out of apartheid to democracy, and his example of flexible and direct negotiations with the leader of his opposition, Nobel co-laureate Nelson Mandela.

We also found inspiration in De Klerk's creative ideas for nuclear disarmament in the Middle East. De Klerk has particular authority to speak of this, as he is one of the few people on our planet responsible for the total nuclear disarmament of an entire country. As he described ordering the dismantling of the seven nuclear bombs in the South African arsenal when he entered office as president, we were deeply moved by the possibility of immediate disarmament among Israel, Iran, and Syria.

The writings of previous and current peacemakers have been a constant source of inspiration: Walt Whitman's poetry and his vision for America, Plato, Herman Melville, Mark Twain, Immanuel Kant, and many other brilliant people are the giants on whose shoulders we stand. We devour the works of artists, business writers, journalists, political science experts, neuroscientists, historians, psychologists, religious writers, and philosophers so that we can constantly inspire, challenge, and inform our work for peace in five years.

We are inspired every time we talk with the people who are working with us to give peace a deadline. At the end of one brainstorming session we held about how to create peace in five years, the same Hollywood actress, who at the beginning said "yeah, right" and "that's a pageant dream," by the end was moved and passionately committed. She wrote out the clear actions in her own life to create peace and helped the rest of us do the same.

All of this adds up to our ongoing practice of inspiration. We take this very seriously, and we feel responsible for our inspiration. You can take the same responsibility: Discover what inspires you, and do it. You are responsible and accountable for your energy and leadership, which makes you responsible for your inspiration.

YOUR SPEECH IS POWERFUL—TRANSMIT YOUR INSPIRATION

The most important resource you can use to take action and to help create world peace in five years is your power of speech. Just by sharing what you are doing, you have the power to persuade others to become involved. Humble conversations can change minds and fire passions. You may not be a powerful orator like Dr. Martin Luther King, Jr., but your simple conversations can create a self-sustaining chain of "peace evangelists," especially if you have taken the time to find your inspiration and align your life with that inspiration. You—and subsequently the people you talk to—are constantly inspiring others with the possibility of world peace and what could become possible for them with world peace—all with your words that carry your infectious inspiration.

Some of the most inspiring conversations are the ones we have with people who do not know about our campaign. The first step in creating world peace is to get everyone talking about it as fun and achievable. This is not as difficult as it may sound. People love to talk. They spend hours talking about sports, kids, school, the news, relationships, TV, weather, food—you name it. Most of these conversations are not purposeful. They simply fill the air with comforting sound. If you make a conversation more useful and interesting, you will find that people enjoy the conversation more. You're contributing to your friends, making their day brighter. World peace is a topic that fascinates and benefits everyone. The world is ready for this conversation right now.

Talking about P5Y doesn't cost anything; to the contrary, it actually adds a huge amount of value to you, your family, and the world. Without productive conversations, world peace will never happen. By talking about P5Y, you inspire support, commitments, and actions. Such conversations inspire others and you. Though we were interested in peace and we attended international peace conferences, we only got inspired to take action when we gave peace a deadline. Once our conversation became specific and businesslike, there was no shortage of inspiration. This conversation rescues peace from vagueness. Your informed, specific conversation about world peace makes it real.

Here is how one conversation went, showing how people make the transition from vague, sometime-in-the-future peace to world peace in five years. Our friend Shannon was in town from Marin County, California, home of hard-core baby boomer hippies. She sat down with us at dinner and asked, "So, what do you mean by world peace?" She We started by telling her everything world peace is not, like all of the ideas of super-happy consciousness. It is not the end to all violence. It is a specific metric of practicing safety from war and nonengagement in violent war among the family of nations. "So, it doesn't mean there will no longer be gang violence in L.A. or anything?" she asked. "No," we shook our heads. We explained more about our strategy and the current metrics for peace. "Oh, I get it," she said, and her eyes brightened. "I mean, for the first time ever! I see that peace is actually possible." Then she started getting really inspired.

For us, the conversation about world peace has opened a deeper world of fun, contribution, and friendship. In many ways, this book is our open invitation for you and the world to join in a productive conversation about world peace.

HOW DO I START THE CONVERSATION?

In the early 1990s, a reporter interviewing Archbishop Desmond Tutu noted that Tutu began his sentences with "When apartheid is over we will . . ." or "When we have integration then . . . " The reporter was hopeful but thought Desmond Tutu was assumptive. A year and a half later, apartheid ended.

Starting the conversation is easy. We began this book by asking the question "Are you willing to have peace by 2014?" The next time you are with friends who know nothing about P5Y, ask them the same question. Or ask them, "What do you think it would take to create world peace by 2014?" Your friends will probably share their views about peace and war with you right away. Whether you agree with them or not, listen to their views attentively. No matter how they react, you will have an interesting conversation.

You will want to start the conversation differently if you are talking with someone who isn't necessarily a friend. The next time you meet someone at a social gathering, and they ask what you do, tell them you are working on a movement to create world peace in five years. Gauge how they react. Tell them about P5Y and about your particular involvement. Your acquaintance will either be intrigued by the idea of peace in five years or will not believe in what you are saying. Certain conversations stay heated, challenging, and interesting while others seem vague and completely uninspiring. You have to gauge whether the conversation is useful or not. No matter what reaction you get, you will have planted a seed of peace.

Even if you are making a more formal presentation to the leaders of an organization, don't hesitate to be straightforward from the very beginning about what you are doing. Tell the group that world peace has a deadline. A strong opening statement is often the key to making a convincing presentation, and there are few stronger opening statements than saying you are working for world peace, and that you intend to finish in a few years.

The main way we start conversations about P5Y is when someone asks what we've been up to lately, we tell them. Sometimes we ask people what they have been up to that really jazzes them—we always love to hear that! Usually they ask us the same question in return. Other times we talk about what inspires us, or where we might have found a nugget of resignation or where we were lying to ourselves, and often that leads straight into world peace. If a conversation is boring, we look to deepen it—honestly, our tolerance for boring conversation is pretty low. We talk about world peace because it is sincerely what we are most interested in discussing. We keep asking the question "How do I create world peace in five years?" and you can too.

Once you have started the conversation, talk about what peace in five years means to you. Talk about your own views of war and the wish you have for the world. Talk about the cutting-edge thinking on peace you have found in this book or from other sources. Talk about peace as safety and war as an illegitimate means to an end that is rarely or never achieved. Speak about your passion and how you would like to make a difference in the world. Describe what you are accountable for. Talk about the people and organizations with whom you are collaborating.

Here are topics and points you can use for your conversation about peace in five years:

- World momentum is toward peace. Point out that despite the nightly news, according to Fareed Zakaria in *The Post-American World* (W. W. Norton, 2008), we are living in a peaceful time.

- Peace as safety: Show how the practice of peace is not vague. Peace is the practice of safety from war. Like many safety practices, peace is multi-layered, including prevention, prediction, intervention, and containment if violent conflict does break out. Incitement, oppression, and human rights violations are global violations of peace safety.

- A concerned citizen can lead peace. We do not have to wait for representatives or institutions to cause peace for us, although we should continue to educate and invite our institutions and governments to practice effective peace safety.

- War doesn't give us safety. The consequences of war are terrible and getting worse. With the growth of technology, terrible weapons under the control of a very few people can cross borders and oceans. The notion of defense as a strong barrier is outmoded and dangerous. The only effective defense is to practice peace as safety to prevent enemies from arising, to resolve conflict without war, and to intervene in violations of peace safety.

- Now is the time for peace. It is possible to create world peace in five years with a determined effort. By focusing worldwide media, getting businesses involved, inviting everyone to take specific actions (or to stop specific actions), we can create peace.

- The resources already applied to peace today are probably sufficient to create world peace in five years. What is new is effective collaboration and planning among all of the forces of peace.

Once you get the conversation started, you will find that talking about world peace is easy.

YOU ARE POWERFUL WITH FACTS

When you know what is going on, you have a lot more influence, so be *informed* about what you are saying. What's going on in the area of the world your peace project relates to? What's the status of the world's conflicts? What's the political news? How is P5Y making progress? You need to have this information at your fingertips. Get it at www.P5Y.org/stats.

Here are two examples to illustrate why this matters:

Example 1:

Joe: Hey, Fred, how's it going?

Fred: Hey, Joe, I'm totally jazzed about creating peace in five years, because I've read this book and people can actually do it.

Joe: It sounds cool, but I don't think it's doable.

Fred: It is. It's right here in this book. There's this big plan for it and everything.

Joe: Okay, whatever. Wanna get lunch?

Example 2:

Joe: Hey, Fred, how's it going?

Fred: Hey, Joe, I'm totally jazzed about my plan for creating peace in five years. I've got a timeline and everything.

Joe: It sounds cool, but I don't think it's doable.

Fred: Well, I'm doing my part. There are seventeen armed conflicts in the world, and the plan calls for reducing that to fewer than fourteen by the end of the year. My project is to help ten former child soldiers from the Congo who are in Uganda to start to live normal lives by teaching them job skills in construction while they are getting trauma therapy. I've got to do it by the end of next month or I miss my commitment.

Joe: Whoa! You are teaching construction to kids in Uganda for world peace?

Fred: Yeah, well that's what my six-month commitment is. I think my next commitment will be closer to home—maybe do some accounting or start a peace team. I've got to decide by the end of next week.

Joe: Dude! That's cool. Can I do it too?

In the first example, Fred is excited and wants to tell Joe something about world peace, but his speaking is neither informed nor specific. Fred may be informed, but he isn't making his passion relevant to Joe's world, and Joe doesn't care that Fred has read a book about world peace. In the second example, Fred is talking to Joe about his life and his own commitments and is being specific about times, places, and numbers. Even if the second example conversation doesn't get Joe excited about world peace in five years, he has just had a much more interesting and energetic exchange with Fred, which gives them both a more enjoyable and educational day. It is pretty likely that Fred's conversation will be the most interesting thing that happened to Joe all day, and when Joe goes home to his wife, he will say something like, "Fred was talking about world peace in five years. I kinda doubt it can happen, but he said he's going to Nigeria or something to help traumatized kids. Yeah, Fred. Who knew?" You never know what will spark interest in someone. Plant seeds of speech and let them grow.

YOU ARE INTERESTING IF YOU ASK PEOPLE QUESTIONS ABOUT THEMSELVES

Once you have engaged an individual in conversation, the next thing you need to do is start asking questions. People love to talk about themselves: what they love, what they hate, what interests them, and what bores them. Ask them how world peace is personally important to them and what they care about. Find out what their ideas about world peace are. Get them to tell you specifically what peace will mean to them. Would it mean the end of hunger? No more organized war? No more terrorism? Or something else entirely? Listen carefully to the answers! The speaker will soon say something important and relevant to your own personal peace process.

Questions you could ask include the following:

- What would be good for you, personally, in a peaceful world?
- What are your passions?
- What are your commitments in life?
- How could your commitments in life work toward world peace?
- What kind of peacemaker are you?

Listen for the point at which someone says that they have given up on peace or are resigned and hopeless about the state of the world. If appropriate, ask what brought about such a feeling of resignation and pessimism. Ask them, "Why do you think we can have peace?" Do they give a legitimate answer, or does it seem that the speaker has given up hope because of something deep within their personality? The point is not to analyze the speaker but to find out what matters most to them so you can engage in a deep, thoughtful, enjoyable conversation.

Remember that a listener yields his or her time to you for a reason. It's not just because they care about you. It's also because they find something of interest to themselves in what you're talking about. Take advantage of their "enlightened self-interest" to engage them at a level that sparks their passion.

We're not suggesting you quiz people like a TV news anchor or Stephen Colbert. We're suggesting that you engage in an honest, open, intelligent dialogue that includes yet transcends political and religious differences. Remember, peace benefits everyone. We all want to live, prosper, and be healthy and happy. Reach out and understand the peacemakers around you.

Peace Action

What you can do today to further peace by 2014

Create a local peace event and post it on www.P5Y.org. Afterward, report the attendance, including details of what was accomplished and how many people decided to become peacemakers.

When you are ready to dive deeper, ask the following:

- What current conflict moves you the most?
- What resources are needed to create peace in this conflict?

There are many complicated dimensions to current conflicts, but keep asking "How do you think we can create peace in this area?" If you keep asking this question, you will keep forcing all people involved in the conversation to reconsider the situation and visualize peace in a new way.

Our point is that as a global community we have the resources, infrastructure, money, maturity, and willingness of people to have world peace within five years. By continuously asking the question "How do we create peace in this area?" and by describing details that could lead to peace, you are taking responsibility, and you are demonstrating that peace is achievable. Your commitment, transmitted by your words, can be contagious.

INSPIRE OTHERS

This is a basic template for talking about world peace. It is designed to help you get started and to guide a conversation, but it is not a substitute for your own natural speaking style, emotional honesty, and commitment.

1. Ask, "Are you willing to have peace in five years?" or "What do you think it would take to create peace in five years?"

2. Most people will answer yes to that first question. If you get a negative response, you might ask why they answered no and get into a deeper conversation.

3. If the person says yes to the first question, you can say, "Great, let me tell you what I'm doing about it." State your commitment, your deadline, and the overall deadline for creating world peace.

4. Tell them what kind of peacemaker you are and help them find out what kind they are. Ask them about their passions, skills, and life, and how they could collaborate for world peace in five years. Usually, adding a greater purpose and sense of cooperation to what we love to do makes it even more enjoyable.

5. Ask them what kind of commitment would be most interesting for them to make for world peace in five years, based on their skills, desires, and what kind of peacemaker they are.

6. At the moment when your friend is ready to take some step toward creating world peace in five years, like visiting the P5Y.org website, joining a peace team, or getting a copy of this book, set a time to follow up with them, and write it in your appointment book with their phone number and email address.

7. Follow up the conversation at the appointed time.

8. Enjoy contributing to such a nobel goal.

GOING PUBLIC

There's no better way to reach large numbers of people, publicize your own projects, and let people know about P5Y websites and organizations than by speaking to groups, such as schools, churches, civic organizations, and businesses. Look at the organizations you are already involved with. Find the core message you want to communicate and connect it to the desires of your audience. How are these people just like you in their hopes and fears? What solution, opportunity, or insight can you offer them? What is the core message that you want to deliver? What is your highest outcome? Do your homework beforehand and brainstorm what materials, technology, or handouts would support your message. Even while you're speaking, listen to and extend your attention to the people in the room.

Public speaking is usually an acquired skill, honed with practice. If you have a talent for public speaking, you probably enjoy it. World peace with a deadline is a topic that is sure to get you in front of all kinds of groups. The visibility and status you gain from speaking confidently about global issues in front of groups can boost your self-confidence and your career.

SPEAK FROM YOUR TRUTH

Many years ago, Nathan attended a weekend seminar that made a lasting impression on him. Close to two hundred people from all walks of life attended. One was a lanky, black-booted rogue truck-driver type. He was the kind of guy who Nathan tended to dismiss or overlook before he learned that every human being has huge potential and gifts.

At the end of the seminar, this man stood up to talk to the group about what he got out of the seminar. What followed was astounding. This aw-shucks, pompadoured smoker spent six minutes delivering extemporaneous poetry with exact metaphor, impeccable logic, and heartbreaking authenticity. Nathan was speechless, awed, and humbled. When the cowboy uttered his closing sentence with perfect timing and emotion, there was at least a full minute of silence before thunderous applause. The audience was awestruck and teary-eyed.

This man was speaking from an honest place, relaying a personal experience. He was aligned with the truth of who he was, and he was completely genuine and unapologetic. We hope that he is still out there in the world, speaking from his truth.

We have seen this happen enough that we have come to believe that powerful speech is an innate human capacity. Have you ever witnessed someone speaking in a way that transfixed you with truth and passion? It might have been a moment in a movie or a play or a great political speech. Or perhaps it was an intimate conversation with a parent, friend, or child. But it changed you. Nothing was quite the same afterward. That's the kind of power your speech can bring to P5Y.

When you speak about creating peace in five years, speak from the personal truth of who you are and your authentic commitment to peace. Speak about what moves you, lights you up, and excites you. That kind of unbridled energy is empowering. When you uncover the wealth of your truth and expression, you will become impassioned. If your audience feels that you are speaking from a deep place of passion and self-expression that they would like to have in their own lives, you'll reach them. Even if you are naturally shy, you will want to speak up, and if you are naturally talkative, you will want to speak with a much deeper conviction. Speaking from an authentic place is at the root of powerful speech. The rest is just refinement.

Let's say your conversation—speaking from your experience and using informed specifics about your commitment to world peace—inspires the people you are talking with. Invite them then to discover for themselves:

- Who they are in relation to creating peace in five years and what kind of peacemaker they are.
- How their gifts and talents fit into the tactical picture of what needs to happen to create peace.
- What commitment excites them most.

Send them to www.P5Y.org or lend them your copy of this book. Both actions can help them find out what kinds of efforts are under way, how they can help, and how to make a commitment.

For a quick reference on how to talk about peace in five years, use the following:

- Ask, "Are you willing to have peace by 2014?" or "How do you think we can create peace in five years?"
- Talk about what you are accountable for in a peace project.
- Speak from your own truth and what excites you most about it.
- Tell the listener what kind of peacemaker you are and find out what kind of peacemaker the listener is. (You will learn more about how to determine the type of peacemaker you are in chapter 12.)
- Be informed and cite specific numbers and times.
- Relax when speaking and listening.

Your words are the most powerful tool you have to inspire others. The expression of those words and the conversations you have about world peace will in turn inspire you. With this inspiration, you will be able to discover the talents in those around you and fully realize your own potential for peace.

DISCOVER: HOW YOU AS AN INDIVIDUAL CAN HAVE A DIRECT IMPACT ON WORLD PEACE

The reasonable man adapts himself to the world; the unreasonable man persists in trying to adapt the world to himself. Therefore, all progress depends on the unreasonable man.

—George Bernard Shaw

WE ALL LIKE to be effective in creating the outcomes we are inspired to work on. Now that we understand how to take responsibility for inspiring ourselves and others, let's see what the next step is in converting our inspiration into perspiration. In common with the great pace of change in our postindustrial world, mankind has never before embarked on a journey of this kind. As we make our way to a world free from war, we will discover new approaches to creating peace, as well as individuals and groups who are currently involved in peace work. We will discover new modes of thinking, new ways of communicating, and new realms of opportunities. As long as we keep our minds open, we will be able to use these discoveries to advance our goal and make war a quaint and horrible relic of the past.

While talking about world peace provides inspiration, making a deep connection with one individual about P5Y is one key to discovering the full potential of the movement. To make this connection and begin the journey of discovery, a peace buddy is an indispensable ally who doubles your fun and your results.

FIND YOUR PEACE BUDDY

Your peace buddy is a friend who helps keep you on track in your contribution, just as you help him or her. Not only is having a peace buddy fun, but finding one is essential for us as we offer our skills and passion for world peace. Only by sharing our commitment and having it reflected back to us through another person can we discover the strength of our commitment to peace and the depth of our willingness to participate in a movement far greater than ourselves. The first person we should reach out to is a peace buddy.

Your peace buddy should be someone whom you trust and respect. Reflect for a moment on the qualities you would like to receive from your peace buddy. The most important thing is that your peace buddy is someone you trust in the areas of accountability and process. Your peace buddy has to be able to share with you your accountability, ideas, successes, and failures. Your peace buddy can help you keep on track with your progress. When you are too hard on yourself or lose steam, your peace buddy is the person who will bring you back to reality. Working with a peace buddy will allow you to discover the skills you have within yourself to connect with others and to incorporate individuals and groups into the campaign for world peace.

Nathan's peace buddy is Mark Mandel, a long-time trusted friend and mentor. Long before P5Y was created, Nathan was looking to discover more about world peace. When he wanted to share a discovery, bounce around an idea, or talk through a stuck place, he found himself seeking out Mark as someone with extraordinary listening skills, who would both challenge and encourage him. After a few conversations, Nathan asked Mark if he would consent to be available long-term for conversations related to world peace. Mark agreed. In order to make it easier for Mark, they agreed to some ground rules—Nathan can call Mark anytime, but they keep the peace part of the conversation to fifteen minutes or less. If Nathan thinks he needs more time, he requests it in advance. They find that fifteen minutes is sufficient for nearly any kind of conversation that is about being "on track" or getting advice on one specific issue. Knowing the time limit helps them both keep the conversation focused. Nathan usually does not call about peace-related matters more than once a week.

Because Nathan and Mark are such good friends, they often speak for much longer, but Nathan takes responsibility for clearly stating when the peace buddy part of the conversation is over.

The process has strengthened an already deep friendship, and both Nathan and Mark gain value from this special part of their interaction.

Take a moment to consider a person who might be your peace buddy. Who would you like to spend more time with? Who inspires you? This is a great way to draw someone deeper into your life, such as an old friend, a coworker, or a mentor.

PEACE BUDDIES

Make a list of all the people you know who may be interested in P5Y. Go through the list and put a star next to the name of each person who is a potential peace buddy and whom you think meets the criteria.

We recommend that you contact your potential peace buddy as soon as you can. Put it on your to-do list or calendar now. Talking with such an individual will help you focus your thoughts about the campaign for world peace and discover what peace truly means to you. Like Nathan and Mark, many of us who are working for peace began working with a peace buddy even before we committed ourselves to a specific action plan.

Don't be shy or intimidated about contacting your potential peace buddy. If you're engaged in something interesting, then you've got something interesting to say. If you're concerned about asking someone, ask yourself, "Just what might so-and-so say to me and how bad could it be?" Writing down fears robs them of their power. Chances are it's not as bad as you think. Most people are genuinely interested in hearing about other people's passions.

In case you are hesitant about talking with your potential peace buddy about something as ambitious as creating world peace, we've included this sample email to get you started:

Hello.

I've become interested in aligning my life with world peace. I'm using a website called P5Y.org to help me make measurable and achievable commitments to creating world peace in five years. P5Y is nonpolitical and results-oriented and has the best ideas on creating peace I have ever seen.

Part of the process is to find a peace buddy, someone to meet with on a regular basis who can help me stay accountable to my commitments, celebrate successes, and find creative ways to overcome challenges. There are thousands of people all over the world doing this.

I'd like you to consider being my peace buddy. Your commitment would be to meet with me once a week for fifteen minutes, sometimes in person, sometimes on the phone. If you are also inspired by this project, we could be peace buddies for each other.

My goal is to have a peace buddy within two days, so if you could get back to me with questions or your response soon, that would be great.

Thanks,

If you prefer talking to writing, here's an example of what you could say during a phone call:

Hi. I wanted to talk to you about a project I've become inspired by to create world peace in five years. There's a whole system that I don't need to go into now, but basically it's a global network of ordinary citizens who are working to create world peace. Together, we're able to make commitments with deadlines that make a measurable difference.

Part of the system is to have a peace buddy, a person who can help me stay on track and who will hold me accountable to the commitments I make to world peace. I called you because I think you would make a good peace buddy for me. The commitment is to meet with me once a week in person or on the phone for fifteen minutes. All you would need to do is listen and give me a bit of feedback on how I'm doing. Is this something that might interest you?

Don't feel intimidated if the first person you call is not interested in being your peace buddy. We actually recommend talking to several potential peace buddies before you decide on someone. Each individual offers you different strengths of personality. Be prepared to discover new depths in your personality and character as you work together to create world peace.

PEACE BUDDY PROTOCOL

To make your time with your peace buddy focused and purposeful, we have created some ground rules based on our experiences. If you use these suggested rules, you will strengthen your contribution and have a more satisfying relationship.

- Set up a regular time to meet or talk. Once a week is good, because if you miss a meeting, you only have a two-week gap.

- Choose a time frame during which to be peace buddies—two months, six months, until 2014, or any other time period in between. When the time is up, recommit or celebrate your accomplishment and find another peace buddy.

- Use a checklist every time that includes the topics you want to discuss. Fill it out before your meeting, if possible, but don't postpone a meeting if you have not filled out your checklist.

- Share the personal contributions that you want to make to peace. Listen to your buddy's feedback. (Of course, if your partner is also committed to P5Y, listen and offer reciprocal feedback.)

- Set a timer and go over your plans for that set amount of time. When the timer is done, be done. If you need more time, ask for it. If your peace buddy says no, schedule more time for your next meeting. Be sure to end on time to preserve your enthusiasm for meeting again.

- Discover what contributions to peace you can make. Once you have developed a personal peace plan, bring that peace plan with you to every meeting.

Peace buddy meetings should typically follow a consistent process:

1. At the beginning of every meeting, state your personal plans for peace.
2. Ask each other how you think we can bring about world peace by 2014. Even if you already think you know the answer or are working on a project, keep asking.

3. Let each other know if you did or didn't do what you promised the last time you met. This is not about making the other person feel guilty if they didn't do what they said. It's providing a way for you to be accountable.

4. Make promises to each other for what you will accomplish over the next one to two weeks.

5. Explore one of the topics from the section that follows, or from the exercises that are available at P5Y.org.

WHAT YOU CAN DO WITH YOUR PEACE BUDDY

Once you've got a peace buddy, try some of these activities to build your relationship. If you think of new ones (and we're sure you will), please tell us about them at activities@P5Y.org.

Remember, creating peace in five years is about connecting your greatest inspiration with *specific effective coordinated action*, so include milestones, measurements, and reporting as part of what you do.

- How could we communicate these new ways of thinking about and accomplishing world peace? Brainstorm for ten minutes about fun ideas to get your community, town, or city inspired.

- How could we contribute right now to one of the many areas worldwide that are experiencing violent conflict? Brainstorm for ten minutes. This is not about coming up with the perfect answer but about freeing your creativity. Write down everything that comes to mind. Don't discard any ideas at this point; just write them down. Turn off your inner editor. Sometimes the crazy ideas are the best ones. As the national plans for peace (from chapter 4) come online at P5Y.org, you will be able to see how your ideas and contributions fit into the overall strategy.

Peace Action

What you can do today to further peace by 2014

Go to P5Y.org and find out which organizations most match your values, talents, and means. Choose one that you are inspired to give to. Make a commitment. Put it in your peace plan.

Here are some activities that will help you and your peace buddy explore your visions and beliefs in greater detail.

- List any obstacles that would prevent or complicate world peace. For each obstacle, ask yourself, "What would have to change about the world in order to overcome this obstacle?" Be specific. Who would have to change? Why might they change? What are the needs that would have to be met in order for people to change? Notice whether this discussion suggests effective actions for peace that you and others might take.

- Bring poster board, colored markers or crayons, scissors, tape, or any other craft supplies. Make a collage or artwork that expresses your commitment to and understanding of world peace. For instance, we made a big sign that says "Peace Room" and put it up in our brainstorming space.

- Pick a place to volunteer and then call and set up a time when you can go in for an hour together.

As you discover the energy and inspiration you give and you get from your peace buddy, you may want to expand the process of interpersonal discovery to include a larger group, a peace team.

THE POWER OF THE PEACE TEAM

By understanding and applying the power of small teams, you can enjoy greater results and hone your contribution around your particular passions and skills. You are able to increase the efficiency of every member of the team. Remember, small teams are powerful, and if you are a member of an effective team, you are more powerful. Margaret Mead famously said, "Never doubt that a small group of thoughtful, committed citizens can change the world. Indeed, it is the only thing that ever has." In the company of others, accomplishments that we could not achieve alone become possible. Even a team as small as two people dedicated to helping each other will stand to have a greater degree of success at any endeavor.

Effective military organizations recognize that there is incredible power in small groups. The basic infantry combat unit is a small group of individuals who rely on each other for mission accomplishment and survival. Historian Francis Fukuyama writes in *State-Building: Governance and World Order in the 21st Century*, "The strongest bonds [among soldiers] are not to large organizations or abstract causes like the nation, rather they are to the immediate group of soldiers in one's platoon or squad . . ."[20] It is human nature to relate most strongly and empathetically to small groups, and there is ample evidence that small teams are among the most emotionally rewarding and sustainable relationships we enjoy.

Business understands the power of small groups as well. The innovative W. L. Gore & Associates, makers of Gore-Tex, is built entirely around the creative problem-solving power of small teams. Teams are given great latitude to accomplish the overall goals of the organization while upholding core values. The result is a company that is made up of nothing but small teams, whose thousands of innovative products and high profit margins have earned the admiration of the world: The company has been in the top ten of the Fortune 100 Best Companies to Work For since the inception of the list.

Huge numbers of unknown people, working together in small, informal groups, have surmounted seemingly impossible obstacles in their time. We know of Gandhi, but we do not know the names of the millions of Hindus, Muslims, Christians, and Sikhs who put themselves on the line through their nonviolent actions just as Gandhi did in order to gain India's independence. The task seemed impossible. That's exactly how it looked, and that's what everyone thought— until it *happened*.

Similarly, small groups of determined people were instrumental in ending apartheid in South Africa and abolishing slavery—an idea that was considered unthinkable. Just as war provides important economic structures that support portions of the power elite, so did slavery. In 1783 six English Quakers—William Dillwyn, George Harrison, Samuel Hoare, Thomas Knowles, John Lloyd, and Joseph Woods—formed a committee to fight slavery. By 1787, this small group had grown into the Society for Effecting the Abolition of the Slave Trade. Although they debated focusing on freeing existing slaves in England, the society made a strategic decision to focus on suppressing the slave trade as the most effective goal toward abolishing slavery—just as P5Y has made a strategic decision to focus on politically organized violence as the most effective goal toward global peace. They hired an energetic researcher and strategist for the group, Thomas Clarkson, who decided that the slave trade needed to be repositioned in the political marketplace in order to gain support for ending it. Author Jim Powell writes in *Greatest Emancipations*: "Clarkson recognized that to win political support for abolishing slavery, he must somehow overthrow the widely held belief

20. Francis Fukuyama, *State-Building: Governance and World Order in the 21st Century* (Ithaca, NY: Cornell University Press, 2004), 137.

that slavery was essential for British national security and prosperity. He had to counter the claim that the slave trade was a 'nursery of seamen'"[21] that provided essential skilled sailors for the Royal Navy.

Clarkson undertook what was probably the first highly researched political documentary. He visited slave ships, talked to crew members, ship surgeons, and other people in the trade. He examined hundreds of records and logs of markets and voyages. Powell writes, "What Clarkson learned about the trans-Atlantic voyages was utterly at odds with accounts offered by slave-trading interests."[22] Clarkson's descriptions of the slave trade are heartrending, but his most interesting and well-documented discovery was that, "far from being an essential 'nursery for seamen' as proslavery interests claimed, 'it was their grave'".[23] In other words, slavery was not only bad for slaves, it was bad for British sailors, who died alongside their suffering human cargo from disease, revolt, and abuse in far greater numbers on slave ships than any other type of ship. Clarkson's research meticulously debunked the soothing propaganda of the slave industry—all because he was supported and encouraged by that small team of six Quakers, also known as Friends of the Truth, who dared to achieve the impossible. Theirs was the power of small teams using effective action toward strategic goals.

We would love to see the name of every woman, man, child, politician, beggar, business owner, priest, teacher, and simple human being who was sparked by their own inner inspiration to bring about audacious change that no one thought was possible. They make up the hands of history that pushed new eras into existence. To create world peace in five years, we must tap into the power of small teams. You as a peacemaker are in a position to either join or lead a peace team.

HOW TO START A PEACE TEAM

The first way to determine what peace team to join or create is to look at yourself. What level of commitment can you make? What are you excited about contributing? What resources do you want to give and where do you need resources?

If you prefer to join a peace team rather than start one, then the first place to look is at www.P5Y.org under the peace team tab. See if there is one in your area. These are independently organized groups that we allow to use our website as a hub to share information. They all have their own frequency and times of meeting.

---

21. Jim Powell, *Greatest Emancipations: How the West Abolished Slavery* (New York: Palgrave Macmillan, 2008), 75.
22. Ibid, 77.
23. Ibid, 78–79.

It may be that a particular group of individuals has an eclectic membership and you wish to add your own talents to that pool. If you still have some distance to go in determining your contribution to peace, joining a peace team will definitely help you.

You may want to start and lead your own Peace Team. If you are acting to realize your own ideas and visions, you are leading that vision. What are you leading? Ask yourself and your peace buddy what you are leading through your actions. It doesn't have to sound grand or global, but it should feel right inside. What you are leading is most effective when it is in alignment with your values, which are then expressed beyond yourself.

Peace Action

What you can do today to further peace by 2014

Talk to your local school board about introducing materials into school curricula that tell the true stories of war and also the plan for world peace in five years. Post your results at www.P5Y.org.

You may have noticed while creating your list of peace buddies that you have written the names of several people with whom you would really like to work for peace. In this case you may want to start your own "peace team." If you want to start your own team, there are many sources of likely members: family, friends, co-workers, community organizations, your place of worship, your yoga class, parents at your kids' school, a men's group or women's group, and so on. Talk to each person about peace by 2014 and engage them in a discussion about what you're doing. If they express interest, there's a good chance they'll join your team.

If you're already leading a group in a manner that inspires many people to want to work with you, you might consider talking with the group about joining you in the campaign to bring peace in five years. If you get a positive response, you may be inspired to create a peace team in your community. A peace team will typically include three to ten people so that everyone can participate and has an important role to play. Everyone in the peace team should have a peace buddy. There's no substitute for one-to-one motivation and accountability.

You may discover that you want to start a peace team in your specific field or area of interest—Teachers for Peace, Scientists for Peace, Lawyers for Peace, Swimmers for Peace, Taxi Drivers for Peace, Men's Group for Peace, Women's Group for Peace, Book Club for Peace. You can take any group you are already a part of and reinvigorate it in the service of world peace in five years. Imagine a

YOUR TEAM

When have you been on a team that you found rewarding? It might have been only for an afternoon, sharing a task like moving a friend or preparing for a party. Or maybe you have been on a sports team, a group of volunteers, or a task force. Focus on your rewarding experiences.

WHAT ABOUT YOUR TEAM WORKED?

_____

WHAT WOULD YOU MOST WANT IN A TEAM YOU JOINED?

_____

WHAT ROLE DO YOU BEST PLAY IN A TEAM—GENERATING CREATIVE IDEAS, KEEPING FOCUS, FILLING IN, LEADING?

_____

WHAT ROLES DO YOU MOST APPRECIATE OTHERS PLAYING?

_____

WHAT DID YOU FIND REWARDING ABOUT YOUR TEAM?

_____

Save your answers to help you find a good place for yourself on a peace team. Join the team that most attracts you, and make your commitment. (Peace team guides are available online at P5Y.org.)

knitting circle whose purpose is for people to socialize and learn to knit. Those same activities can be made more rewarding and enjoyable if you are knitting hats and scarves for children in refugee camps, and you are able to share pictures of children wearing them in the winter months.

Then perhaps the whole knitting circle gets inspired to travel to the camps, bringing hope and care to people who are desperate and have lost their homes, people who might otherwise be ripe for arguments in favor of war. Then perhaps the knitting circle members help those people build new homes, along with a school, and they support a teacher in the school for five years at a total cost to the entire knitting circle of a few thousand dollars. See where this can go?

HOW YOUR PEACE TEAM CAN OPERATE

As with your peace buddy relationship, you want your team to be effective and successful. Once you have joined or created a peace team, you will begin to discover the power of small groups to bring about change. People are fundamentally creative and inventive. When asked, "How do you think we can bring about world peace by 2014?" the average person in the street will probably have some kind of answer. So why hasn't peace come to the world? Ideas need to be followed by execution, with accountability systems and resources behind them to bring them into reality. Providing that infrastructure is the purpose of the peace teams and P5Y.

Your peace team will have its own personality and vision. Compete for peace if your peace team is competitive. Argue if it is argumentative. Cooperate if it is cooperative. No matter what style of discussion your peace team adopts, always act with humor, love, and respect. Be constructive. Don't think that because it is a peace team you have to "be nice" and tolerate what is not working. Your time, attention, and energy are very precious—value yours and that of others. Speak up, lead, get results. You should leave every peace team meeting on time and with a lot of energy, looking forward to the next one.

The following suggestions are some guidelines for getting the most from your peace team:

1. **Have a leader and rules:** Select a peace team leader who is responsible for starting and ending the meetings on time, keeping to the agenda, and moving things forward. Your leader will enforce the protocol for the meetings, or have the authority to delegate roles like timekeeper and agenda tracker. This protocol should include rules by which to run the meeting and rules for the activities by individual members as well as the peace team as a whole. Have your leader look at www.P5Y.org/teams and review the list of forms, agendas, and ideas to keep your peace team fun, interesting, and challenging for everyone in it.

2. **Set a time:** Every group is different. You may want to meet for one hour or three hours. Some people like to do full-day sessions once a month to explore deeper topics. Decide on a time frame and stick to it.

3. **Set a place:** Make sure everyone knows where to meet. Some people like to switch houses every time, other people like to meet at a consistent location such as an office, conference room, or coffee shop. If you change the location of your meeting, make sure everyone knows about the change. Be mindful of each other.

4. **Agree on how to communicate:** Many groups use email, but your group may want to use a phone tree, text messaging, or an Internet group. P5Y.org will be developing tools so that team members can set their preferences for team communication; meanwhile, communicate clearly and frequently to avoid confusion and disappointment.

5. **Choose a name:** Pick a name for your peace team. The name can be inspirational, funny, or even self-deprecating. Most of all, everyone in the peace team should like the name, or at least not dislike it. Some colorful names of existing peace teams are Peace Angels, the Warthogs, Beat Five, Namaste Bitches, Christ's Wingmen, and Lamas Lemmings.

6. **Discuss interesting topics and participate in exciting activities:** The key to discovering the power of your peace team is to hold substantive, exciting meetings that enrich and reward all the members of the group. The most important element of your peace team meetings should be the discussion topics and the group activities. Below we have listed several discussion topics that have inspired various peace teams we've interacted with.

- What is the most effective contribution we can make to peace by 2014?

- What new opportunities will be available to you and people close to you when the people of the world have chosen to no longer engage in war?

- What will be available and possible for the world?

- Share team member commitments to peace and their progress. Are people meeting their commitments? Are the commitments clear? Are they measurable, doable, inspiring? Do they have deadlines?

- Discuss the peacmaker roles of peacemakers from www.thirdside. org/roles.cfm. Decide what role your team wishes to play, and figure out a way to do it. As the national plans for peace come online at P5Y.org, this will become easier.

- Create ways to publicize and popularize the Global Peace Treaty and P5Y. Create a news event around the treaty or the goal, and report your team's progress on the P5Y.org website.

- Have one member or a committee within the team report on how the peace team can contribute directly to one or more specific needs described in the Peace Plans for the various areas of the world. Choose a contribution.

- Use role-playing tools for conflict resolution. Draw on ideas for nonviolent communication found at www.cnvc.org/, or other resources.

- Create a shared peacemaking goal. Make it measurable, accountable, and specific, and give it a deadline.

In addition to discussions, it is important that your peace team engage in activities that will inspire and inform future activities.

- Ask everyone to silently brainstorm for three minutes innovative ways to create sustainable world peace. (We recommend using big sheets of paper or EZ-charts). In the larger group, everyone shares their ideas.

- Close your eyes and imagine where you will be on New Year's Eve 2014. What is your age and the age of the people around you? Imagine the specific location. Look back at what you've experienced up to that point. Who have you been? What principles have you lived by? What could people count on you for? Who is around you? Open your eyes and write down what you saw. Now design your ideal place to be on New Year's Eve 2014. What do you need to change in your life to bring this about? What new purpose or commitment do you need to take on? Share your vision with the group for two minutes.

- For four minutes silently write down the principles and values that reflect how you believe people should act. How do you like to treat people? For two minutes, look at any area of your life where you have broken this principle. Share this with the person next to you in the circle.

We would like to share two activities that our peace teams have enjoyed. One team is in New York City, the other in southern California. The New York team has created a VIP trip with a peace theme to Prague and has invited philanthropists and thought leaders. The purpose of the trip is to raise money for an international peace conference, to educate philanthropists about P5Y, and to launch P5Y at the peace conference. The idea came about from describing to different people our specific objective of launching P5Y. The team came together through these conversations, and we are now working toward a common purpose.

The other activity was a peace brainstorming session in La Jolla, California. Our team gathered about thirty people with diverse backgrounds, from Academy Award–winning directors and producers, and documentary filmmakers, to philanthropists, activists, and artists, among others. We took an afternoon to lead our team and their guests through a process to clear out our concepts of peace and war, free our creativity, and generate ideas and follow-up action to create peace in five years. Although we set out to have a brainstorming session, for many people it turned out to be a much deeper exploration of life and their relationship to the world than we expected. Overall it was a big success, and we are using many of the ideas that came out of the session.

Just as you will discover new perspectives on creating world peace from your peace buddy, by working with your peace team you will be able to discover the power of a small group of individuals to create change. As P5Y grows, and as you grow with P5Y, it is essential that you preserve and expand the power of small group action out into a larger group. If our larger P5Y group can act with the same focus and determination as a smaller group, there is no end to the discoveries we, and the world, will make about the realities of war and peace.

COMMIT: YOU AND YOUR BUSINESS'S LONG-TERM PROFITS OF PEACE

Until one is committed, there is hesitancy, the chance to draw back . . . Concerning all acts of initiative (and creation), there is one elementary truth that ignorance of which kills countless ideas and splendid plans: that the moment one definitely commits oneself, then Providence moves too. A whole stream of events issues from the decision, raising in one's favor all manner of unforeseen incidents, meetings, and material assistance, which no man could have dreamed would have come his way.[24]

—William Hutchinson Murray, mountaineer

WHY COMMIT? Commitment creates the movement from where you are to where you are going. It is putting your contribution toward something that energizes you. The act of being committed moves you beyond resignation, laziness, or depression. Commitment beyond oneself is attractive. Your view of the world is made up of your commitments: If you want to expand your view, then expand your level of commitment. The key to creating world peace is effective commitment. We have committed ourselves to the goal of peace in five years, and consequently, we are committing the resources necessary to achieve

24. W. H. Murray, *The Scottish Himalayan Expedition* (J. M. Dent & Sons, 1951).

that goal. In order to attract the level of commitment needed from millions of people around the globe, as well as organizations and nations, we must make a high level of commitment worthwhile. Your commitment is part of a synergistic combination of commitments.

Although world peace is desired by the great majority of people, it is a big step to trust a method to achieve peace and commit to it. Our spiritual and compassionate sides yearn for peace, but our business sense rightly demands a potential and believable return on our investment of effort. The best way to prove to individuals and the world in general that a commitment to world peace is worthwhile is to describe the benefits of that commitment in sound business terms. We have already said that our overall approach is to treat peace as a practical business goal.

THE PROFITABILITY OF PERSONAL COMMITMENT

The overall benefit of peace in five years is blatantly obvious: Peace will be rewarding to every person on the planet. A world free from war, a world at peace, is a world that is safer for each of us. With safety comes the potential to focus our energies and our efforts on activities that benefit ourselves and humankind. To put the situation in business terms, all of us will profit from world peace.

Peace in five years will be an economic boon for all of us, as we reap the rewards of peaceful economies, tourism, trade, and larger markets. All of us will profit economically from world peace as the resources used to maintain large standing armies and to fight wars are repurposed. How would you want those resources reallocated: lowered taxes, more education, aerospace research?

Monetary profit, however, is only one potential form of satisfaction. The people who will profit most from world peace are those who commit to making it happen. We profit personally from the inspiration and discoveries that are part of the work. We profit from the connections we make both with individuals who are working on P5Y and with the people and organizations with whom we collaborate. We profit spiritually from the peace work itself as we grow in our understanding of peace and we internalize the processes by which world peace will be established in five years.

Many people yearn to be part of something bigger than themselves, something that feels like a significant contribution. Commitment beyond oneself is understood by psychologists, therapists, and many individuals as a common element of a happy life. When our "problems aren't big enough," as the saying goes, we fritter away our attention on inconsequential matters. P5Y offers participants an opportunity to participate in the transition to a peaceful world, one of the great challenges of our time. In committing to such a huge and important undertaking, our lives naturally "straighten out," and we easily find the courage to solve previously daunting challenges so that we can get to the interesting challenge. (This topic is more fully addressed in chapter 13.)

The authors have benefited enormously from P5Y already. Our lives are more full, intense, and focused. We have met dozens of fascinating, intelligent people, multiple Nobel Peace laureates, philanthropists, diplomats, peace experts, business people, and government leaders. We are doing what we love, and we are inspired to do it. Our lives work because they have to. Any area of our lives that is not handled impeccably reflects back negatively on our commitment. Our lives are far from "perfect"; as we write this Nathan's eldest son has just returned from three days in the hospital following a vehicle accident. Despite this crisis, it is still a blessing and a pleasure to continue to focus on world peace.

THE PROFITABILITY OF NONPROFIT COMMITMENT

Commitment helps give us a vision of what success looks like. When a nonprofit organization has a clear commitment with a deadline, the organization becomes much more attractive to give resources to. Nonprofit organizations that are already involved in peace work gain from their commitment to P5Y by receiving access to a global network of peacemakers, worldwide marketing exposure, and collaborative resources to supercharge their own efforts to create world peace. At present most peace organizations are locked into a cycle of isolated projects and fund-raising. Under the P5Y plan, NGOs and peace organizations can seamlessly plug into the coordinated peace plan for their region of operation and into collaborative, financial, and volunteer resources for maximal effectiveness in their mission.

For example, Dr. Jim Gordon, founder of the Center for Mind-Body Medicine in Washington, D.C., runs a program called Healing the Wounds of War, which has trained hundreds of healthcare professionals to "deal successfully with the stress and trauma of war—in themselves and the populations they serve." Dr. Gordon's programs are effective, and the function he serves as the healer is an essential part of the practice of peace safety: It prevents war from recurring by healing damaged relationships.

We asked Dr. Gordon what would help him be even more effective. His reply was typical of peace leaders. He wanted a policy framework that did not undermine his work; he was handicapped by cycles of projects and fund-raising, instead of simply being allowed to focus on delivering the healing function to Serbia, Gaza, and other areas where he works. He said that his work would be more effective if combined with job training, economic development, and education. The position he described is known as the provider, the person who helps provide the most basic needs—food, safety, identity, and freedom. In collaboration with P5Y, we see Dr. Gordon as having the opportunity to make commitments in collaboration with other providers, gaining access to increased levels of funding and qualified volunteer commitments, and particularly benefiting from policy changes in the United States and elsewhere that are more supportive of peace. Dr. Gordon, who is expert and effective at healing the psychological wounds of war, can profit by applying his expertise more broadly and continuously, thereby increasing the safety of everyone on the planet by preventing war.

There are many organizations like Dr. Gordon's, with their various peace missions. Through the planning, collaboration, and resources of P5Y, these organizations can profit by being more effective at whatever role they play in peace safety.

THE PROFITABILITY OF CORPORATE COMMITMENT

What is probably more surprising is the fact that for-profit corporations stand to profit handsomely from their commitment to world peace. As philosopher/economist Adam Smith put it, "Either goods and services cross borders, or armies do." Your customer base increases in a secure and safe market. Your company can complete projects faster with global efficiency and increased trust in the market. Your company needs educated employees and customers whose professional development is undisturbed in a peaceful environment. Any corporation that takes the long view must consider action for peace a good investment, for security and prosperity go hand in hand. Corporations have immense resources, organizational intelligence, and influence. Corporations as a form of human organization have both benefited and hurt humanity, just as governments have both benefited and hurt humanity. In both cases, shortsighted and narrow policies have done the most damage.

Until now, global corporations have been largely left out of the supposed "peace party," but without them, world peace will not happen. As world peace is repositioned into the mainstream, P5Y offers a new, more interesting proposition to corporations to help create world peace that does not involve regulation, browbeating, or tax demands; rather, it offers significant bottom-line and social values.

War and the threat of war have a direct impact on the profits of many corporations. Energy in particular affects businesses as higher fuel prices cut into the bottom line, hurting profits and stock values. Then there's the impact of losing key personnel to military call-ups as highly skilled, experienced people are taken away from their jobs. The cost of hiring and training replacements can run into the tens of thousands of dollars per individual. Hiring skilled people from foreign countries becomes more difficult and costly as visa requirements are tightened. Billions of dollars flee to safer havens, making capital more expensive and scarce, further restricting business growth. Government bonds that are used to finance war suck hundreds of billions of dollars out of the economy, further restricting credit and even hitting consumers with high interest rates, which can drive down demand for products and services.

The spending on war takes capital away from other areas where it is badly needed. According to Nobel Prize–winning economist Joseph Stiglitz, the massive spending on Iraq—fifty to sixty times what the government initially estimated, which could end up topping $1.6 *trillion*—is a major cause of the subprime banking and housing crisis. War spending affects business's ability to operate and grow. High taxes and crumbling infrastructure put downward pressure on demand for products of all kinds. The burden on corporations is felt by everyone in higher prices, stingy services, tighter budgets, and lost jobs.

The corporate cost of war is so high that the business world is beginning to understand that a commitment to peace is one of the best long-term investments possible.

Peace Action

What you can do today to further peace by 2014

Organize and hold your own "Peace Aid" festival with musicians from your community, using all the money raised to support your own peace efforts or those of favored organizations. And of course, publicize and promote the event on www.P5Y.org.

YOUR BUSINESS ANALYSIS OF PEACEMAKING

Now that you are starting to understand how you can profit from peace, here is how you can express your higher impulses inside of your business instead of quitting to join a nonprofit. In order for the business community to join in our efforts to create world peace, we must demonstrate clearly that the commitment to peace will be profitable for corporations. In the business world, decisions are based on information and analysis. Why would a rational, profit-maximizing corporation take steps to create world peace? Because changing conditions make an investment in world peace an opportunity for creating shareholder and stakeholder value. Increasing globalization and the increasing impact of corporate social responsibility (CSR) make it easier than it ever has been in the past to quantify the business benefits of a commitment to peace.

Increasing globalization makes peace more valuable, and war more disruptive. Global supply chains are catastrophically disrupted by both warfare and asymmetrical threats. Increased peace and security create disproportionately more opportunity for creative business partnerships and cost savings. Many global corporations would be fatally disrupted by a global war, something that was not true just fifty years ago. Corporations have both a great deal to protect and a great deal to gain from more secure globalization. This ought to be factored into any consideration of investment in safety from war.

Risk is something that corporations make a huge effort to understand and manage. They buy insurance, they have risk-assessment departments, and they assume and minimize risks they are particularly expert at and in control of. War is a risk that is unpredictable in the long and medium term, but it is predictable in occurrence. In other words, in the present world without an effective practice of war prevention, we know that war will occur, but we don't know what it will affect. Aside from the predictable casualties and mayhem, for instance, key resources can be nationalized, trade barriers can go up overnight, shipping lanes can be closed or mined, market access can be denied, and travel can be restricted. Globally reducing the risk of war is very much in the interest of business, except those that are directly profiting from arms sales and military contracts.

Another consequence of globalization is that a large corporation's employees are often from all over the globe. As these highly educated professionals travel, interact, work, and learn in other cultures, they become natural ambassadors. From their perspective as citizens of the world, war is unappealing. Even if you have never left your country, but you work for a foreign corporation, or your job depends on imports or exports, your enthusiasm for war will tend to be minimal if you know that it threatens your job.

CSR is a business trend that is on the increase and encourages corporations to commit to peace. CSR has become, if not the heart and soul of corporate life, at least an important consideration in both marketing and the creation of a corporate culture. There have been many successful CSR campaigns, where success is defined as an image and sales benefit to the company and a contribution to a humanitarian cause. One of the most successful has been Bono's (RED) campaign (so named because red is the color of emergency), which has benefited dozens of partners, including American Express, Gap, Inc., and Motorola. Bono's idea is to channel a percentage of (RED) merchandise sales to causes, particularly AIDS and malaria treatment and prevention in Africa. Corporations would not increase their investment in CSR unless it made good business sense, which it does. CSR is profitable. Effective CSR is also important to attracting and retaining global talent, which is a fierce and ongoing battle among corporations.

CSR doesn't mean finding any good cause and supporting it with a regular donation. Though better than no involvement at all, that's barely a beginning. We propose that CSR be aligned more directly with the corporation's core mission and values. When CSR integrates with a company's values and capabilities, it authentically benefits employees and customers. Instead of being viewed as a marketing expense, an enlightened CSR program can be seen as an investment.

Creating world peace as a CSR project has significant advantages over other CSR programs. Consider the enormous challenges of today's marketing environment. Every corporation faces a struggle to be both relevant to customers and to project authenticity. A CSR program that ties the core values of the corporation to a global project to create world peace accomplishes the main business goals of CSR: it is inspiring, fresh, relevant, and beneficial to every person on the planet. The powerful PR and word-of-mouth positivity generated by such a commitment extends well past traditional consumer and business-to-business relationships. Imagine a company receiving a goodwill award from a whole nation in gratitude for a commitment to world peace. In other words, world peace can be profitable for corporations. When the CSR program is itself a powerful global brand, as P5Y will be, and as Bono's (RED) campaign is, then the CSR benefits are maximized, because the company participates in the recognition and credibility of a well-known program. The only question they have to answer is what their peace project is, and how it fits into the larger collaboration to create peace in five years.

THE QUESTION OF PURPOSE

Beyond the ordinary consideration of investment and profit lies a deeper question of our purpose on the planet. Just as individuals have ordinary concerns as well as deeper questions of life and meaning, so today it is reasonable to ask the same of our systems of organizations, both public and private. Corporations are founded and operated by individual people, and these people share common values and a common purpose.

At W. L. Gore & Associates, founder Bill Gore stated the mission of the company very simply: Make money and have fun. He saw the primary purpose of his business as having fun while making a contribution. He would often say that the only reason to make money was to keep having fun.

Often the default purpose of a corporation is just to make money. However, for a corporation to say that its *only* purpose is to make money—or "enhance shareholder value"—is like a person saying that his or her only purpose is to eat. It is necessary but not sufficient. Making money as the only purpose is shortsighted. It is an unworthy goal and provides no incentive for individuals to cooperate for a higher purpose. It falls short of a goal worthy of the time and attention of educated, intelligent people.

It used to be sufficient to be a conqueror, a titan of industry, a hugely profitable enterprise, but that's no longer enough. The CSR movement is communicating to business the hunger for a higher purpose that includes and even improves profitability. Corporations who discover how to integrate their higher purpose will thrive, and what purpose could be higher in this moment of history than committing to world peace?

DEVELOPING PEACE AS CSR VALUE

In a recent conversation with the CEO of a leading corporation, we discussed the common misconception that corporations have to have a CSR program that is different from their business's core competency. It's fine for a steel company to benefit Toys for Tots, for instance, but what they are really good at is steel. The goal should be to align the company's core competency with its values for CSR.

By following a basic six-step process, any corporation can create a CSR program that is both authentic and woven from the fabric of the corporation itself. This process will assist any corporation in determining what kind of peacemaker it is. As we meet with corporate leaders and talk to them about committing to world peace, we work through the program with them, discussing these six steps.

SIX-STEP CSR PROCESS

1. **Core Competencies:** What does your company do best? What do people count on and expect from your corporation? Don't get mired in details. This is a big-picture overview.

2. **Skills:** What skills are highly developed in your company, and how are they applied to do what you do? For example, a company that sells appliances might have highly developed engineering skills. Does your company excel in logistics, innovation, project management, engineering, or rapid execution?

3. **Mission and Values:** Gather any previously written charters, mission statements, value charts, strategic branding materials, and founding principles. What are the core values of the company? What were the intentions of the founders of your company?

4. **Current Giving:** Is there a current CSR program? Do you donate time or materials to community projects? Do the founders have any philanthropic involvement? Is there an industry standard? For example, in the medical industry there is a standard of compassionate use of medical products that are donated to treat people who would normally not have access to them.

5. **Wish for the World:** What is the company's wish for the world? If you look at your mission, products, customers, marketing, employees, and values, what are you already promising? If you took your marketing promise and pushed it all the way, what would it say? What is it moving toward? For example, Club Med promises a happy vacation. Taken all the way, their wish for the world is for people to be happy. A company that makes plumbing supplies promises quality products delivered on time. Taken all the way, its wish might be for every person to have clean water. This is not some new direction. It is something you discover that the company has always been moving toward. What is your company's ultimate wish for the world?

6. **Corporate Image:** What is the CSR program that would align with the company's competencies, skills, values, and wish for the world? What CSR program would inspire your employees? What would you want to see reported in the news about your CSR program? What CSR program would take advantage of your core competencies? What would you want to be telling prospective talent?

How does your CSR fit into P5Y? How is it relevant to our times? Developing a CSR program that commits to world peace is a lot like developing a normal, profitable business project. It takes planning, resources, and commitment from top leadership. It is strategic, and it delivers value in the form of marketing, employee motivation, customer goodwill, perception of leadership, talent retention, and recruitment. Corporations will find that a commitment to world peace in five years is not only profitable but also feasible if approached in a businesslike manner.

As P5Y and other efforts move world peace into the mainstream, it will become easier for corporate leaders to formulate and discuss their world peace projects openly. The present cultural and political trappings of the practice of peace have reached the end of their usefulness to humankind. Peace has outgrown being just for saints, hippies, angry young activists, dreamy-eyed New Agers, academics, and ultra-dedicated underpaid professionals. Those pioneers have shown us the way and brought us to the brink of peace; now it is up to the rest of us to take it the rest of the way. Corporations can make a huge contribution to world peace simply by making it "normal" and achievable. While talking to a corporation, remember that an effective discussion of world peace with anyone demands respect for the contributions that are possible. Whether we are talking to individuals, nonprofit organizations, or regular corporations, we always remember that a commitment to world peace is possible and in the best interest of everyone.

Corporations that conduct business with the military have, until now, often been painted as obstacles to peace. "Military contractors" and "the military-industrial complex" have been regarded as warmongers. Maybe not, maybe so—it is just as easy to point a finger at NGOs who waste aid budgets in multiple layers of home office expenses, or subcontractors or government agencies who prioritize ineffective policies over peace, and so on. From any point of view, the present system is broken, and the result is war and misery.

Corporations with military business have some of the most potent contributions to make to the practice of constructive conflict. They have deep experience in chaotic areas, huge logistical capabilities, understanding of politics, and the capacity to manage and undertake large projects with large budgets. They have engineering expertise to create technical solutions to difficult problems. They can effectively collaborate with military organizations. They have lobbying power. They are experts in key components of peace safety—physical security, construction, deterrence, and intervention.

As P5Y gets under way, military contractors will be invited to profit from peace. We don't yet know the exact form this will take, but we suggest that peace contracts can be as profitable and perhaps more long-term than war contracts. Military hardware is not disappearing anytime soon. Countries may reduce their arms purchases when the need for them is seen to diminish—probably after a few years of world peace. Meanwhile, the people who work for these contractors, and the businesses themselves, can be creatively helped to make the transition to a peaceful world, just as many other industries have navigated change. What follows is a list of possible solutions to reorganizing current military contractors:

- Security contractors may be doing similar activities, but with a mission that is structured to create functioning states, reduce corruption, build essential services, and train local security and police forces.

- Engineering and infrastructure companies could be put to work repairing decaying roads and bridges or reinforcing levees and other structures critical in natural disasters.

- Weapons makers may continue to supply militaries around the world, but as orders diminish, they may channel their design and manufacturing capacities into creating sophisticated, reliable, robust, cheap, and usable solutions to energy, water, and transportation use throughout the world.

- A wide range of companies could work to bring clean water, roads, schools, and sustainable farming to undeveloped regions.

We don't know all the solutions, but we do know that there are no losers in world peace, and we are just as certain that everyone has important contributions to make. We also recognize that the traditional trappings of national security are part of a peaceful world, and that in its best moments, the military represents some of the highest ideals of humankind. The new global reality that we must either adapt to or perish from is that the only strong defense lies in intelligently and compassionately preventing the creation of violent, organized enemies in the first place, and in defusing conflict before it becomes war.

Here are some specific commitments you and your business can take action on now to promote P5Y:

- **CSR Programming:** Go to the P5Y.org website and download the manual for creating an authentic CSR program that generates genuine benefits for your company and for the world. See how the principles of your CSR program can be applied to P5Y. Strongly consider participating in the P5Y brand to benefit world peace and to create high recognition among consumers, similar to Bono's (RED) campaign.

- **Marketing and Advertising:** Co-brand P5Y and include P5Y in your advertising and marketing campaigns. If your group is international, create an international collaboration. Go to www.P5Y.org/brand and download a logo and link to put on your print materials and website. If you want a customized P5Y program, please contact us at CorpRelations@P5Y.org.

- **Sponsor:** Sponsor contests for innovations, ideas, and projects related to P5Y, offering prizes for the most creative or effective ideas. Or sponsor an NGO that correlates to your core mission and competencies. A company can also sponsor a principle of conflict resolution, such as understanding needs, building trust, or relationship healing.

- **Employee Peace Fund:** Fund peace projects, or create a scholarship or grant to provide resources to employee or member peace projects.

- **Lend a Skill:** Your company could help out other P5Y groups by lending its skills. You can assign one or more of your employees to dedicate themselves to a project full time, or designate a time each week to donate skill sets.

- **Register Commitments:** Take on P5Y commitments from people in your organization. Put a "Projects for Peace" poster in your lobby, building elevators, employee cafeteria, or teachers' lounge, and encourage people to commit to their own projects.

CORPORATIONS FOR PEACE

Take a moment now to think about corporations and world peace. Try to imagine what the corporation would do, what its commitment might be. What corporations would NOT commit to peace? If they did commit, what would their contribution be? What could a company do that would make you want to buy from them, or that would make you feel positively about them? If you work for a company, write down what they could do that would make you feel prouder to work there. Write down the names of various corporations that come to mind:

_____

_____

_____

YOUR COMMITMENT TO PEACE IS PROFITABLE

P5Y takes a businesslike approach to world peace. We understand that to succeed in creating world peace in five years we need commitments from both individuals and corporations. With corporate commitments to world peace, P5Y will have the resources and the support base we need to replace war with the practice of peace safety.

Looking around the world, we can see how peace has had a positive impact on the business community. Northern Ireland has seen a huge increase in prosperity since the end of "the troubles." Areas of Africa that were previously desperately poor because of their involvement in war are thriving markets today. It is easy to imagine that a persistent global commitment to peace would allow trade and commerce to thrive and corporations to efficiently market to hundreds of millions of newly prosperous customers.

Creating world peace is a large endeavor, too much for any one corporation, however large, to undertake alone. The business benefits of peace accrue to all businesses, not just the ones who invest their planning, expertise, and money in creating peace. Therefore, businesses interested in committing to peace and making investments that secure their markets, supply chains, and customers from the threat of war can best do so in collaboration with other corporations, governments, and NGOs. Even if some corporations work hard for global peace, and others benefit from their efforts, we suggest that the goodwill, market access, and expertise gained from the process will continue to be a significant business advantage for those corporations who commit to peace now.

Any corporation will need to make its own calculation of the return on investment of world peace and make its own determination as to whether or not to participate. Although the returns may appear uncertain or difficult to calculate, they are doubtless enormous. You and your business can profit from peace.

COLLABORATE: ADVANCE HUMANITY'S NEXT EVOLUTION

I think that people want peace so much that one of these days government had better get out of their way and let them have it.

—Dwight D. Eisenhower

COLLABORATION IS POTENT because you give of your greatest gifts and skills and also receive of the greatest gifts and skills of others. In this chapter you will discover the quantum leap in collaboration inherent in a movement toward world peace. Each previous increase in collaboration marked a radical shift for humanity: agricultural, industrial, and technological knowledge economy (the Internet). Today, massive global collaboration requires constructive conflict. Wars are not fought alone. We get war when people collaborate on violence, many times under the guise of higher ideals—for protection of human rights, for cultural and religious freedom. Humanity is a meta-organization and our huge leaps forward happen from people collaborating. Now we can collaborate to organize our international agreements to prevent war and engage in active peace-as-safety practices. When you understand the importance of collaboration, you can actively usher in a new era for humanity. You need to know this because it is already happening one way or another. P5Y is just speeding it up. The practice of collaboration makes your organization more effective because it builds trust, knowledge, and communication. Fundamentally, collaboration produces exponential results for your personal commitment and mission that you could not accomplish alone. It simultaneously produces exponential results for the mission of your organization. Leading-edge businesses have known and practiced this for years. The engine of prosperity is human ingenuity; the engine of innovation is collaboration; and collaboration requires safety. Safety creates a global environment where we can collaborate to meet everyone's needs.

Most likely you are already collaborating if you're part of a business, group, community, church, synagogue, mosque, prayer circle, school, university, Little League team, or activist group. One attribute of P5Y is that we are approaching peace from the perspective of aligning one's life with core values and innate strengths to foster effective collaboration among private, governmental, and corporate organizations for world peace. You may be thinking about how your organization can contribute to peace by 2014. Organizations, religious groups, communities, schools, counties, and states can all become part of our campaign.

You've already discovered the roles of peace buddies and peace teams in creating world peace. As we progress toward our goal, we must learn to collaborate not only with individuals and small groups but with larger groups as well. Collaboration is sometimes easy and sometimes difficult, but it is always essential for peace. While asking the world to give up war and adopt a more collaborative and cooperative attitude toward conflict resolution, we must be prepared to collaborate and cooperate with a great number of diverse organizations as we learn to work together for peace.

The organizations you are part of can be a vital part of this movement for one obvious reason: They bring together people who tend to be of like mind and similar passions. One person who belongs to a church, a large civic organization like Kiwanis International or Rotary International, or a political group like the Green Party can inspire an entire organization to strive for world peace by 2014.

A few highly motivated people can change the course of a large organization. For instance, in 2008 a group of fourth-graders in Watertown, Massachusetts, were assigned a task by their teacher: Take charge of a project to contribute to the fight against global warming by getting the city to reduce the size of the margins on their computer printouts. The class calculated that if everyone in the United

States did so, it would save more than six million trees per year. The result was a letter-writing campaign to the city, a commitment from their school to change their margins, a lobbying effort at the Massachusetts State House, and a feature story on NPR. It's not directly related to peace, but this story shows that a small group of passionate activists can change the attitudes and behaviors of large organizations.

This book would not have been written without collaboration, the advice of dozens of multidisciplinary experts, each offering diverse experiences. P5Y already has collaborators ranging from Internet marketers, broadcast stations, and microlenders to journalists and stand-up comedians working with artists.

BECOME A SUCCESSFUL PEACE COLLABORATOR

On the surface, collaboration may seem challenging, but it is actually easier and more efficient than working from your strengths and passion alone. Independent-minded individuals are powerful collaborators who make distinct, strong contributions. The best way to collaborate is to do it. Collaboration starts with an invitation. Collaborate with people you trust and from whom you can learn. Complement each other's strengths. Great collaboration takes delegating, trusting, forgiving, changing what hasn't worked in the past, communicating, and following up—regularly. Most of us collaborate in some way or another every day. For example, we collaborate on school projects, car pools, neighborhood block parties, and work projects. As we discussed earlier in chapter 6 about the power of small teams, successful collaborations bring improved results for all the parties involved.

The elements needed for successful collaboration include what Jon R. Katzenbach and Douglas K. Smith, two senior McKinsey and Company partners, identified for high-performing groups in their book *The Wisdom of Teams* (Harvard Business School Press, 1993).

- Common purposes for working
- Specific performance goals that are commonly agreed upon
- Complementary skills in group members
- Mutual accountability among all members
- Shared working approaches
- Small numbers of people—typically fewer than twelve

For high-performance collaboration you also need trust, transparency, and an infrastructure for shared communication and follow-up. Once you have learned how successful collaborations work, you can begin to work on your own to expand the P5Y campaign for world peace.

YOU ARE LEADING THE WAY

Let's take a moment to apply this by considering the organizations you participate in. As you go through the following exercise, consider how you can work with others within the organization to launch a truly collaborative effort for world peace.

ORGANIZATIONS

WHAT GROUPS AND ORGANIZATIONS ARE YOU A PART OF?

_____

_____

_____

_____

_____

Here are some vital questions you can ask yourself as you launch a collaborative effort with your organization:

- What kind of potential peacemaker is this group/organization? What are its strengths, and in what areas can it contribute?
- In what effective and fun ways can you see this group getting involved with P5Y?
- How committed is the organization to world peace?
- What leadership role might you take on?
- What actions could you take?

One of the most important things to consider is the political dimension of any collaboration. To make a collaboration work, you must understand the organizational structure that will be collaborating. Get to know the decision makers within the organizations and familiarize yourself with the systems that support the organization. Do the organizations have a history of collaboration? They may be experts at internal collaboration yet this may be their first time collaborating with another organization, business, NGO, or individual. Know your strengths and communicate up front what you are willing to contribute.

If you are moved to get your organization to collaborate with P5Y, convene a meeting of your group and let them know beforehand that you want to share the possibility of working on a potential project. Prepare well for this meeting to help guarantee its success. Here is a list of things you should do before the meeting:

- Consider fun ways your organization might get involved that are aligned with its purpose.
- Write an effective invitation for people to attend, especially key leaders.
- Make sure you have a good place to meet, one that is quiet and convenient.
- Prepare handouts with key information.
- Consider making a presentation with your peace buddy or a partner.
- Share what you're doing with P5Y and what you've taken on as your personal commitment to peace.
- Consider what your group, and the people in it, can gain from P5Y.
- Have a specific project suggestion ready that outlines these benefits.
- Plan to explore with the group what they would be most excited to do for peace by 2014.
- Plan to wrap up your meeting by asking for and promising next steps. What are the next steps? Decide what the best outcome of your presentation would be.

Schedule a follow-up meeting soon after the initial meeting. Set a deadline for making a decision about collaborating on P5Y and make sure that your organization holds to that deadline. Work hard to secure this

Peace Action

What you can do today to further peace by 2014

Envision the dream team you need to help you fulfill on your commitment. Consider peace groups already active in your community. Set up a time in your schedule to talk with them about collaboration.

collaboration. You cannot overestimate the importance of collaborating even with one organization.

THE POWER OF ONE ORGANIZATION IN THE WORLD

Just consider, for example, one Unitarian church with a congregation of about five hundred people. This community has the ability to reach out to thousands more among family and friends. It has a built-in fund-raising capacity. It has a cross-section of skills and professional training ranging from lawyers and physicians to craftspeople, teachers, law enforcement officers, and political officeholders. It has a mailing list. It has a built-in infrastructure for peace teams and peace buddies. Most important, it has clear values and a mission that align with world peace. A traditional strength of religious groups is to uphold the highest values of humanity. Churches are just one example of an organization that can collaborate with P5Y. Every organization has particular strengths to offer peace by 2014.

Some organizations are collaborating publicly with P5Y and some privately. For instance, ideocore, a Santa Barbara–based branding company, offered to collaborate with branding the P5Y movement. Media One of San Francisco has taken on P5Y as their core cause. DharmaMix media is making voice-over music available free online of the message of this book. Numerous diplomats and international political advisers are publicly and quietly collaborating with P5Y.

ACTIONS YOUR ORGANIZATION CAN TAKE

The best way to keep the organization engaged with world peace is to act. Once your organization has agreed to collaborate with our campaign to create world peace in five years, start work immediately. Capture the enthusiasm of your organization for world peace and never let it waver. Remember that this is a multi-year project, and to maintain your organization's enthusiasm for collaboration throughout that time, create early success and celebrate milestones. Design activities suitable for your organization that deliver anticipated outcomes according to a definite time frame. Such activities will of course depend on the kind of organization you are working with, and the types of activities that it normally undertakes.

If you are working on collaboration with a religious or spiritual group, register prayers, meditations, contemplations, candles, ceremonies, and spiritual studies for peace. Measure the number of prayers, hours, etc., and put it in as a project. There is an increasing body of research that suggests that the mental intention of groups of people can affect the material world in measurable ways. For example, author Lynne McTaggart, working with Dr. Gary Schwartz at the University of Arizona, has conducted an ongoing series of "intention experiments" to test the effect of human intention on everything from plant seeds to the molecular structure of water. In her book, *The Intention Experiment*, McTaggart discusses this intention experiment involving seeds:

> Human intention appears to have made a group of seeds grow eight millimeters more than a control group of seeds . . . The odds of that happening by chance are approximately one in one million. Intention really can affect the outside world, so intensely committed groups sending intentions of peace can accomplish wonders.[25]

An effective action for any organization collaborating with P5Y is to create displays. Put up "Peace by 2014" or "I promise peace" signs around your locales. Give out stickers, T-shirts, bumper stickers, posters, and flyers that say "I promise peace." No matter what your organization does, you can create a physical structure or display in your office or building that reminds people of your commitment to world peace by 2014 and to help spread the word about P5Y. Your organization can provide volunteers, skills, communication networks, co-branding, updates in your newsletter, and specific projects within national plans for peace.

Collaborating with other organizations can be an effective way for your organization to pool resources. The following are some examples of how organizations can collaborate with other organizations: a steel-manufacturing company can collaborate with effective NGOs working under the P5Y plan to provide materials to build bridges; a textile manufacturer can collaborate with clothing designers; and business adviser groups can offer high-level strategic involvement with local groups working within the national plans for peace.

Finding an existing organization to get behind P5Y in a practical manner is an efficient way to create peace. Groups have power and resources to get things done. Your organization standing for peace by 2014 can serve as a beacon to the whole community in which it is located. As we learn to collaborate with organizations all over the world, we will build a base for a world at peace.

Everyone wants to be effective. People do not have to agree on religion, politics, or how they live their lives in order to collaborate. Collaboration is the antidote to the ills of specialization: lack of communication, conflicting agendas,

25. Lynne McTaggart, *The Intention Experiment: Using Your Thoughts to Change Your Life and the World* (New York: Free Press, 2007).

mistrust, jargon, and defended expertise. The present situation is a nadir of those ills: uncoordinated policies, agendas, projects, budgets, and goals. We have the resources now to create world peace: processes, skills, money, goodwill, brainpower, and all the answers except for effective collaboration—the piece that is missing but will make all the difference in the world.

The most fundamental cooperation is for every country that needs it to have a comprehensive plan for creating a functioning government, with all of the NGOs and foreign aid in that country conforming to make it effective.

Collaboration for peace requires a mature human willingness to put aside differences voluntarily; fortunately we have millions of world citizens doing just that today. Increasing collaboration decreases the possibility of war in the future, so your act of collaboration is an act of peace.

MEASURE: HOW YOU CAN SEE THE IMPACT YOU'RE HAVING ON WORLD PEACE

What gets measured gets done.

—Tom Peters

MEASUREMENT GIVES YOU credibility and power. Using measurement feels exact and empowering. When you are talking to others, measurement is convincing because you are communicating a fact, not an opinion. Measurement is surprising, valuable, and specific. It is accounting, the basis of accountability. Measurement removes all vagueness. "Peace" is vague. "The end to politically organized deadly conflict by February 14, 2014" is definite. It is a milestone, a specific measurement of human welfare to be accomplished by a specific time. There are many measurements to be made along the way and communicated to those collaborating. Bottom line: You enable success through implementing a system of consistent measurement and accountability. What you measure, you change.

Our invitation to you is to know what measurement is relevant to your commitment. Today's technology offers you a huge choice of information to store at the top of your mind. Choose information that is important in helping you meet your goals.

YOU CAN KNOW WHAT'S GOING ON

If you are interested in world peace, and wish to talk about it with authority, then you must know the state of the world in numbers. On our website, P5Y.org/state_of_the_world, there is a table called "the state of the world." Inform yourself. We also recommend sipri.org and icg.org. The Stockholm International Peace Research Institute (SIPRI), an organization funded by the Swedish government, conducts scientific research on cooperation and conflict. You can find databases of information on past and current conflicts and resolutions at sipri.org. We think the International Crisis Group is the most comprehensive private international organization working to understand, anticipate, and prevent violent conflict. Visit their website at icg.org to keep abreast of global news.

As we write this, the Iraq War is still under way. And as we read in chapter 7, estimates are that the direct costs of the war plus the cost of healthcare for veterans could end up exceeding $1 trillion—that is one thousand billion dollars!

In 2007 the British polling company ORB surveyed Iraqi households, asking how many extended family members had been killed since the invasion. Using accepted statistical techniques, the poll estimated that nearly 1.2 million individuals were wiped off the face of the earth for being in the wrong place at the wrong time. If you want to make an impact in a conversation with someone about P5Y, know facts such as these.

If you are American, you may be interested in how your personal participation in financing our government relates to the number of Americans and Iraqis killed. Each Iraqi death came at a financial cost to the United States of about $400,000. Each average household has paid more than $4,000 for the Iraq War. One could say that each American household owns about 1 percent of an Iraqi death. Your household. If you paid more in taxes, you

Peace Action

What you can do today to further peace by 2014

Compile measurable war statistics that apply to your local community, business, and family. Research costs and measure the direct impact to the groups you are involved with.

bought more death. American deaths from the Iraq War, more than 4,100 as this book went to press, cost about $200 million per death. The average household has participated in 0.00002 American deaths. If you count the wounded, add about another 30,000 Americans. Then the cost per casualty drops to about $16 million per American, or 0.0003 American casualties purchased per household.

Whether you agree with the logic of this calculation or not, it is only because of measurement that we can make it. The point here isn't that war is bad; that's obvious. The point is that every tax-paying American is financing death, and we are personally responsible for that. It is especially challenging if we disagree with the U.S. government on its policy of war and even more disheartening if it violates our moral values. We are NOT saying that you should feel personally guilty; we are saying, however, that citing specific measurements of casualties and expenses allows you to ask others the following question: How much of your taxes go to violent human death and what are you going to do about it? As an individual, as an organization, as a family, as Coca-Cola or Pepsi—does that match your values? This isn't to make you depressed but to empower you.

This is the power of measurement we evoke in creating world peace in five years. Until now, the peace business has been managed to "make a difference." Well, it has made a difference. We are grateful for each life that has been touched and saved by peace movements. But this work has taken place mostly under a set of assumptions that did not include deadlines and the possibility of complete success. In order to meet those deadlines and achieve success, we have to measure reality as it exists and use measurements to keep an accurate record of our progress. By using the power of measurement, we can create peace in five years.

THE BEST MEASUREMENTS ARE EASY AND RELEVANT

Simple relevant measurements help you achieve your goals and collaborate. When the people you are collaborating with understand your measurements you can be more effective. Temple Grandin, author of *Animals in Translation* (Simon and Schuster, 2005), has some cogent thoughts on the subject. She has created a five-point animal welfare audit for meatpacking plants. If the plant fails on any one of the five points, the plant fails the audit. Each of the five points is readily observable and is directly concerned with an animal's welfare.

Grandin makes the point that she is looking at the *animals* in the plant, not the people, equipment, records, or procedures. Her goal is to increase animal welfare, so that is what she measures. That's because a plant could receive a score of 95 out of a 100 and pass certain audits, yet it could still be a place where animals unnecessarily suffer. Therefore, one of Grandin's audit points is "Do cows fall down?" Looking over the feedlot, it is immediately obvious whether cows fall down or not. So "cows fall down" is an easy measurement to make. Grandin says that cows hate falling down; it is a major source of stress and suffering for them. So "cows fall down" is directly relevant to their welfare. She goes on to point out that cows falling down can have any number of causes, all of them directly related to their welfare: they could be on slippery flooring, have poor nutrition, not enough space, illness, neglected hooves, and so on. Grandin's point is that all of those causes are the responsibility of the experts at the meatpacking plant to identify and solve.

The meatpacking-plant people are *accountable* for the welfare of their animals. One *effective measurement* of their accountability is "Do cows fall down?" It is up to the people at the plant to sort out the complex causes of cows falling down, find the particular problem at their plant, address the problem, and test the solution by measuring again.

This is a key point about creating peace in five years. What about human welfare? There has been a lot of press in the last few years about happiness—what it is, how to measure it, and so on. Happiness and well-being are tricky to measure quantitatively, at least at the present time. But war is obvious. It is easy to observe and measure in terms of dollars, casualties, duration, refugees, bullets shot, bombs dropped, personal invasions of homes, and so on. Because of the chaotic and political nature of war, exact numbers are sometimes hard to come by, but the fact of war is blatant. Even though the causes of war are complex, the measurement of damages, costs, and harm to humans is obvious.

War is our "cows fall down" obvious measurement. When cows don't fall down, they are better off. When humans don't fight wars, we are better off. Cows falling down is obvious, and war is obvious. The causes of cows falling down are many and specific to each plant. The causes of war are many and specific to each conflict. Meatpacking-plant experts are accountable for the welfare of their animals by law, as measured by cows falling down. Who is accountable for the welfare of humans, as measured by war? Are you?

We are aware that this measurement excludes other measures of human misery, like the rights to free speech and liberty. It doesn't include labor exploitation. It doesn't include the diverting of aid supplies by corrupt governments.

We have to draw the line somewhere, and this is where it lies: war, or deadly politically organized violence. When we see that, we know that the safety mechanism of peace has failed. We also know that other factors of human welfare are not being taken care of. Since war is predictable, we usually know this is coming well in advance.

OUR METRIC

Our metric for P5Y is a measurement of the number and severity of politically organized armed conflicts globally. According to the 2007 Global Conflict Trends report, despite a dramatic drop in armed conflicts since the end of the Cold War, twenty-eight countries engaged in some form of armed conflict in 2007, including more than 300,000 "child soldiers" under age eighteen, displacing or making refugees of approximately 35 million local inhabitants. SIPRI cites seventeen politically armed conflicts. SIPRI is the overall metric we are using for P5Y. There are many metrics to apply to P5Y, depending on your project, that will integrate with the implementation tools.

The best way to become familiar with a measuring system is to use it. By applying a measurement you're going to become better and better at it. Applying our measurement system to conflicts around the world as we were writing this book, we noticed the number of politically organized deadly conflicts rose from sixteen to seventeen with the Russian invasion of Georgia.

MEASUREMENT AND ACCOUNTABILITY

Your accountability is the external view of your commitment. Being accountable can be empowering, fun, and an expression of your highest values. When your accountabilities are aligned with your inner truth, a well of resources opens up. Your accountabilities are the promises you make to others who are trusting you to meet your commitment. We have a commitment we have made to ourselves and the world, and we align our actions with that commitment.

One of our accountabilities in P5Y is to monitor continually the measurements of peace in the world and notify our network of an increase or a decrease in warfare on a worldwide basis. By measuring conflicts we can work to keep governments accountable for their actions. But the welfare of humans cannot be left to governments alone. We all have individual desires, interests, companions, families, beliefs, and ideals. We are all neighbors. Measurement has shown us that we are personally participating in war on our planet. With a little reflection, even noticing that we purchase products from or own the public stock of Coca-Cola, Whole Foods, Google, Hasbro, Apple, the Gap, or any other company that pays taxes to a country that participates in war makes us realize we are participating in war.

We are accountable for our personal role in war and in killing. As we work for world peace, we must realize that this accountability is not a burden; rather, it is a blessing. In order to understand our attitudes toward accountability, it is important for each of us to discover what we are naturally, happily accountable for.

To begin to understand your attitudes toward accountability, work through the following exercise. Be honest and open as you list the things you are accountable for and your feelings toward each one.

ACCOUNTABILITY

Write down at least twenty things you are accountable for. When you are done, write a number from one to ten about how much you enjoy being accountable for each item. Ten represents great enjoyment; one is pure drudgery.

1. _____	11. _____
2. _____	12. _____
3. _____	13. _____
4. _____	14. _____
5. _____	15. _____
6. _____	16. _____
7. _____	17. _____
8. _____	18. _____
9. _____	19. _____
10. _____	20. _____

Nathan came up with the following list of personal accountabilities in no particular order.

Nathan's List

Accountable for	Enjoyment/Energy/Motivation on a Scale of 1 to 10
American foreign policy	8
My kids' welfare	10
Managing my finances	5
Living each moment to its fullest	10
Writing this book	9
World peace in five years	10
Government representing my values	6
Resolving a family dispute	8
Love	10
Teaching circus skills to kids in school	3
Paying alimony and child support	9

Nathan's biggest and most satisfying accountability area is in terms of his global responsibility. He is able to internalize the measurements of war and accept accountability for war making in various areas. Perhaps you feel oppressed or resigned in some area, rather than accountable. What would it be like to feel accountable for clean water in your community, or for the way your boss treats some people, or for creating world peace in five years? Does it feel different to feel accountable? How does it feel to be voluntarily, personally responsible for changing whatever needs to be changed? Imagine if you changed your biggest ongoing complaints into accountable actions. For example, instead of saying, "The homeless problem in my city is just terrible," change that to "I'm going to volunteer at a homeless shelter and offer a hand to people who need it to get off the streets and back into productive life."

Or how about asking yourself what you would like to be put in charge of. Imagine you could put yourself in charge of anything at all just by saying to yourself and others, "I'm in charge of such-and-such."

If you were acting on your accountabilities, whom would you be working with? What would you be saying? Where would you be going? What arrangements would you make for the rest of your life to make room for these accountabilities?

What would you stop doing because you no longer have time? Would you keep all of your current social obligations? Reflect for a moment.

Having done this exercise, perhaps you can feel the freedom that accountability and responsibility confer. Accountability is not a burden; it is a choice for freedom. Feel how you are supported by others who choose to accept their accountabilities and responsibilities: your spouse, the electrical company, the local fire department, the grocer who stocks the store's shelves, and so on, branching into a vast network of interconnecting accountabilities, contributions, and responsibilities that you trust with your life every day.

ACCOUNTABILITY FOR PEACE

It is our point of view that every one of us is accountable and responsible for the total well-being of the planet. In our time, that well-being is measured in part by the obvious "cows fall down" metric of deadly organized armed conflict. The question of this time and place in human affairs is precisely the question of how we can remove the context of war from our planet, establish dignified resolution of our conflicts, and move on to secure for all people the benefits that safety from war promises.

To create peace within five years, we are counting on enough people with aligned values to take personal accountability for peace. In order to create this ground swell, it is essential that everyone understand the importance of accountability at just this point in time.

Ballerina Gail Visentine taught Nathan that *timing is everything*. The timing is right for a great wave of success in creating peace in five years. The ebb of history in America and elsewhere has turned to a flow, and we are ripe for the "Fourth Turning" Howe and Strauss have spoken of, which we mentioned previously. This will be a radical change in national and world affairs, "a fierce new dynamic of public synergy." The opportunity for a Fourth Turning comes only once in every four generations (about every eighty or a hundred years), and the time for historical

Peace Action

What you can do today to further peace by 2014

Enlist friends or family who have been in the military to become champions for peace in five years. Ask them to speak at public forums and to invite still others to get involved in P5Y. Post speaking schedules and video clips on www.P5Y.org.

evolution is now. Furthermore, now is the first time in history that we have both the cultural understanding and the networked technology to work globally and accomplish universal goals.

There are thousands of worthy causes in the world, from liberation movements to breast cancer research to ending the war on drugs to child nutrition to clean water programs. No matter what cause you feel accountable for, it suffers from ongoing war. Whatever your cause, it will be served by world peace.

Our friend musician John McLaughlin said to us as we were planning an anniversary event for the United Nations Universal Declaration of Human Rights, "Cosmic weapons require cosmic consciousness." He didn't mean that in some mystical sense. He meant that because we have nuclear weapons capable of destroying our global civilization, we have to think about the whole world when we think about how to deal with them. We have to think cosmically.

YOUR ACCOUNTABILITY

Write your name below and read the sentence out loud:

I, _____, AM PERSONALLY, SPECIFICALLY RESPONSIBLE FOR THE VIOLENT DEATHS OF ONE OR MORE IRAQI PEOPLE THROUGH EITHER PAYING TAXES TO THE U.S. GOVERNMENT OR BUYING THE PRODUCTS OF COMPANIES THAT PAY TAXES TO THE U.S. GOVERNMENT.

You may or may not feel accountable through this exercise. Nevertheless, you may feel the urgency and necessity of world peace and that you are in charge of that. We Americans, as well as anyone who participates in the global economy, are each responsible and accountable for financing a government that acts in a way that contradicts our values.

YOUR NATIONAL ACCOUNTABILITY

As more and more citizens take responsibility for efforts to create and lead peace, their governments will come to reflect this leadership. These civil leaders are empowered by measurement. Information used to be the provenance of government. Today anyone with access to a computer can wield the power of measurement.

Our friend Lekha Singh, a provocateur and photographer, is committed to finding a way for every mother in the world to be able to feed her child. Her first inspiration was to combine best business practices with the broad capabilities of the Internet to touch the lives of 50 million people by 2005. She is the founder of Aidmatrix and has touched the lives of more than a billion people. She is a civil leader chronicling desperate areas of the world through her photographs, which are featured in *National Geographic* and her book, *The Making of an Activist*.

You can find a plethora of statistics, blogs, documentaries, and reliable sources to integrate into relevant measurements for your project. Civil leaders are emerging through their use of blogs. With the dawn of inexpensive digital technology, you can see on-the-ground footage of human rights violations and empowering messages from people working in the field. Now citizens can lead past their government. (In the next chapter you will find out more about media and how you can use them to communicate and educate your community.)

YOUR SPIRITUAL ACCOUNTABILITY

From churches to yoga mats the time is right for religious and spiritual leaders to become truly accountable for peace as well. A survey conducted in sixty countries by the Gallup Organization Poll found that 87 percent of respondents consider themselves to be part of some religion. Every major religion teaches tolerance, peace, and understanding; yet in the mix of the complex causes of war, religion has been used for thousands of years to reach political ends. It is time for the leaders of each of the great religions to insist on peace. It is not time to blame the past; it is time, however, for each adherent to take responsibility for the greatness of his or her tradition. Ask yourself what resonates with you from this list of quotes from the great faiths.

> "The fruit of the Spirit is love, joy, peace, patience, kindness, goodness, faithfulness, gentleness and self-control. Against such things there is no law."
> —*Galatians 5:22*

> "The Holy Prophet Mohammed came into this world and taught us: 'That man is a Muslim who never hurts anyone by word or deed, but who works for the benefit and happiness of God's creatures. Belief in God is to love one's fellowmen.'"
> —*Badshah Khan, as quoted in* Nonviolent Soldier of Islam

"What is hurtful to yourself do not do to your fellow man. That is the whole of the Torah and the remainder is but commentary."
—*Talmud, Shabbat 31a*

"Better than a thousand hollow words is one word that brings peace."
—*Siddhārtha Gautama, the founder of Buddhism*

"And if they lean to peace, lean you also to it; and put your trust in Allah; surely He is the Hearing, the Knowing."
—*Qur'an 8:61*

"May the Lord of day grant us peace.
May the Lord of night grant us peace.
May the Lord of sight grant us peace.
May the Lord of might grant us peace.
May the Lord of speech grant us peace.
May the Lord of space grant us peace.
I bow down to Brahman, source of all power.
I will speak the truth and follow the law."
—*Taittiriya Upanishad*

Mark Twain wrote the poem "The War Prayer" as a response to the Philippine-American War; the poem was published after his death due to its controversial nature. Twain describes how a prayer for victory in war contains an unspoken prayer for death and destruction. In the poem a mysterious man addresses a congregation:

When you have prayed for victory you have prayed for many unmentioned results which follow victory—*must* follow it, cannot help but follow it. Upon the listening spirit of God fell also the unspoken part of the prayer. He commandeth me to put it into words. Listen!

"O Lord our Father, our young patriots, idols of our hearts, go forth to battle—be Thou near them! With them—in spirit—we also go forth from the sweet peace of our beloved firesides to smite the foe. O Lord our God, help us to tear their soldiers to bloody shreds with our shells; help us to cover their smiling fields with the pale forms of their patriot dead; help us to drown the thunder of the guns with the shrieks of their wounded, writhing in pain; help us to lay waste their humble homes with a hurricane of fire; help us to wring the hearts of their unoffending widows with unavailing grief; help us to turn them out roofless with little children to wander unfriended the wastes of their desolated land in rags and hunger and thirst . . ."

Unless we pray for peace for all, we are not praying for peace. You can be a spiritual leader for peace through whatever accountability calls to you. Once we have become accountable for peace, we can invite our religious family to actively lead the world to peace as a beautiful religious expression. You can talk to your religious leaders, form peace teams with like-minded people, and write articles for the journals and newsletters of your tradition. The world's largest religions have more influence and local infrastructure than many governments. Religion is transnational and has been very powerful in creating both war and peace, but at heart, all religions teach peace. If you are practicing your religion sincerely, then you are actively creating peace. Note that in this chapter on measurement, religion can have one of the most measurable effects in stopping war and promoting safety from war. Religious and spiritual groups can measure their effect by signing on at P5Y.org and registering their collaborative efforts as a group and individually. In any local area you could measure the number of children educated, hospitals built, farms tilled, agricultural classes given, or job skills taught, as just a few examples among many worthy projects.

Just as you can realize that accountability is rewarding, so too the world's religious organizations and nations find that becoming accountable for creating peace is a rewarding experience, both for their own citizens and for the entire world.

MEASURING MONEY AND TIME

We have looked at measurement in many aspects, especially as it leads to powerful communication and accountability. Measurement allows you to set goals and track your progress. Along with measuring peace, we almost always measure two other things: money and time.

With overseas development assistance equaling $50 billion a year, and over $30 billion in private funds, we believe there is sufficient money already being put toward peace. As we have stated earlier, the *how* is more important than the *how much.* An example of foreign aid misuse in Afghanistan has been cited by UN advisers Ashraf Ghani and Clare Lockhart:

> All in all there were five contractual layers, and at each one, 20 percent of the financing was lost to overheads. The villagers said that only a small proportion of the original donation remained with which to buy wood . . . From the people in refugee camps in Darfur to those in hamlets in Rwanda and Cambodia, every cent that is wasted affects their lives.[26]

With additional coordination and a focus on results, the current hodgepodge of aid programs, peace programs, peacekeeping efforts, and humanitarian aid can be replaced with collaborative plans that you can contribute to. What has been largely missing is measurement of time. Now peace has a deadline.

We are inviting you, as an individual, to know your greatest commitment to humanity, then find out what information you need to measure in order to fulfill your commitment and to collaborate in creating peace in five years.

26. Ghani and Lockhart, *Fixing Failed States*, 94.

COMMUNICATE: UPDATE YOUR DEFINITION OF MEDIA

Doing terrible things in an organized and systematic way rests on "normaliza-tion." This is the process whereby ugly, degrading, murderous, and unspeak-able acts become routine and are accepted as "the way things are done"...
*It is the function of defense intellectuals and other experts, **and the main-stream media**, to normalize the unthinkable for the general public.*

—Edward S. Herman, excerpt from "The Banality of Evil" (Emphasis added.)

IF YOU UNDERSTAND the power of the media to affect you, then you will under-stand how crucial the media are to causing world peace. If food makes up your body, then media, in the broadest sense of experience, constitute your mind. We literally become the media we consume.

The whole medium of our life, our environment, our friends and relatives, our careers, our travels, and what input our brain receives from all of our senses may be considered the media we consume. Mass media can be used to propagate stereotypes, normalize good or bad actions, or promote useful ideas. The mirror neurons in our brains, which cause us to emulate and synchronize with the behavior of others (they're one of the reasons that laughter and other moods are contagious), compel us to take on the characteristics of the people and ideas we see in print, radio, and television.[27] The more unexamined repetition we allow ourselves to be exposed to, the more we accept the ideas as normal and acceptable. For the majority of people, and for all of us in some areas, what is normal and acceptable is simply what everyone else does, or what is presented with the most authority. For a minority of people who have activated their inner truth and critical faculties, many mass media communications appear laughably false. Nevertheless, the power of the media to represent the mainstream, and to make ideas seem normal and acceptable, is undeniable.

Peace Action

What you can do today to further peace by 2014

Watch one substantial news program and consider what is not being said, or what might have been reported instead. Talk to your friends about it. How does the program relate to world peace?

We are inviting you to update your definition of *media*. As we read in chapter 5, the brain does not distinguish between internal or external experience, or between "real life" or "media" in terms of processing experience. Degrees of reality relative to our purposes are assigned to these experiences, but the experience itself is just an experience,[28] and it changes us to the degree we repeat it with alert attention. Neuroscientist Norman Doidge, in his 2007 book, *The Brain That Changes Itself*, says: "What we have learned . . . is that neuroplasticity contributes to both the constrained and unconstrained aspects of our nature . . . it renders our brains not only more resourceful but also more vulnerable to outside influences."[29]

Even if we think that our critical faculties are activated, it is most likely that we are simply agreeing or disagreeing with previous media we have consumed and taken in as part of ourselves. Cutting-edge brain research confirms what is called "confirmation bias," in which we reject valid evidence against our existing conclusions and amplify corroborating evidence.[30] As early as 1620, Francis Bacon wrote in *Novum Organum*, "The human understanding when it has once adopted an opinion . . . draws all things else to support and agree with it. And though there be a greater number and weight of instances to be found on the other side, yet these it either neglects and despises . . . in order that by this great and per-

---

27. Marco Iacoboni, *Mirroring People: The New Science of How We Connect with Others* (New York: Farrar, Straus and Giroux, 2008).

28. Franklin Merrell-Wolff, *The Philosophy of Consciousness Without an Object* (Julian Press, 1973).

29. Norman Doidge, *The Brain That Changes Itself* (New York: Viking, 2007).

30. Michael Shermer, "The Political Brain," *Scientific American*, June 2006.

nicious predetermination the authority of its former conclusions may remain inviolate."

Communication with the media is a two-way affair. As peacemakers, we send out information through the media, and we absorb information from the media. It is our job as world peace communicators to understand thoroughly the impact that the media has on the world and the impact that we have on the media.

The media to which we expose ourselves does a great deal to determine the acceptable range of our reality. When we absorb and retransmit messages repeatedly and uncritically, we become the inertial enforcers of the status quo. Many messages of the status quo are useful and positive: eat more vegetables, buckle your seat belt, don't shake babies. Others are very questionable if not downright false: pork is the other white meat, brain damage is irreversible, war is part of being human. But if we do not examine the truth of these messages, we will not know the difference. We agree on what reality is as a culture—some topics are on the table for debate, and some are not. These topics change all the time, and the media does a great deal to influence the collective reality by propagating ideas, new and old, throughout our culture. But the media does not decide our reality. "War is part of being human" is a common idea that many people believe and have not yet questioned.

What makes this time in our history both more perilous and more promising is that with instant communication, we can transmit ideas globally in seconds, shaping opinion for better or worse. The Internet is the world's most powerful communication tool. It is renowned as an echo chamber for people who seek to have their opinions repeated back to them by those who agree with them. But it is also a tool for research, inquiry, and connection with people of disparate opinions and backgrounds all over the world. For instance, you can use the Internet to help answer the question for yourself whether or not war is part of human nature.

Peace Action

What you can do today to further peace by 2014

E-mail the editors of at least three media outlets in your area and tell them what you're doing to promote peace in five years. Offer to give them an interview, and obtain the rights to rerun the piece on www.P5Y.org.

IF YOU WANT TO EXPAND YOUR LIFE, CONSUME EXPANDING MEDIA

Anyone today can responsibly choose media influences. The Internet also gives us the power to transmit our own influence into the culture. With great power comes great responsibility. As we become more skilled in both choosing and critically examining all of the ideas and assumptions that enter our awareness, mass media and propaganda become less influential on us, and we become more influential on them. We shift from being receivers to being transmitters. Mass media will always be capable of shaping minds, especially uncritical minds.

Look back at what kind of peacemaker you are and the values you bring forth for world peace. What music, films, books, advertisements, radio stations, magazines, speakers, concerts, plays, theme parks, and plays support your values and commitments? This is not about finding media you agree with. This is about choosing carefully what you consider to be true, and about your sources of information. Consuming facts and thinking rigorously rather than uncritically accepting emotion, opinion, gloss, and fluff makes you more potent. Don't get too serious—but if you consume media for pure entertainment, make it really fun and inspiring.

We have personally avidly consumed all kinds of media, depending on what we need. Family films, works of philosophy, war movies, documentaries, and many, many books. We have consumed transformational workshops, meditation retreats, peace conferences, museums, opera, dance performances, Broadway shows, zoos, business meetings, rock concerts, and strategy brainstorming sessions. We are agnostic about what we consume, but we have varied and specific reasons for consuming what we do: to learn, to find out firsthand what the messages are out there, to contribute, to move our goals forward, to have fun and recharge, to enjoy an experience with our friends. The point is that the media you consume should help meet your needs and your purpose: information, entertainment, new perspective, beauty, art, and fresh ideas. In all of these areas, you can be responsible for exposing yourself to the highest quality media that meets your conscious purpose.

All the media each of us consumes affects our ideas, words, and actions. It's our responsibility to consume our media with awareness. When you consider our broad definition of media, this responsibility becomes an issue of moment-by-moment awareness.

One way to practice being more aware is to ask yourself, What is the intention of the creator of this piece of the media pie? To entertain? To sell advertisements? To educate? To enrich? To influence? Do I agree or disagree with the intention? Notice the unquestioned assumptions that the story depends on. Are those assumptions true? This is about you becoming your own authority and exercising your critical faculties. If you stand for women's rights, then be aware of what music, articles, and films support that. If you are watching a film that reinforces subtle oppressive stereotypes, be aware that it is affecting you. The veil is very thin and easy to see through in media if you ask yourself just a few questions.

MEDIA EXPOSURE

LIST THE DIFFERENT MEDIA YOU ARE EXPOSED TO EACH DAY: TV, RADIO, PRINT, WEB, BILLBOARDS, FILMS, MOBILE PHONE ADS, COWORKERS, CONVERSATIONS, ETC.

_____

_____

_____

_____

_____

WHAT MEDIA DO YOU NOW SEE THAT WERE "INVISIBLE" TO YOU BEFORE DOING THIS EXERCISE?

_____

_____

If nothing else, we want you to be an aware consumer of media so that you will know that the random story you are watching on television or the conversation you are having colors your thoughts.

Imagine you have just watched a movie in which a daughter and a mother find reconciliation, or a movie in which a man betrays his best friend and kills him. The movie leaves you in a state that influences your subsequent behavior (any parent knows this if their child has watched *Star Wars*). This lingering effect is called "priming," a well-known phenomenon in psychological and neurological studies.

Priming describes the process of activating particular possibilities of behavior. For instance, asking people to describe their favorite vacation before they meet a new person is likely to make them like that person more; having someone write down words for violent action—shoot, kill, maim, bruise—will lead them to act more violently immediately afterward. Priming is a big part of media, and it is both subtle and powerful.

> Whether subjects perceive primes consciously or not, they're unaware of any influence or correlation between primes and their behavior. These influences are rapid, automatic, and unconscious, apply both to goals and means, and don't depend on subjects' volition or having independent goals that would rationalize their primed behavior.[31]

In other words, we do not get to choose whether or not we are influenced by media. With regard to priming and its effects, we only get to influence what media we consume. Knowing this makes us responsible for the media we consume, and it also gives us hope in spreading the message of P5Y. With such a compelling message, the media effect is amplified.

ADVERTISERS CAN HELP CAUSE PEACE IN FIVE YEARS

Media and their messages are greatly influenced by advertisers, who provide most of the revenues for many of the media companies. One of the larger media companies, Clear Channel Communications, owns more than 1,200 radio stations in the United States, making it a powerful influence on the public's perception of reality. To bring about the shift that makes peace by 2014 possible—to alter the current, agreed-upon reality that says war is an acceptable means of dealing with nations or groups we don't agree with—we must do two things: first, influence the existing media to carry messages of peace to the widest possible audience; second, create new media expressions that reach into people's consciousnesses and communicate truths about war and peace to people who are more selective in their choice of media consumption. We can do both of these things—indeed, we must do both of these things if we are to reengineer collective reality to make world peace in five years a dominant idea.

We saw from earlier chapters that corporations have an important contribution to make toward world peace. One of the most important contributions is

---

31. Susan Hurley, "The Shared Circuits Model: How Control, Mirroring, and Simulation Can Enable Imitation, Deliberation, and Mindreading" (Chapter to have been published in *Behavioral and Brain Sciences,* 2007, by Cambridge University Press).

to influence media outlets to be more consistent with a corporation's mission in regard to world peace. If this sounds strange, remember that peace is very good for business, that corporations are made up of people who benefit from peace, and that corporate social responsibility (CSR) is a huge movement. This does not mean that Clear Channel needs to carry liberal messages to its well-developed and loyal conservative audience, but messages of peace are highly consistent with safety and family values. It is also important that advertisers shun programs that are inconsistent with their carefully crafted CSR policies.

You don't have to create media yourself to have a transformational impact. You can convince other organizations to communicate for the campaign. For example, it would be a powerful transformative media tool to convince the largest corporations to add P5Y logos to all of their billboards and advertising, from small villages in Morocco to Times Square. Imagine the message on the sides of buildings in Hong Kong, on stadiums in Los Angeles, on TV commercials during the Super Bowl, all saying, "Peace by 2014 is possible and it's for real."

In this game of peace, international conglomerates like Coca-Cola, Nike, British Petroleum, and thousands of others all have an opportunity for mass global reach through creative projects, advertising, sponsorship, special events, and much more. As the idea of peace by 2014 spreads, the world's largest advertisers will realize that peace benefits them as much as everyone else. We expect corporate advertisers to get behind the new "peace media" with enthusiasm.

What you can do to help corporations is tell them that you welcome their participation in world peace, and that it means a lot to you as a consumer. Look for alerts through registering at P5Y.org so we can focus our efforts on each corporation in turn at the crucial, effective moment.

ADDING OUTCOME AND MEASUREMENT TO ENTERTAINMENT

How do we create media, marketing, and art that transform our old thinking about war and peace into the new? How do we create media to support world peace?

Peace with a deadline is dramatic. Let's look at the story line. We now have a character: a world that wants something badly enough to do something about it. Our character as an individual, a nation, or a world has tactics to achieve its goal by 2014. Will we succeed or fail? We need compelling movies, stories that show the transformation of a person into a peacemaker and the challenges he or she faces. We need filmmakers to tell us stories of what the world could look like;

stories that produce a dissonance between where we are now and where we are going; stories that inform, inspire, and open up new possibilities. Look for ways to collaborate to accelerate the creation and distribution of your film.

Are you a musician, singer, producer, rapper? Are you making the next big hit for peace with a deadline? We'd love to see Peace by 2014 concerts and records as our movement from a world with war to a world with peace safety gains momentum.

Collect stories about your peace journey and those of others, and publish them—if you don't have compelling, wild stories yet, you will soon if you are serious about P5Y. Get a group together to create a P5Y quilt. Use your cooking skills to communicate and hold a bake sale for peace. Or if you have a home business, incorporate effective communication about world peace in five years into your business. If you have a skill that's especially useful for people who are working to create peace, write a concise, illustrated manual of how to do what you know.

Do you run a magazine and could you donate ad space? Are you a journalist who could cover P5Y projects in the media? Do you own, manage, or work for an advertising or marketing agency? You can make things happen in print.

Start the process yourself: download the logo from P5Y.org, print it out, and put it in the window of your home or business. Get people talking. Tell the story.

If you are inspired to create media that transform, here are some avenues:

- Start a blog.
- Write a book.
- Make a short film.
- Tape a radio documentary.
- Create an art installation.
- Launch a website.
- Write a play.
- Do a puppet show.
- Post a YouTube video.
- Write a song.
- Make a music video.

- Make a DharmaMix vision board for peace at dharmamix.com and post it in your workspace.

With the Internet, YouTube, mobile media, independent film, satellites, magazines, advertising, iPods, podcasting, blogs, Twitter, Facebook, and more, the media have never been more powerful or more wide open. Media are indispensable for peace by 2014, so let's use them right. We have been marketed into tolerating war, and we can market each other into constructive conflict. So how can we use media to inspire peaceful ideas, promulgate principles of peace safety, and collaborate on fruitful projects and effective actions?

This is about giving your time, your talent, your vision, your PR experience, your marketing expertise, your broadcasting experience, and your passion to transform the world's media into a force for peace. What media could you produce for P5Y? Brainstorm in the space below.

MEDIA MATTERS

WHAT OTHER WAYS CAN YOU THINK OF THAT THE MEDIA COULD BE USED TO CREATE PEACE BY 2014?

_____

_____

_____

_____

Next consider the desired outcome. New thinking, nonviolent communication, ending a specific conflict, forgiveness? What is the ideal outcome of a script, commercial, film, or music recording session? Working from outcomes backward is very powerful. Consider the specific outcome for your project that most inspires you. For each outcome, decide the measurement that you can use to tell whether or not you have achieved your outcome. Here are some examples of what your outcomes might look like:

- One thousand people will become aware within three weeks that peace has a deadline. Measurement is achieved by calculating the foot traffic past my art installation and using standard billboard metrics.

- Twenty people will register on the P5Y website by Friday. Measurement is achieved by using the P5Y.org referring member tool on the P5Y home page.

- Five social workers will volunteer to work as peace safety workers in Kosovo under a corporate sponsorship program by the end of the month. Measurement is achieved by counting signed commitments.

- Fifteen local companies will agree to include principles of P5Y in their marketing and packaging materials; actual materials appear in public within one month. Measurement is achieved by making follow-up calls to the companies.

- Within two months, ten members of my church group will go through a one-day "principles of peace" training workshop and the group will agree to finance one teacher for two years in Afghanistan for $3,000 per year. Measurement is achieved by tallying how many people go through training and the money raised for the Afghani teacher.

Now consider how you might measure the effectiveness of your communication efforts.

We've talked about the importance of measurement. Measuring the impact of the media peace project you create is vital for feedback. Knowing if viewership or readership is up or down is one measurement. These are some possible measurements to use to determine whether a communication effort is effective:

- How many times has a song been downloaded?
- How many people said you registered them at P5Y.org?
- How many people saw my public access TV show?
- How many packages with peace inserts did a company send out?
- How many tickets does a documentary sell?
- How many households are viewing an ad?
- How many people have read a blog?
- How many people signed a petition at a concert?
- How many people registered their commitment after viewing a movie or sitcom?
- How many times has a music video been viewed or downloaded?

- How many impressions are there of "World Peace by 2014" on every network per hour? Per day? Per week?

- Based on key words and phrases, how many news stories on P5Y run in the mainstream media in a given period?

- What is the traffic and readership of key P5Y websites and blogs?

Action taken, times viewed, Internet response, money raised, debts forgiven, schools built, volunteers recruited—choose your measurement. How do you know you've been successful?

Whatever inspires you in media, understand your intended outcome and measure the result. We invite you to report your results at www.P5Y.org.

WAYS YOU CAN ACT NOW

We have been involved in the media for many years, and we understand the power of media activism. For a campaign like P5Y, it is sometimes more effective to use nontraditional methods of media communication rather than relying on the standard approach to get out the message. The following is a list of goals for media actions that we are undertaking at P5Y:

- To feature the "World Peace by 2014" logo on at least 10 percent of all advertising on television, in print ads, at the end of film credits, on the back of CD cases, in newspapers and magazines, and on the product labels in grocery and department stores. We'll do this by creating a cultural tidal wave of people who have made peace their number-one factor in deciding what to buy and who to buy it from. The power of the pocketbook will influence the media companies and advertisers.

- To create and maintain one or more weekly television shows dedicated to asking the question "How do we create world peace in five years?"

- To create a line of original products built around the logo: T-shirts, hats, handbags, and hundreds or thousands of licensed products, all carrying the peace logo and specific messages that help accomplish peace in five years.

- To beam messages of peace pledges and action plans into the mobile phones of the world's most wired nations—Japan, China, Korea, the United States, and the European Union.

- To produce a documentary about the effort to create peace by 2014, along the lines of *An Inconvenient Truth*, and gain worldwide release.

- To promote "Peace by 2014" music festivals around the globe—synchronized through using the Internet—that will feature the top rock, country, hip-hop, and alternative artists making music centered on creating and promoting peace among cultures and religions. The recordings would become the "Peace Music" for the generation and the proceeds would benefit the P5Y campaign.

- To create a DharmaMix event featuring celebrities and thought leaders talking about world peace over music.

- To launch a series of P5Y blogs, all dedicated to following the activities of peace-committed individuals, that will track breaking war- and peace-related news, holding leaders immediately accountable for their actions and debunking misleading stories in the mainstream media.

We are looking for interested peacemakers to join us in these efforts. We are looking forward to progressing with all of these communication projects and monitoring their effectiveness for creating world peace.

OUR CURRENT MEDIA PARTNERS

The Economist Intelligence Unit, sister company to the famous weekly news magazine, is working with us to develop metrics to measure our progress toward peace and to publish these metrics on an ongoing basis. This is an example of how the media can work cooperatively with the peace movement.

Another media partner is Media One, based in San Francisco. Owner David Levy is keen to promote peace and a worldwide culture of generosity. He has suggested that P5Y be the lead cause of Media One. We have been offered TV shows and documentaries about P5Y.

We founded a for-profit social venture media company, DharmaMix, which is for P5Y. DharmaMix is a hip, cool combination of music, self-inquiry, self-development, and social networking features that lets you harness the power of small teams to achieve your goals and to help others achieve theirs. A DharmaMix is a three-to-five-minute song of spoken word over lounge, acoustic, or dance music with a specific outcome in mind.

GOOD INFORMATION IS THE BASIS OF YOUR EFFECTIVE ACTION

One of the most powerful effects of media is to report activities that people wish to keep secret. Until the advent of ubiquitous and cheap recording and transmitting devices like digital cameras, small camcorders, cell phones, and public satellite images, it was easier to keep compromising or embarrassing information out of the public eye. Today, governments, corporations, and individuals must operate within the reality that there is little or no privacy, and that it is very easy to collect damning evidence of secret activities and release it to the media.

Remember, transparency was key to abolishing slavery. The propaganda of the slave traders—slaves are treated well, the slave trade is important for the British Navy, slave owners have the best interests of their slaves at heart—was exposed as lies.

A more recent example is "secret prisons." Although the United States and other countries have tried to maintain a shroud around their practice of maintaining secret prisons, it is simply not possible on the scale they are attempting. On June 2, 2008, this news story appeared in the British newspaper *The Guardian*:

> The United States is operating "floating prisons" to house those arrested in its war on terror . . . Details of ships where detainees have been held and sites allegedly being used in countries across the world have been compiled . . . from the U.S. military, the Council of Europe and related parliamentary bodies, and the testimonies of prisoners.[32]

U.S. human rights violations create more problems for the United States than these violations solve. Every violation has repercussions around the world. If the world's shining example of democracy is egregiously violating human rights, that gives license to every oppressive regime to do the same. It gives effective and powerful tools to those who wish to foment terrorism, and these violations ultimately are a practice of destructive conflict, because they sow the seeds of future wars.

We attended the Forum 2000 peace conference in Prague in 2007. Attending the conference was Grigory Yavlinski, a member of the Russian Duma, or parliament. Mr. Yavlinski spoke with us strongly about the negative effect in Russia of U.S. human rights violations. Although we did not explicitly record his words to us, he is quoted in the conference transcripts as saying: "Believe me it is very difficult to speak in Russia about human rights when five times a day in news you have reports from Iraq or from Guantánamo. It is very difficult to convince Russian people about human rights in Europe when all the time you have reports about secret prisons all over the Europe and secret CIA deals: it is very difficult to give real arguments."

Since that time, former President and current Prime Minister of the Russian Federation Vladimir Putin has consolidated his power in Russia, and the country is becoming increasingly more belligerent and uncooperative with the United States and Europe. Along with giving propaganda ammunition to terrorists, this is another consequence of U.S. violations of peace safety. In the current atmosphere, it is possible that war could break out between Russia and former Soviet bloc countries, that the war could escalate, and that the United States could be drawn into it through NATO. Even nuclear war could result. While this is a pessimistic scenario, it is the current direction of affairs. This is a consequence of the United States operating under the old paradigm of how to create security: create barriers, defend them, go after your enemy, kill him, and keep the nasty stuff secret. But in today's world, barriers do not stop weapons; the "enemy" is impossible to find and kill; and in the new world of transparency, the nasty stuff does not stay secret—it comes out and exacerbates precisely that problem the United States is trying to solve by violating human rights in the first place. Not only that, it is also just plain wrong to violate human rights.

The United States is not the only country that is suffering recently under the new reality. Many regimes are embarrassingly exposed in the media: China, Egypt, Myanmar, and Libya have all been exposed more fully as violating human rights.

In her report on the Forum 2000 in the year 2007, Christiane Amanpour spoke about the challenge of transparency in the media.

It came into sharp focus in Bosnia, because there it was evident to all of us, who were reporting and who were in the city of Sarajevo with the civilian population and other besieged cities, it was quite clear what was going on. Our governments, the Western governments, United States, Europe did not want to intervene or take a position. So their public propaganda was that this is an ethnic conflict, this is just inevitable, these are years of ethnic hatred and we are faced with 'How do we report that?' We knew that, actually, that was not the case, we knew that, actually, there was a group of people heavily armed, who decided to carve out their powerful, ethnically pure state and that others based on their religion and ethnicity were being slaughtered. Men, women, children. On our watch, in our backyard in the television and satellite age. So what to do about it?[33]

Sometimes a failure of transparency creates war. A friend of ours lived in Nigeria for some years. There, the oil companies are known for treating the local villagers badly, polluting their fields and rivers, and failing to share any of the oil revenues. Although the villagers have been complaining for years, they have not had a voice for their complaints. According to our friend, the direct result of this lack of transparency and the ongoing peace violations have led to the recent spate of pipeline bombings and kidnappings of Western workers that have been reported in the news.

P5Y's goal is to use our modern technological age to expose the realities of war and unite the world under new practices of constructive conflict. In the end, the tactical module of P5Y communications has seven major goals:

- Inform people about peace in five years so they can become involved.

- Reposition world peace as culturally mainstream.

- Promote safety practices of constructive conflict.

- Promote a Global Peace Treaty among the family of nations to resolve conflicts nonviolently.

- Inform those who are already involved about progress, new projects, resources, and needs.

- Report on the activities of governments, media outlets, and individuals so their actions are transparent relative to creating world peace, or not.

- Celebrate the milestones of world peace.

There are many different ways to communicate peace. Remember, even a simple smile or a short conversation with a friend or someone on the bus uses communication to help create world peace.

---

33. Christiane Amanpour at Forum 2000, October 8, 2007, Prague, http://www.forum2000.cz/en/projects/forum-2000-conferences/2007/transcripts/panel-3--freedom-and-responsibility-in-media/#christiane_amanpour

HOW YOU CAN JOIN US

11

GOVERNMENT 2.0

When America does what was promis'd . . .
When through these States walk a hundred millions of superb persons . . .
I announce natural persons to arise,
I announce justice triumphant,
I announce uncompromising liberty and equality,
I announce the justification of candor and the justification of pride . . .
I announce splendors and majesties to make all the
previous politics of the earth insignificant.

—excerpt from Walt Whitman, "So Long"

FROM READING THIS chapter, you will get a glimpse of the shift that Walt Whitman claims will "make all the previous politics of the earth insignificant." It is the shift from war to constructive conflict, a shift that we promised to make when we gave peace a deadline.

We cannot fulfill this promise by ourselves. We need the help of millions of people around the world, starting with supporters here in the United States. While all countries have their essential roles in creating world peace in five years, America has a leader's role, the key to world peace. Without America's leadership, we will not have peace in five years. We Americans have a special responsibility to our country and to the world to remember our promise and fulfill it.

Since its founding, the United States of America has been the land of promise. And what is America's promise to the world? Simply this: *America promises freedom*. This promise does not come from some inherent virtue in the American character. It comes from our audacious political system and the culture that has sprung from it: open, democratic, independent, creative, forceful, entrepreneurial, and powered by free markets and an open exchange of ideas. To be fully American, one need only participate in the American set of agreements.

In many moments we have not fully lived up to those ideals, but the potential remains and is expressed powerfully at times. May this become one of those times? May we lead the world to peace by our example?

In the recognition of our freedom, a natural humility and responsibility arise: To fulfill our promise to the world, we must learn to act like true leaders. We are not talking about behaving like an adolescent, blustering, ham-handed world policeman. No, we are talking about embodying the deeper promise of America, the unique spirit, history, generosity, and humility of our people, our form of government, and the energy of possibility that is ready to come forth at the slightest inspiration.

PARTICIPATE IN THE SHIFT TO GOVERNMENT 2.0

There is a radical shift happening in America and the rest of the world, a gigantic maturation of feeling about politics and participation in government and the world. John F. Kennedy famously said, "Ask not what your country can do for you—ask what you can do for your country." His next words, less often quoted, were, "My fellow citizens of the world: ask not what America will do for you, but what together we can do for the freedom of man." JFK was interpreting the promise of America for his times, and he inspired a generation.

JFK's exhortation was an invitation to make a trade-off between selfishness on one hand and generosity of civic spirit on the other. According to the interpretation of Howe and Strauss in *The Fourth Turning* (Broadway Books, 1999), President Kennedy was asking the question at a time when America was experiencing a peak of material comfort for individual Americans and declining interest in working for the good of society as a whole. JFK wanted, as many people did, a return to the spirit of cohesion and sacrifice that won World War II, even as the early baby boomers and silent generation were beginning to reject that cohesion.

Today we are in the opposite position: a period of economic instability, with a high demand for material well-being, much like the period leading up to World War II. A simplistic call for sacrifice such as JFK's is suspect, and rightly so. We need a more deeply nuanced, more satisfying definition of government and our role in it, and our identity and place in the world, both as Americans and as world citizens. We need government 2.0.

The most common question Americans ask about their government is, "What can I get from it?" Perhaps you have progressed to the question, "What can I give to—or what difference can I make in—America, my country, the world?"

Both of these questions remain in the realm of the politics of the ordinary. Both presume a separation between an individual and his or her country. Both presume that the individual acts to get something from or give something to the nation as a separate entity. In truth there is no separation between individuals and their country. It is time we understood this essential truth and adopted the politics of government 2.0. Continuing to splash about in the muddy middle of the politics of the ordinary is unworthy of America, unworthy of the world, unworthy of you, and definitely unworthy of peace in five years.

In the chapter on communication, we discussed the importance to the individual of a broadly defined collective reality. Inevitably, our government is an extension of who we are as individuals. Just as we often like some parts of ourselves and not others, so too is our relationship to our government. Still, many of us continue to believe in the fictional idea that government exists outside of ourselves. We wrongly imagine that government has power over our souls and may be dangerously influenced by wrong thinkers and wrongdoers. The belief that others have power over us through the government is a cause for a great deal of anxiety. We can alleviate this anxiety when we realize *as* the government, when we accept the government as a part of ourselves, then even though we may suffer the same previous indignities of bad, cruel, or corrupt government, we are in a position of authority in ourselves, and our anxiety eases.

KNOW YOURSELF, KNOW YOUR GOVERNMENT

You don't know whether the government is representing your values until you create your vision for government. You may have a low level of anxiety or a feeling of excitement and inspiration—but where is that coming from? What is it based on? Do the following exercise to know what your highest vision of government is and to give it personal relevance.

MY HIGHEST VISION OF GOVERNMENT

WHAT WOULD MY GOVERNMENT VALUE MOST?

_____

HOW WOULD MY GOVERNMENT FULFILL MY NATION'S PROMISE TO THE WORLD?

_____

HOW WOULD MY GOVERNMENT REPRESENT ME GLOBALLY?

_____

HOW TO REALLY GET REPRESENTED

To give peace a deadline, we must uncover the underlying reality of the politics of the individual. As quantum physics both transcends yet includes Newtonian physics, the new paradigm of the politics of the individual transcends yet includes the politics of the ordinary. Like quantum physics, the politics of the individual, once put into practice, offers us new and previously unimaginable powers and properties. Just like Web 2.0 makes media a self-expression, so government 2.0 makes government a self-expression. Although Web 1.0 applications still work, with Web 2.0 whole new realms of application become available: social networking, business collaboration, virtual meetings, blogs, webinars, and real-time cross-platform communications. Just as Web 2.0 expands on yet includes Web 1.0, so government 2.0 expands on yet includes government 1.0. The revolution in technology supports and enables government 2.0, but the real revolution is deeper than that. Government 2.0 is based on the individual. The politics of the individual allows for the splendors and majesties that Walt Whitman predicted would make all previous politics insignificant.

The following table is a brief overview of the new politics of the individual as comprared to the politics of the ordinary:

Politics of the Ordinary	Politics of the Individual
What can I get, or what can I give?	Who am I as my government?
Government is outside of me.	Government is constituted inside of me.
Government has authority.	I am authority itself.
Government is out of control.	Government is a self-expression.
Government does not reflect my opinions.	I contain all opinions. I express opinions as art.
Government is imposed.	Government is chosen.
There are things I don't accept about my government and other governments.	I accept everything exactly how it is, as a manifestation of myself and how I have allowed my values to be expressed.
Government is unfair.	I contain both fairness and unfairness; I am the sole authority on fairness.
Government is by compromise and consensus of various interests and powers.	Government is a perfect unfolding expression of human consciousness, mysterious and beautiful.
Government is about power.	What can be bound is never free.
Government is illegitimate.	I am the sole arbiter of legitimacy and illegitimacy.

YOUR AUTHORITY IN BEING GOVERNED

From the point of view of ordinary politics, the language in the previous overview appears to be highly self-centered and egotistical. For example, take the assertion, "I am authority itself." To assume authority as an individual bent on exercising that authority upon an external world is indeed egotistical. But where can authority authentically exist? Notice that for yourself, you specifically grant authority or withhold it according to your choosing. How else could it be? Even if you are handcuffed, you are free to grant authority, or not, to the person handcuffing you. Force is not the source of authority inside you; many political dissidents and non-violent activists have demonstrated that.

Nelson Mandela is one such example. What was true for him was that the South African system of racial discrimination was wrong. What was possible was for him to nonviolently oppose that system and be put in jail for decades, yet Mandela did not grant any authority whatsoever to the system that jailed him. Although there was no guarantee that his protests would effect change, his politics did triumph in the end. What was then possible was for Mandela to become the first black president of South Africa.

The process of granting authority is either unconscious, based on your culturally relevant programmed cues of what constitutes authority (a stethoscope, a business suit, a commanding voice, gray hair), or conscious, based on your decision to grant authority in a given situation. In either case, you have the power to either grant or deny anyone else authority over you by your actions and attitudes. No one else possesses this. You are a sovereign.

YOU CAN BE RIGHT WITHOUT SOMEONE ELSE BEING WRONG

The impact of recognizing your own inviolable sovereignty is that you can be right without someone else being wrong. Your politics become a fully free expression, both completely accepting of others' opinions, working with what is possible while simultaneously resting sovereign, unswayed in your own truth. Mandela shook hands with his jailers when he was freed. He knew he was right.

The politics of the individual works from the individual on up. If you notice that government is constituted within your awareness, you can freely choose your relationship to it as a part of yourself, literally. It's not a part that you "control" like you seem to control your hands, but there are many parts of your life that are "you," yet they are not under your control. For instance, your health or your job are parts of you that you influence but do not control.

The understanding that we are united with, not separated from, one another is essential for creating peace. Suppose you are in a conversation with someone close to you, and they express something you disagree with. Now, under the politics of the ordinary, they are wrong, and you are right. Inside yourself, you have the feeling this person is wrong. So where exactly is that wrong feeling? Is it in the other person? Well, *they* feel that what they just said is right, so *they* are not feeling wrong. So who is feeling wrong? *You* are feeling wrong. What is the first thing anyone does when they feel wrong? Of course, they try and fix the wrongness. You argue to try and persuade the person who is wrong to accept your right point of view. Or perhaps you listen to the other person, and give up your point of view for theirs, allowing yourself to be persuaded. If you don't come to an agreement with the other person, maybe you yell a bit. Perhaps you sulk, give up, get angry with yourself, or withdraw from the challenge.

However, if you are able to disagree with someone with the understanding that their opinion is a part of your sovereign reality, then you can listen to that other person's opinion without fear that their idea will contaminate or dominate you. You can be much more free with humor, flexibility, and centeredness. Their opinion arises just as naturally as yours does. The impact of noticing your sovereign reality is your freedom to express what is true for you and also to listen to the truth of others. You are free to attempt to persuade another, yet your internal well-being does not depend on convincing them that you are right. Because you don't have to defend yourself against any verbal expression of the other, you are free to do as you like: You may understand where they are coming from, argue vehemently, leave the room, or feel compassion for them. You will probably have the chance to have a deeper conversation, since underlying concerns, needs, or feelings only come out in a relaxed exchange of ideas.

Like you, the consciousness of a nation can undergo a similar shift in its center of gravity. Nations can be right without others being wrong, and from that place, have more productive conversation about their needs, desires, and national interests. The quality we call "sovereign" in a nation has been traditionally considered physical control of borders and territory, along with general acceptance into the international order of things, to make treaties, international loans, and, unfortunately, war. The true source of national sovereignty, though, is in the indomitable spirit of the people. The actual borders and territory of a nation can be destroyed, their people killed and humiliated, but the hidden source of sovereignty may remain untouched, the spirit unbowed. There are many examples of this, some tragic: both the Israelis and the Palestinians have an indomitable spirit, as well as the Kurds and the tribes of Afghanistan. All of these peoples have lost their nations at one time or another, but their source of inner sovereignty remains. As more individuals recognize themselves as constituting their governments and nations, and not the other way around, their nations can operate from more inner power. It is time now that the adolescent spirit of dominance among nations give way to a more spiritual and pragmatic expression. If not, we face a dire future.

The politics of the individual may seem counterintuitive, or contradictory. How could I be right without someone else being wrong? Doesn't rightness only exist in the context of wrongness? What if someone just comes up and whacks me in the face with a shovel? Isn't that wrong? Do the politics of the individual allow me to defend myself? Is all of this just New Age doublespeak?

All we can say is, look into it for yourself. The politics of the individual cannot be transmitted in a series of intellectual or even emotional lessons. It is not a system or an ideology. It is a realization that is understood one person at a time. This realization can often be felt as a quality of being. If it has a principle, it is that you are the sole authority on what is true for you.

YOU CAN BE POWERFUL FOLLOWING OR LEADING

Realizing the politics of the individual is a fundamental shift that entails reexamination of our relationship to politics. For instance, we have to look at the roles of followers and leaders in a different way. Just as we grant or deny our authority to governments, we cannot abdicate our responsibilities when following a leader. Nor can we see ourselves as separate from our followers when we ourselves are acting as leaders. You can fulfill your mission by following or leading; in some sense, you are always leading yourself. Let's explore these changing roles in more detail.

POWERFUL FOLLOWING

Whom do you follow? Write their names in a list. These people could be dead or alive, near or far. Your pastor, imam, group therapy leader, parents, a team leader at work, a PTA leader, the head of your company, your mentor, a head of state, a philosopher, your friends, authors, and your doctor are examples of people you might include on your list. What are the qualities of the people you follow? For instance, do you follow intelligence, wisdom, and friendliness? Maybe you follow what could be considered inappropriate qualities, such as aggression, indifference, or selfishness. List the qualities of the people you follow.

_____

_____

_____

What does it mean for you to be a follower? What specific actions do you take to follow these leaders? Do you listen to them, ask their advice, or practice what they preach? Wait to make decisions? Is being a follower a passive role for you? I suggest that it is not. Being a follower is an active engagement of energy, time, and resources. You are making a personal decision to follow your inner guide, which directs you to follow an outer leader.

Where do you feel the qualities you listed previously? You experience them inside yourself, right? If you do not feel the greatness of a leader, do you nevertheless follow him or her just because everyone says that leader is great? Hopefully, your answer is no. Earlier we spoke about mirror neurons. These brain structures power our empathy and identification with those who reflect qualities we would most like to see in ourselves. Great leaders spark the desire in our minds to be part of their greatness, but great followers also go where their empathy and identification lead them. You follow because the leaders reflect your values.

Are you a high-quality follower, giving energy and competence to what you are following? As you share the goals of your leader, do you take on those goals for yourself, and do your part, or do you wait to be told what to do? Do you make artful suggestions for improvement, or do you complain without suggesting how to change or what would make it better for everyone? What changes might you make to your experience of being a follower to make it more artful and more aligned with your highest values?

For instance, Nathan volunteers to manage the concession stand at his daughter's high school volleyball games. He understands this role is not just to roll out the concession cart and sit there. His role is to support the volleyball program—so it includes welcoming the out-of-town parents, noting when the concessions are running out, cheering for the girls—in short, doing the job as it was meant to be done. He is following the lead of the volleyball program with his quality time and energy.

Powerful Leading

How about leadership? Whom or what do you lead? Make a list of things or people that you lead, like your family, your company, your friends, your men's group, a hike, anything at all. Is your leadership an expression of your values?

Would you as a leader express your values by supporting violent conflict if there are workable alternatives? The proper practice of peace safety provides those alternatives.

The politics of the individual and the policy of being right within ourselves mean that we can speak as individuals and nations without turning disagreements into personal affronts. Constructive conflict becomes a natural expression. This means we can be ultimately accountable for the systems and organizations that act in our names. The entire dynamic of personal and national relations can be transformed in this way.

PUTTING YOUR POLITICS INTO ACTION

After doing these exercises, you will have a clear understanding of a government that represents you as an individual. The politics of the individual is not an abstract philosophy to be debated among policy makers. Instead, it is a vital tool for our daily lives. By applying the politics of the individual to our own individual circumstances, we take steps toward creating a world of personal responsibility, a world that practices safety from war.

Here's an example of the politics of the individual. In Jefferson County, Iowa, Nathan's brother Joel noticed that a proposed county zoning regulation was not expressive of his values of freedom and private property. He had doubts about whether he could do anything to affect the regulation's outcome, but he wrote a pamphlet opposing the regulation and mailed it to every resident of the county. The response was very positive. Many other people shared his values. Joel went on to organize a series of meetings to oppose the regulation. At the county Board of Supervisors meeting, four hundred fifty Jefferson County citizens appeared to express their values of freedom and private property. The zoning proposal was voted down. All three supervisors lost their posts in the subsequent election because of their support of something that was not in alignment with the values of the people in the county. Joel's expression of his values altered his government.

So what would the government look like if it represented your values? Where are your values being expressed—or not expressed—through your government? Let's get into some exercises and see. Be honest with yourself. Say whatever is true for you. Don't censor yourself if your answers seem trite, or too big, or unusual, or different from what your friends might write. This is about having a moment of honest reflection.

HOW DO YOU FEEL REPRESENTED BY YOUR NATION?

For example, Nathan feels represented by our system of checks and balances, democracy, the open and competent character of Americans, the diverse ethnic backgrounds of Americans, and our military participation in UN peacekeeping. Amber feels represented by democracy, freedom of speech, freedom of religion, the intention of our founders that we are created equal, and capitalism.

I FEEL REPRESENTED BY:

_____

_____

_____

HOW DO YOU FEEL YOU ARE NOT REPRESENTED BY YOUR NATION?

Nathan does not feel represented by secret prisons, Guantánamo Bay, waterboarding, agricultural subsidies and trade barriers, and American support of foreign dictators. Amber does not feel represented by non-principled foreign policy and inefficient foreign aid spending.

I DO NOT FEEL REPRESENTED BY:

_____

_____

_____

_____

WHAT ALLOWS YOU TO FEEL REPRESENTED IN THE WORLD?

Nathan feels represented by the beauty and genius of human achievement. Amber feels represented by the human spirit; the innate altruism of individuals to contribute to family, community, friends; and the deep teachings of brotherhood, tolerance, and oneness of every religion.

continues

I FEEL REPRESENTED IN THE WORLD BY:

_____

_____

_____

_____

WHAT KEEPS YOU FROM BEING REPRESENTED IN THE WORLD?

Nathan does not feel represented by narrow-minded bureaucrats and unethical corporations. Amber does not feel represented by the abuse of women and children, our men and women being sent to war, and the lack of an infrastructure to meet basic needs when we have the resources to do that.

I DO NOT FEEL REPRESENTED IN THE WORLD BY:

_____

_____

_____

_____

Now, consider for a moment: How would you create local, regional, national, and global governments that reflect your values? Again, go past what you think is the "right thing" to say and be honest with yourself.

You have just written what government can be as an expression of yourself. Now, is there any part of that vision that excites you to make it an actual reality? Write your most thrilling commitment about the possibility of your vision. This could be something you change about yourself, something you learn, or someone you talk to. This is *not* about what the world *should* be or what you *should* do with your awesome powers of commitment, or about impressing anyone. If it makes you feel excited, then write whom you might collaborate with to accomplish your vision. There are entire teams of trained professionals who love doing the things you hate to do and are probably better at it. This is about enjoying yourself and committing to what lights you—not anyone else—up.

**WHAT THRILLS ME MOST ABOUT
MY VISION OF THE WORLD IS:**

_____

_____

_____

**WHAT I AM MOST THRILLED TO COMMIT TO
IN THE REALIZATION OF THAT VISION IS:**

_____

_____

_____

I COMMIT TO IT IN THE FOLLOWING WAYS:

_____

_____

_____

Congratulations! You now have practiced the politics of the individual, and you have created a vision for the world that reflects your values. You understand what most thrills you to accomplish for that vision. You have discovered what is worth committing to in your life to make your nation a direct reflection of who you are. Now it's time to act toward realizing this vision and aligning your life with the vision of peace.

WHAT KIND OF PEACEMAKER ARE YOU?

The question also arises in any democracy—as in any life—what will we use
our freedom for? Will we preoccupy ourselves with selfish interests—or dedi-
cate a portion of our time and energy to helping others? Will we squander our
liberty in pursuit of the frivolous, or engage in the kind of serious work that
lives on in the hearts and minds of future generations? Some say it is a mis-
take to try to place public policy within the context of morality and values.

—Madeleine Albright

IN THIS CHAPTER, we are going to lead you through a process that will help you
discover your most joyful contribution to world peace. Working with us for peace
will energize the other parts of your life rather than drain the resources you commit to them. In the process of determining what kind of a peacemaker you are,
you will also learn more about yourself and the difference you want to make. We
are going to walk you through a model and typology of peacemaking developed
by William Ury so you can get an idea of the kinds of contributions that are effective in preventing and containing conflict. After you gain that understanding,

we will take you through a personal process to discover what kind of peacemaker you are.

"I'm just one person with skills to contribute. How do I know what to do?" We hear this all the time. We believe that joining our five-year mission and committing yourself to peace must complement the rest of your life in order to be fully realizable. In fact, everything that you are already doing can be for peace in five years if you are able to focus your efforts and understand your skills and motivations. Once you find out what matters most to you and how you can find the time to do it in the service of peace in five years, you can identify the specific activity that is most effective and needed in order to create world peace.

The process looks like this.

First, you will explore your activities and how they reflect who you are and what your values are. Second, you will look at your skills. Are you a good poker player? Organizer? Knitter? Musician? Number-cruncher? Finally, and most important, you will determine what you are most passionate about, what you cannot get enough of. We will see where these three areas overlap, which will reveal what kind of peacemaker you are. Let's get started.

WILLIAM URY'S THIRD SIDE MODEL

The model is described on the website www.thirdside.org.

> Conflict does not come out of nowhere but proceeds from latent tension, develops into overt conflict, erupts into power struggle, and from there crosses the threshold of destructive conflict and violence. As Thirdsiders, our aim is not to suppress conflict altogether but simply to keep the trajectory of escalation below this threshold. In addition to being a perspective, the Third Side is a systemic approach to handling conflict. We have at least three major opportunities to transform conflict from destructive fighting into constructive change.
>
> The first is to prevent destructive conflict from emerging in the first place by addressing latent tensions. The second is to resolve any overt conflicts which do develop. The third is to contain any escalating power struggles that temporarily escape resolution. What is not prevented is resolved; and what is not resolved is contained. The motto of the Third Side is thus: "Contain if necessary, resolve if possible, best of all prevent."

In difficult conflicts it's often not enough to use one mode. Many of these conflicts can best be transformed by using all three modes.

The Third Side model also provides a typology of peacemakers. These types are helpful in determining what kinds of methods and resources need to be used in the practice of peace safety. They also help you understand how your contribution fits into the peacemaking role. We reproduced the diagram of types here, but for more complete descriptions of the ten roles, visit www.thirdside.org or read *The Third Side* (Penguin Books, 2000).

TEN ROLES OF THE THIRD SIDE

Prevent		
provider	teacher	bridge builder

Resolve			
mediator	arbiter	equalizer	healer

Contain		
witness	referee	peacekepper

YOUR ACTIVITIES

Now that you have an idea of what kind of peacemakers there are and how they contribute, take a look at yourself and how you spend your time. By looking at how you spend your time and energy, you can notice what commitments you are serving. Do you bicycle, knit, write, cook, clean, paint, communicate, travel, type, direct, teach, journal, negotiate, farm, fix things? Do you play a sport, an instrument, video games, cards? Many of us live compartmentalized lives of work, home, family, hobbies. What activities do you do between the major areas of your life? Do you read books, listen to music, ride the bus, fly a plane? What activities occupy you?

Inside the circle below (or on another piece of paper or in your journal), write in your activities. For instance, maybe you drive a lot, running errands. What are the errands in service to? Does this service reflect your values and where you want to be contributing? Perhaps some of your activities serve your commitments weakly: for example, eating potato chips might be a way for you to meet your commitment to yourself to relax and rejuvenate, but it might not work as well as taking a brief nap.

Some of your activities might serve your commitments, but they might not be a good match for your skills or what you like to do. Put a rating next to each activity you list related to how much you enjoy it, and another for how good you are at doing it.

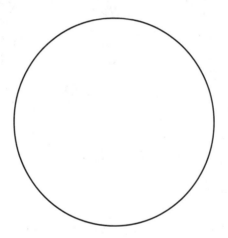

YOUR SKILLS

What are you already doing in your life? What have you done in the past? What talents do you have that your friends and family or coworkers acknowledge you for? If you don't know, go ask them. Are you a teacher, lawyer, student, businessperson, programmer, farmer, mother, cashier, writer, philanthropist, nurse, pilot?

Your contribution doesn't have to be your day job or relate to your area of training, but if that's the most valuable skill you have, then we encourage you to use it. A friend of ours is a lawyer who is also starting a raw chocolate company on the side. He generally dislikes being a lawyer and loves raw chocolate. But for bringing about world peace in five years, he's invigorated to offer his legal services for writing contracts and even doing business operations. He also can't get enough of meditating daily, painting, having friends over, and asking fundamental questions about reality, but he still makes time for his peace work. He's an artist-lawyer-entrepeneur for world peace in five years.

Write your skills in this circle, or on the same piece of paper you wrote your activities:

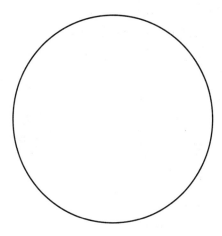

There is no wrong skill or wrong profession in the work for peace. War affects everyone in every line of work, and so peace must include everyone. P5Y is a cross-partisan, cross-religious, cross-ethnic, cross-cultural, cross-disciplinary collaboration. We need all types of peacemakers with all kinds of skills. The list would include, among numerous others:

Truck Drivers for Peace	Writers for Peace
Prisoners for Peace	Artists for Peace
Mothers for Peace	Fathers for Peace
Seamstresses for Peace	CEOs for Peace
Teachers for Peace	Dictators for Peace
Students for Peace	Children for Peace

Gangs for Peace   Jewelers for Peace
Monks for Peace   Pilots for Peace
Songwriters for Peace   Nurses for Peace
Welders for Peace   Politicians for Peace
Hairdressers for Peace   Ministers for Peace

Peace in five years also needs journalists, marketing experts, executives, managers, heads of state, skilled networkers, strategists, fund-raisers, engineers, Web programmers, and accountants. It needs people with experience in alleviating poverty, developing communication tactics, and negotiating. Jews and Arabs could take on specific projects. Doctors, therapists, judges, builders, epidemiologists, soldiers, transport specialists, infrastructure experts, diplomats . . . the movement needs people from every walk of life to set examples, help local leadership, exert pressure, help in negotiation, and direct peacekeeping missions.

SPECIAL SKILL: PROBLEM-SPOTTERS FOR PEACE

If you mostly see the problems and obstacles, then you might be a "problem-spotter peacemaker." That's great. Your efforts are needed by the rest of us to keep us focused on results and what might go wrong. Contribute by pointing out where things need to be filled out in the plan. Answer "What resource is still needed to create peace in this area?" There are many complicated reasons for conflict, so keep asking the question "What would it take to create peace in this region?" Let us know what resource, tactic, or solution is still needed.

Problem-spotters are a very valuable part of our plan. They tell us where we still need to look, what we still need to fix. We have a cynical friend who prides himself on the hopelessness of humanity. He's very logical and enjoys being right about the fate of the world. But often, the deepest cynicism and pessimism hide an extreme optimist who at some point gave up hope on something very important to them. Some trauma made them develop protective armor, and now they

Peace Action

What you can do today to further peace by 2014

Call the CEO of a local company that has taken actions to promote peace and justice in the world. Tell the CEO that you praise the company for its actions and have shared your approval with friends in order to bring the company more business. Post these "P5Y Good Guys" at www.P5Y.org.

say and find humorous evidence for "why it's not possible." We all have the potential for extreme pessimism and optimism. We need them both to help world peace happen by 2014. People with an orientation as to what can go wrong help keep us grounded and help strengthen our plan. If you are a cynic for peace, then you can identify problems and help us find the solutions. We want you on the team.

YOUR PASSION

Causing a revolution in how we choose to resolve our differences can actually be fun instead of a struggle. We assert that we are in a much better position to enjoy the revolution when we come from our strengths and passions. In this section we will look at what your deepest, most enjoyable, most passionate contribution to world peace can be. As you may already know, Amber founded a media company that produces voice-over inspirational music and music videos. She loves what she does. Why? Because it combines dancing, music, truth inquiry, and making a difference. We want our parents, siblings, friends, and everyone to similarly live from the truth of who they are and to know their awe, power, and magnificence.

Before we created P5Y, we were already asking ourselves these questions: what do we love in life more than anything else, and how can we use it to make a difference? For both of us, our passion is exploring the truth. We love seeing a person find the courage to live their truth.

You can turn your passions into contributions to P5Y. Whether you love photography, playing with your children, taking walks alone, playing an instrument, strategic planning, or watching a television show, all of these can be applied to a contribution to world peace in five years. Take a moment and brainstorm about how many ways your passion can be applied to world peace in five years.

Write your passions in this circle.

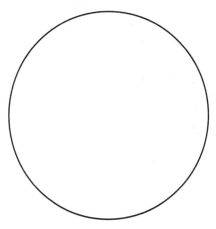

PUT IT ALL TOGETHER TO DISCOVER
YOUR GREATEST CONTRIBUTION

Now that we have examined our activities, skills, and passions, let's see how they all fit together. Look at the following diagram. Think about the activities, skills, and passions that involve you the most. Next to each circle, write down three specific items that come quickly to mind. Now, consider the lists you made and choose one item from each list that you feel would inspire you most to make a strong contribution to world peace. For example, you might choose the activity gardening, the skill organization, and the passion living in the moment. Take the three items you choose and write them down in the center of the diagram.

This is an intuitive exercise to help you better feel your inspiration, and to make it concrete. Choosing your activities, skills, and passions is an individual process. You can't get it wrong, and you can change it later if you like, so just pick what seems best to you. You may find you forgot a skill or passion, so write it in.

Go ahead now and fill in the diagram below (or do it on another piece of paper).

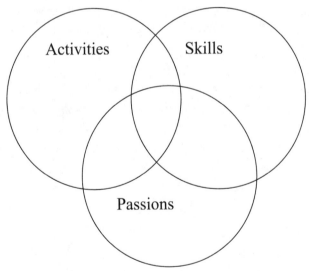

Now write a "peacemaker statement" using your center activity, skill, and passion. The form of the statement goes like this:

"I serve world peace by doing (*activity*) using my skill of (*skill*) in service to my passion for (*passion*)." Substitute your own personal activities, skills, and passions for the italics in the template. You may have to tweak your peacemaker statement to get the grammar and meaning to reflect your truth. Go ahead and write out your peacemaker statement now. Share it with your friends.

You have just identified the most powerful part of your life, the part that means the most to you and will mean the most to the cause of world peace by 2014. This is a key step in determining what kind of a peacemaker you are. One of the benefits of this exercise is that you have found the contribution you can continue to give without burning out. Because you are serving your passion, acting according to your peacemaker statement is likely to give you more energy than it consumes. It is a sustainable commitment. This might be what you have wanted to do your whole life but haven't known.

Now, let's move from the specifics of your day-to-day existence to the overall trajectory of your life.

YOUR WISH FOR ALL PEOPLE

In chapter 5 we discussed how your wish for all people connects you to your inspiration. Write it down now if you didn't do so earlier. Let's connect this to the large purpose of your life. We believe every person is born with a unique gift to offer the world. You may know what yours is, but let's take a moment to reflect. One way to consider this is to look at the following question: What would you wish for every man, woman, and child on the planet? Give yourself permission to offer anything to humanity. What is most honest and genuine? Write your wish for humanity here:

_____

_____

_____

Now look at how your life activities, skills, and passions fit inside your wish for humanity. For example, Amber's wish for all humanity is for people to live from the truth of who they are, and consciously create their lives, community, and world from that place. She believes world peace would be a result of more people living from the truth of who they are.

Examine how the activity, the skill, and the passion you selected for peace fits into your overall wish for humanity. Can you see how your wish inspires the rest of your life? Basing your activity, skill, and passion in your wish will anchor you in strength as you work for peace and in other aspects of your life's work as well.

As a final exercise in this chapter, think about yourself and your own commitments. What matters more than anything else in the world to you? It might be family or money. It might be revenge. It might be universal love or finding enlightenment or union with God or doing God's will or being happy. Sit with this question for a while. Notice what you feel in your body, and where you feel it, and what your breath does as you ask yourself this question. Allow any emotion to come through. Does your answer make you proud or ashamed or confused or certain? Acknowledge that emotion and stick with the question.

If you feel stuck, come at the question in a different way. What do your friends say you're committed to? How do you spend your time, and why do you spend it that way? What are the moments in your life when you have felt most fully aligned with your commitment? What were you doing? Take a moment to consider this.

Write what you are most committed to here, or on another piece of paper. You can start with "I am most committed to . . ."

_____

_____

_____

HOW CAN WORLD PEACE HELP FULFILL YOUR WISH FOR HUMANITY?

To contribute to every person in the world you have to have access to them. You have to be safe to touch them in some way, or communicate with them, or send them something using global transportation networks. World peace is most likely a prerequisite to fulfill your wish for humanity.

Is there room in your deepest commitment for peace in five years? Does world peace help advance what you are most committed to? For instance, if your passionate commitment is to revitalize your own neighborhood and help create a stronger sense of community, would spreading the practices of constructive conflict and mutual respect aid that goal? What would you do to make peace in five years happen, knowing that your maximum commitment is for five years? This is an ongoing question. Think about this one and keep thinking about it. Is peace possible as a part of your deepest personal commitment? Can you incorporate peace into the personal mission you're working for today?

Now you're starting to get to the core of what kind of peacemaker you are. Our artist-lawyer-entrepeneur friend's wish for all people is that they know their true essence and experience unconditional love. So whatever project or task he's doing for world peace, it's actually in service of people knowing their true essence and experiencing unconditional love. His projects, discipline, and being take on vibrant power now that he knows what he is really working for. A greater strength radiates out of him whenever he is doing what furthers his deepest wish.

CREATE YOUR MISSION AS A PEACEMAKER

So now that you know what kind of peacemaker you are, you might consider the type of peacemaking activities that most appeal to you. You can choose the activity that you acknowledged in the previous exercise, or, upon further reflection, you might choose other activities. Some activities are much better suited for a five-year commitment than others. Be open to all the possibilities and your own interior motivations.

Refer to the diagram of types of peacemakers from William Ury on page 183. Now that you have made a deeper exploration of your gifts, this diagram will have more meaning and relevance. Which area of peacemaking most appeals to you of the three major areas—prevention, resolution, or containment? What peacemaking mission would you be thrilled to accept? Write your mission here, even if it seems like the circumstances and other commitments of your life are not currently arranged to make it possible. Just let yourself imagine for now. The form of your mission statement goes like this:

"The peacemaking mission I am most thrilled to accept is in the area of (prevention, resolution, containment, other—write it out). My mission is to (put your actions here) by collaborating with (group or people) in (geographical area) for (period of time starting on a specific date). The outcome of my mission is that I (your accomplishment here)."

Here are two examples:

"The peacemaking mission I am most thrilled to accept is in the area of **prevention**. My mission is to **foster young entrepreneurs who help lift their communities out of poverty** by working with **Ashoka, a social-venture NGO,** in the **West Bank of Palestine** for **six months starting in January 2009.** The outcome of my mission is that **six entrepreneurs start sustainable businesses that give jobs to at least 24 people.**"

"The peacemaking mission I am most thrilled to accept is in the area of **peace software.** My mission is to **make peace user-friendly** by creating **Internet software that helps peacemakers connect, collaborate, and measure,** in **my home in India** for **six months starting in January 2009.** The outcome of my mission is that **one million people are using my software by June 2009.**"

Write your peacemaking mission statement here:

_____

_____

_____

PERSONALIZING YOUR PEACE PROCESS

Now that you know what kind of peacemaker you are, and you have chosen an activity, you need to finalize your own mission as a peacemaker. The best way to do this is to personalize our process action plan. This is the process:

Inspire➔ Discover➔ Commit➔ Collaborate➔ Measure➔ Communicate

How can you begin to develop your own strategic action plan? Perhaps it will be easiest to understand if we use an example. The following personal course of action is based on a composite of people we know.

1. I am *inspired* to work for world peace in five years. I am inspired to help build roads for world peace because I want peace, and I am a civil engineer.

2. I *discover* exactly how that fits into the overall effort. I go to P5Y.org and see what projects are happening.

3. I *commit* to spend three months in Kenya on leave from work building roads with the appropriate organization. I understand that I am part of a multidisciplinary team preventing civil war.

4. I *collaborate* with others using proven methods to bring peace and add my own resources to their work. I learn how to communicate and cooperate with the locals.

5. I *measure* how many roads I build and the positive effect for peace.

6. I *communicate* the results back to the person I gave my commitment to and to P5Y.org. My results are collected as part of the overall metrics for preventing civil war in Kenya.

Perhaps the most surprising element of this strategic action plan is the measurement aspect. As we discussed in the earlier chapter on measurement, the difference between P5Y and other peace campaigns is that we help you and everyone gauge effectiveness by measurement. Measurement ties inputs to outputs and gives us verifiable data to prove our progress toward peace. The measurement of your personal effort for peace is just as important as our organization-wide measurements.

There are as many different ways to measure your progress as there are activities to undertake. For example, a student for P5Y may measure how many conversations about P5Y she has each day with people. You could measure how many posters you put up, stickers you give out, or blankets you sewed, or how much time you spend giving advice in your field for a P5Y project. Part of our measurement process in creating this book was to count how many words we wrote every week. Later, we will measure our progress by other metrics such as how many P5Y-related commitments we have, or how many P5Y media videos are being watched. We will also measure how many foundations are creating initiatives for world peace by 2014.

Now it's your turn. Complete the following exercise to see what your personal action plan for peace will look like.

ARE YOU INSPIRED?

How can you personalize the P5Y strategic action plan? Take some time to complete the following exercise and discover your own path as a peacemaker.

WHAT AM I INSPIRED TO DO?

_____

I HAVE DISCOVERED HOW TO ACT ON MY INSPIRATION IN WHAT WAY?

_____

WHAT DEADLINE WILL I COMMIT TO?

_____

WITH WHOM WILL I COLLABORATE?

_____

HOW WILL I MEASURE SUCCESS?

_____

HOW WILL I COMMUNICATE MY RESULTS?

_____

WHAT MIGHT I GAIN FOR MYSELF FROM THIS PROCESS THAT I REALLY WANT?

_____

CAN I ADJUST MY PLAN TO GET MORE OF WHAT I WANT?

_____

With a strategic action plan integrated to fit your activities, skills, and passion, you are poised to begin working for peace in five years. Just like a diver poised to plunge, it is necessary that you align yourself properly to achieve the best results for your efforts.

ALIGNING YOUR LIFE WITH PEACE

Peace has to be created, in order to be maintained. It is the product of faith, strength, energy, will, sympathy, justice, imagination, and the triumph of principle. It will never be achieved by passivity and quietism.

—Dorothy Thompson

ALIGNMENT, CONGRUENCY OF ALL PARTS, is what gives you consistent power and flow within any endeavor. When your life is aligned, you experience uncommon energy in your actions. The breakdown of one part in a watch will stop the entire mechanism. In human beings we call this discomfort, pain, or extraordinary effort with disappointing results. You know what kind of peacemaker you are and where you are moved to make a commitment. Now it's time to look at how you might further align your life with the ambitious goal of peace in five years.

GIVING FROM YOUR ABUNDANCE

When you give from abundance, it feels generous and natural. Our philosophy about world peace, and all contribution, is that you can *only* give sustainably from what you have in abundance. If you feel depleted in a certain area, you're probably not going to be giving in that area. For instance, we don't have an excess of time, but we have an abundance of vision and experience, so we're writing a book. We have abundant writing capacity, inspiration, well-being, rigor, empathy, enjoyment, intuition, skill in facilitating large groups, and helping people discover their deepest contribution. Thus, we're giving from our abundance. When our health is off, or maintenance on our house or cars is required due to poor management, or our travel schedule gets crazy, then most of our attention goes to the problem. We call this arrested attention.

Often in the haste and business of life, we don't take the time to reflect on why we are doing what we're doing. We don't understand what lies behind most of our actions. Acknowledging the underlying values that drive us and bringing them to the surface actually give our lives more vibrant purpose. In our key moments of decision, the clarity of our values helps us make the choice that is truest.

In order to achieve our maximum potential as peacemakers, we must align the areas in which we have abundance with the campaign for world peace in five years. The only way we can do this is by digging deep into ourselves, examining our core values, and aligning our values with peace action.

HAVE MORE OF WHAT YOU VALUE

Knowing your values helps you get more of what you value. Instead of haphazardly enjoying or expressing what you value and feeling more or less happy about it, when you know your values, you can arrange your life to enjoy and express what you most value. Now, let's discover what you value most in life. Ask yourself, "What's most important to me in life?" Is it a person, a state of being, an experience, or an area like work, family, or play? Let yourself explore and be honest. Then ask the question again, "What's the most important thing to me in life?" Keep going. Be as specific as you can, but also true—if you most value a bubbly feeling in your chest, be true to that, but also look at what might give rise to that feeling.

Now, complete the following exercise. List what you value most, starting with the most important.

WHAT I VALUE MOST IN LIFE (PART 1)

1. _____

2. _____

3. _____

4. _____

5. _____

How do your own values find expression in your life? We can explore this through the second half of the exercise. Next to each thing you value write a description of how that value finds expression in your life. What activities, people, and structures relate to it? Write the expression for each of your five values now. For example: "Love in my life expresses itself as spending quality time with my spouse, children, and close friends."

The list Amber made looks like this:

1. Truth: Looking at what is essential here and asking "what is true?" and sorting out life from that place.

2. Connection: Which includes friends, family, community.

3. Vibrant Presence: Am I actually experiencing this moment, the people around me, beauty, this thing called "life" fully so I don't miss them?

4. Contribution: Making a difference, listening, seeing people's greatness, and working together to cause something, using the canvas of life to create it any way I want.

5. Discovery: Learning new things, stretching my mind, giving up everything I think I know already to look at life with fresh eyes.

As you compile this list of values, you will probably be surprised at what you discover. In many, our values are well aligned with our activities, but in others, the various parts of our lives do not express or represent our values.

WHAT I VALUE MOST IN LIFE (PART 2)

Describe how each of the five things you value most find expression in your life. What form do they take? What do you do to experience them?

1. _____

2. _____

3. _____

4. _____

5. _____

HONEST EVALUATION

Sometimes we would rather deal with our anxiety than have an honest look at where our life is or isn't aligned with what is true for us.

This may be a challenging process, because those areas of our life where we have not aligned with our truth are precisely the ones that are difficult for us (otherwise we would have aligned already—see how it works?). Or perhaps the ground of your truth has shifted underneath the form and structure of your life, and making changes that reflect your evolution feels daunting or impossible.

On the other side of discovering and articulating your truth is relaxed contribution. There is also a sense of relief at reducing your own suffering. Usually, however, we have to go through something that feels scary or makes things worse. Now that you have dug a little and articulated your deeper values, let's do an honest evaluation of how your life is currently reflecting those values. You don't need to perfect yourself in order to have world peace by 2014. However, when you are out of alignment with your values, it causes internal pressure, anxiety, and resentment, and it takes away from your effectiveness.

Let's examine various areas of your life to see how aligned each area is with your values. To see how well you are aligned, work through the following exercise. For each of the areas in the following table, rate how aligned the area of your life is with the values you wrote previously. Use a scale of one to ten, where ten is completely aligned. Put another number to indicate how workable this area of your life is: ten is completely workable, while one is chaotic. By "workable" we mean that it feels reasonably dealt with and is not likely to erupt into crises. After you've put a number, if it's less than seven, write any truth you haven't come to terms with in the space next to it. Pain and lack of alignment tend to come when one knows or initiates a truth that isn't acknowledged fully. For example, if someone asks you to volunteer for a bake sale and you feel anxious after making that agreement, then there's some truth about that bake sale you haven't expressed. You might need to be paid for the ingredients; you might be behind on another project you committed to and are feeling harried as a result; or you might not believe in the cause the bake sale is for. Until you know what this truth is, and come to terms with it, you're going to feel that anxiety.

We all have areas that are out of alignment. This is not a time to be hard on yourself, just honest. The human habit is to beat oneself over the head with criticism. There's nothing wrong with you. Hopefully, there's no one looking over your shoulder checking your answers. If you need more privacy, then write this exercise on a separate piece of paper and burn it afterward. The most important thing is that *you* are honest with *you*.

MY AREA OF LIFE	MY ALIGNMENT RATING	MY WORKABLE RATING	WHAT I NEED TO BE HONEST ABOUT
MY FRIENDS			
MY FAMILY LIFE			
MY INTIMATE RELATIONSHIP			
MY COMMUNITY INVOLVEMENT			
MY POLITICAL INVOLVEMENT/ OUTLOOK			
MY NATION			
MY WORLD			
MY ATTITUDES			
MY EMOTIONS			
MY ANGER AND "NEGATIVE" EMOTIONS			

MY JUDGMENTS OF OTHERS AND MYSELF			
MY BODY AND HEALTH			
MY ENVIRONMENT			
MY FREE TIME AND HOBBIES			
MY ENTERTAINMENT			
MY CAREER			
MY FINANCES			
MY SYSTEMS OF ORGANIZING MY LIFE			
MY TECHNOLOGY USE, INTERNET, PHONE, COMPUTER			
MY MEDIA: INTERNET, TV, MUSIC, LIVE EVENTS			
MY RELIGION/ SPIRITUALITY			
MY:			
MY:			
MY:			
MY:			
MY:			

Have a lot of compassion for yourself as you look over this exercise. Everyone has areas they are aligned with and not aligned with. This is not about right or wrong, good or bad. Each area that is under seven is an opportunity to discover more happiness and fulfillment in your life.

In order to align your life with your values, we recommend taking two powerful steps. First, recognize and acknowledge activities or strategies you undertake that are indicators of misalignment. Second, rely on your values to overcome traits that inhibit you from alignment.

MISALIGNMENT IS LEAVING YOU CLUES

When we suffer misalignment in various aspects of our lives, we often fall back on certain activities. These activities keep us from attempting to bring our lives more into alignment with our values. They ultimately result in pain, not only for ourselves but also for those around us.

In order to align our lives properly, we must stop indulging in these misalignment activities and instead focus all of our actions on aligning our lives with our values. There are numerous behaviors that impede our alignment. We have chosen to examine two.

WHAT ARE YOU NOT SAYING?

Anything you are not saying is taking up your attention and life. It's what gives you ulcers and heart attacks and insomnia. The benefit of speaking your truth is that all this stops immediately.

A friend of ours, call him Dean, told us the story of how he was having a secret affair for two years. During that time he went to the emergency room twice with terrible welts on his body and face, and the doctors had no idea what was causing it. Four months after his second trip to the emergency room, Dean finally told his wife about the affair. Although it was a painful time for both of them, all the welts went away. Under the burden of his secret, Dean had thought he was going to lose all of his friends if they found out. Now he has a lot to deal with in his life from the repercussions of his truth-telling, but as he told us, "For the first time in my life I feel loved—because I am not lying to anyone." Dean also said that for the first time in years he could have an honest relationship with his wife.

The benefit of his honesty is intimacy and working something out together, but the number one benefit is relief.

You might be withholding affection, your opinion, or support from someone close to you. Who are you harming by holding back? How can you work to overcome your hesitancy to provide those around you with what they need?

For example, you may be withholding love from your spouse because it feels like he or she would not receive it. You feel it would feel good to just love them without worrying about how they would receive it.

Or perhaps you are lying to your boss when you say you enjoy doing projects with a coworker. You lie because you are afraid of looking bad at work and of your coworker finding out that you don't like how you work together. There is probably a deeper truth than "I don't like my coworker" underneath your general feeling of dislike—for instance "I don't like how my coworker doesn't do work up to my standards." It would feel good to tell your boss the truth and try and communicate constructively with your coworker.

YOUR RESENTMENTS

Looking at your resentments gives you access to your underlying truth. A resentment alone is like anger with no action. It doesn't move anything forward. Clearing up a resentment is a relief and unlocks your energy where you have been stuck. Clearing up a resentment also opens up a chance to create a new form of relationship to the object or person of resentment.

Make a list of people or circumstances you have any resentment toward and why you resent them. Remember, no one ever needs to see what you have written. If it makes your writing more free, use a separate piece of paper and burn or shred it when the exercise is complete. Be honest about even your tiniest resentments. The following are some examples:

- You may resent paying taxes because you don't agree with the way the government uses your money.
- You may resent you neighbor because he has a nicer car than you do.
- You may resent your body because it doesn't look the way it did when you were younger.

Reflect for a moment on how these areas of discomfort and misalignment are affecting your life and the lives of those around you. How much do you think about it? How much energy does it take? How much money or intimacy has it cost you? What have you missed out on? Consider how you can align your life in such a way that you no longer spend time on these misalignment behaviors.

YOUR VALUES CAN OVERCOME YOUR FAULTS

Writing a list of wasteful behaviors might seem counterintuitive. Doing this is important, though, because it gives you a chance to gain strength and humor. If you know, for instance, that you hate completing projects, you can have a moment of hating to complete your project, laugh about it, and then complete it. Or, knowing your fault, you can find someone to work with who hates starting projects but loves completing them.

If you know you are impatient and don't like listening to people past the first sentence, then you can catch yourself in a moment of interruption, and remind yourself to listen. By telling people around you about your habit, and what you would like them to do when you express it, you will neutralize some of the negative effects of your bad habit. This can also help you overcome it.

Misalignment of our lives with our values not only leads us to wasteful behaviors, but it also, at times, causes conflict between our values and traits in our character. These negative habits can inhibit the alignment process. Knowing your values and your traits lets you head your bad habits off at the pass.

KNOW YOUR CHARACTER TRAITS

Take a moment to complete the following exercise. Write down a list of five traits that you have that might inhibit you from aligning your life with your values.

1. _____

2. _____

3. _____

4. _____

5. _____

Reconsider your values now as you look over your list of character traits. Choose the highest value that would inspire you to overcome actions rooted in a particular character trait. This trait that you wish to overcome may be stubborness, procrastination, impulsiveness, righteousness, laziness, or entitlement. This can be a very difficult moment, but look at the price you pay for compromising your highest values. Do you really want to keep paying it?

What follows is a composite story drawn from people we have talked to. Karen J. of Topeka, Kansas, says, "I am not at peace with my mother. I am angry because when I got married on May 28, 2000, she promised to give me money for the wedding and didn't do it. I expected her to give me at least $2,000. I am angry and disappointed. The way this affects me is that I feel distant from my mother. It gets in the way when I talk to her. It is also typical of other times my mother has hurt me by breaking promises."

Karen later chose to overcome her character trait of entitlement that her mother would pay for her wedding. She worked to grow into accepting her value of unconditional love in order to forgive her mother. It felt like a real sacrifice until she made the decision, and then she felt great relief.

Karen wrote: "The next time my mom called, I told her I had been holding the wedding thing against her for eight years. I said I was sorry and told her I loved her. My mom broke down crying and said she was sorry too. She told me how worried she was about money and how bad she felt about her broken promise. I feel closer to my mom now more than ever. I felt so light and happy when I got off the phone! I hadn't realized how important this was to me."

Karen came to terms with herself before she took action. She then talked with her mother. You do not have to take external action to obtain the rewards of alignment. The greatness barometer is whether you feel aligned inside.

Now take a look at your own life. Think of a character trait that you need to sacrifice for a higher value in order to alleviate a situation. For example, Karen would have written, "I'm choosing to sacrifice my character trait of entitlement for my higher value of unconditional love."

Notice if you feel more true to yourself. Is there any action you need to take? If yes, put the action in your calendar now or go do it now. Don't feel you have to take action immediately. The greatest reward of this exercise is acknowledging the traits that inhibit your alignment and determining the values that you must rely on to overcome those traits.

GET IN ALIGNMENT

Write your alignment statement here:

_____

_____

_____

In our own lives, some of the most excruciatingly difficult moments have been transitions to greater alignment. It shakes things up, which is not necessarily comfortable or enjoyable. However, there is a deep satisfaction in the whole process that can only be known once we have taken this courageous step. Alignment is definitely worth it.

We've tried to help you look deeply at aligning your life with your values. Aligning with your values frees up your ability to use your gifts and emotional energy more efficiently. Another way of aligning your life is by identifying your strengths. Giving from your strengths is more joyful than trying to improve your weaknesses. Tom Rath, Donald Clifton, and a team of scientists at the Gallup Organization created an online strengths assessment test at strengthsfinder.com. The latest version of the book from Gallup, *Strengths Finder 2.0*, dispels the superhero myth of being extraordinary in all ways. "You cannot be anything you want to be—but you *can* be a lot more of who you already are."[34] Instead, the authors emphasize building strengths from where you are already talented. Knowing your strengths allows you to collaborate effectively. You can work with people whose strengths complement your own.

Some people have an easier time noticing the strengths in others than in themselves. If you need to ask your friends and family what you are good at, this is not a moment to be shy. Look back at what you wrote about your skills in the previous chapter. Our wish for you is that you live in alignment with your highest values, and that you contribute from your strengths in collaboration with others to achieve a goal worthy of you.

We found out by experience that it takes time and effort to align yourself with your values. When we first started traveling together it became apparent that Nathan's brilliance could be better used in some areas more than others. Most

---

34. Tom Rath, *Strengths Finder 2.0*, (New York: Gallup Press, 2007).

obvious to Amber, based on years of friendship, was that he had tremendous skills in logical analysis, precise vocabulary, viewing situations from new angles, and communicating complex ideas to varying groups of people.

We both have a strong commitment and years of practice in what we call "truth culture," which is looking at what is true, both eternally and in the moment, and speaking honestly about it. Upon discovering and articulating a deeper purpose for our lives, we put our truth culture into practice. We had an honest conversation about his life and how aligned various aspects were with his deepest truth. This was a difficult but powerful conversation. It made his choices very obvious and practical, although not easy.

Nathan realized he could free up more of his genius by handing over more details of his life to competent support staff and various assistants. This was a tough task, because he's very talented at getting things done himself and is often faster than someone else who is asked to do it. The hardest part was implementing new structures and having tough but necessary conversations with people close to him who were affected by his prior commitments.

As a result, Nathan's eyes were opened to a whole new way of implementing his vision. Amber was deeply moved and inspired in her own life by witnessing Nathan's shift, which is a gift we unwittingly offer our loved ones when we deepen our own lives. Nathan took other steps to align his life more fully with his deepest purpose. Some of them were painful. The payoffs to aligning one's life is peace of mind, happiness, clarity—even better sleep. When you align your life you stop doing things that waste your time and you're not good at. You also stop dissipating your emotional energy on habitual complaints. Your genius is freed.

GIVE SOMETHING UP TO BE MORE EFFECTIVE

You can avoid being overwhelmed through consciously giving up something that takes your time and attention. Sometimes the key to effectiveness is not doing more, but doing less. Is there anything you think you need to stop doing that will enhance your effectiveness as a peacemaker? Perhaps you have wanted to reclaim your energy and attention from this area for some time. Again, this isn't about right and wrong. We all have areas we think we can improve on or habits that don't propel us in the direction we want to go. Examples might be watching too much TV, unproductive communication, engaging people in inflammatory political conversations, and so on. Earlier, we mentioned our crazy travel schedule, but we've given up complaining.

Instead of grumbling about not getting enough exercise and high-quality foods, we looked at where we could take an action to nurture ourselves. Sometimes you might reduce an activity to bring it into balance—for instance, you might benefit from exercise but only need to do it three times a week instead of every day.

HOW TO BE A BETTER PEACE ADVOCATE

What could you stop doing or do less often that would help you become a better advocate for peace by 2014? List three things:

_____

_____

_____

Pick one of these three things and work on eliminating it from your behavior. It will probably affect different areas of your life as well. You will have more energy to work on other areas that are important to you.

Sometimes the most important thing you can do in your life is to create space for reflection. Time alone, meditation, taking a long bath, or getting out in nature can allow you to experience spacious feelings and thoughts. Creating a breath of personal space, even from the ones we love the most, can rejuvenate and realign our lives. Time alone with no agenda except reflection or some intention of clarification allows for realizations of larger patterns that we otherwise lack the perspective to see. The creativity required for creating peace in five years may only come through spaciousness in your schedule. With clarity inside yourself, you gain energy and efficiency in your actions.

IMPLEMENTING YOUR ALIGNMENT

Now is the time to get very practical. If practicality isn't your strength, then find a friend to help you. Knowing what you know, what could you do to create an aligned lifestyle that supports your strengths? Where are you wasting your time trying to improve your weakness instead of working with your gifts? Are your life and mind aligned with this wish? Do you have a nagging feeling of having overlooked something that is important to you? Is this something you feel that you really need to communicate to people, something you need to pass on? Is this a wish you've been dying to grant but didn't know how? What would you have to do in order to grant that wish to the world? Don't worry if it seems impossible, just write it down.

GETTING ALIGNED

THE MOST USEFUL ALIGNMENT FOR ME TO MAKE IS:

_____

THE EASIEST ALIGNMENT WOULD BE:

_____

ACTIONS I COULD TAKE TO BRING THEM BOTH ABOUT:

_____

The outcome from all the work you've done in this chapter is that you have discovered what is most important to you in life, and you can now consciously create all aspects of your life from that place. We want your life to be aligned so you will find uncommon energy in all of your actions and bring that energy to world peace. We want you to discover the magic of making commitments from your truth. We want you to align your life with peace.

ALIGNING YOUR LIFE WITH PEACE

When you read the words "aligning your life with peace," what do you think of? What do you think it would look like in your life? We are not here to espouse any dogma of what alignment with peace looks like for you. Can you remember a time when you felt off, like you did something that wasn't up to your standards? Or a time that you felt good inside because you were proud of how you acted? Everyone knows deep down what alignment is. Trust yourself. How do you think you need to be to align yourself with peace? What is true for you? What is your peace code of conduct?

ALIGN YOUR LIFE WITH PEACE

WHAT DO YOU THINK ALIGNING YOUR LIFE WITH PEACE WOULD LOOK LIKE?

_____

WHAT IS YOUR PEACE CODE OF CONDUCT?

_____

Again, this is not about right and wrong; it's about coming from the place of power that emerges when we know we are personally aligned with peace. No one else can give this to us. Once we have aligned ourselves with peace we can work for peace from our strengths supported by our values. This allows us to pursue our personal action plan and fully contribute to the campaign for world peace in five years.

YOUR PERSONAL ACTION
PLAN FOR PEACE

*The gift turned inward, unable to be given, becomes a heavy burden, even
sometimes a kind of poison. It is as though the flow of life were backed up.*

—May Sarton

WHEN YOU HAVE completed this chapter, you will know what to do next in order
to give your gift, and why you are doing it. A large project like creating world
peace in five years breaks down into individual plans. By creating this plan for
yourself, you are helping to create world peace. What becomes available to you is
a clear road map to your contribution: you will know what you are contributing,
who you need to collaborate with, what resources you need, and how your contribution integrates into your overall life.

Now that you've defined what government looks like when it reflects your
values, discovered what kind of peacemaker you are, and aligned your life with
peace, what naturally comes next is wanting to create that vision. How do you
close in on that vision? What do you need to do to accomplish your final goal?
The first step is committing. Our definition of commitment is promising to take

on a project and being accountable for that project. Your commitment requires five steps:

- Identifying a commitment that is true for you
- Making a promise to someone who will hold you accountable
- Setting a deadline for accomplishment before 2014
- Measuring the result
- Reporting the result back to P5Y on or before the deadline

As we work through each of these steps, keep in mind that a commitment must remain true to your core being and be aligned with your orientation toward peace. The first step to making a commitment is to define the action that you are willing to commit to. You have identified a commitment in chapter 12 that is true for you. Look that up now.

YOUR NEXT STEP

What is a commitment that is true for you? What area of P5Y most inspires you to take part in? Is there another area you know you could make a difference? This could be volunteering for team support in a distinct conflict area, creating an art show to raise awareness of peace-safety violations, or talking to the head of your company about implementing a portion of your vision. Some examples of what people have committed so far: connecting P5Y with their company mission, creating music albums, making financial contributions, and researching effective conflict resolution systems.

Look over the peacemaker statement you developed in chapter 12. Do you believe that this action still works best for your schedule, your lifestyle, and your attention span? If not, brainstorm a list of possible actions you could take on, or use the top three you wrote in the exercise to determine what kind of peacemaker you are. Look at any groups you're involved with and see what actions you can collaborate on together. Write down three possible actions that you can commit to:

_____

_____

_____

Before moving ahead, let us take a look at what obstacles might come up that would hinder your commitment. Have you been excited about doing something in the past and then your enthusiasm dwindled? What was your "good" reason? What do you usually say to yourself or others? You forgot about it, your kids, your job, the traffic, finances, or just not interested? Sometimes they are very valid reasons, and we all have at least one that is our favorite. It is valuable to know what might come up along the way.

COMMIT, COMMIT, COMMIT

Take a moment and reflect on your favorite excuse for not doing something and write it down.

_____

_____

What will you do instead if this comes up?

_____

_____

If you are sure that you can make the commitment, and that your enthusiasm for the project will not dissipate over time, write down your chosen action.

I promise to undertake the following action for peace: _____

_____

_____

Now that you have defined your commitment, you have to validate the confirmation with another individual.

Get the Support You Need

We are all human, and we all share the same human frailties. One of the most human of our frailties is our need for support when we undertake difficult tasks.

We have already discussed the importance of peace buddies and peace circles. When it's time to take action it is even more important that we enlist the support of another individual.

Whom should you choose to be the custodian of your commitment? You could choose your peace buddy, but it might be better to choose someone else. If you rely on one individual too much, you will burn out that individual and your relationship will suffer. In choosing this individual, make sure it's someone you like and respect, and someone who will take you to task if you fall down on the job. Every week Amber has a call with the CEO of World Peace through Sports. We both make our weekly promises to each other. We say what we did and did not do, see if there is any support that would make a difference, and make commitments for the week. The call usually takes about ten to twenty minutes. We both hold each other to account, so if one of us doesn't follow through we know the other person will notice and not let it slide. Amber chose someone who would hold her to account.

Set up a regular time to discuss the progress of your action with the person you have chosen. You will probably want to meet once a month or so—not as often as with your peace buddy, but often enough for your partner to stay up-to-date on your activities.

SET A DEFINITE DEADLINE FOR COMPLETION OF YOUR ACTION

We have discovered that the best way to maintain enthusiasm for a project is to set deadlines. The most effective deadlines are those that we can clearly visualize. Reflect for a moment. Where are you going to be in 2014? How old will you be? How old will your friends and family be? What would your ideal outcome on that day look like? Close your eyes and look at what you've dedicated your life to. Your time? Your resources? Open your eyes and write down the answers to those questions.

_____

_____

Looking back from 2014, are you happy and fulfilled with how you've given of yourself? Was it life and business as usual for you or has anything special happened? Will you be able to accomplish your action for peace by 2014? If not, what part of it will you be able to accomplish?

Now that you have an idea of the action you wish to commit to and the time for its completion, it's time to start setting your milestones on paper. If you have a computer calendar system, open it up to February 14, 2014. If you have a paper system, see if you can order that far ahead. If you don't have a calendar system, get one and use regular 8½ by 11 sheets of paper for now. Let's start with the result in mind at 2014 in your calendar. Write or type, "February 14, 2014: A new era of World Peace as measured by *The Economist* magazine!"

Now take your action and work backward from 2014, being sure to focus on what you need to achieve in each period to meet your goal. In other words, if the goal of your action is to have created a micro-loan program for indigenous peoples in the Amazon basin by the fall of 2013, you would have to get financing sources in place by the spring of that same year. This is about progress, and there are building blocks to each achievement.

Depending on how much or how little time you have, you could break down your peace action into six-week to six-month subactions. How will you begin taking action? Do you need to learn something by a certain date? Meet someone in a specific area of expertise? What subactions do you need to take to accomplish your action?

The best way to organize your action is to break it down into smaller steps. For example, if you want to create "World Peace in Five Years" clothing, you will need to make a design, source your manufacturing, check trademarks, and consider the marketing possibilities. No matter what your action may be, it will require certain substeps. The best way to measure progress is by marking these substeps with measurable milestones. Make notes about your measurements and milestones. Determine as best you can what milestones you can predict and the associated dates. Then write them down, working forward from today to the date on which you anticipate completing your action.

Fill out a form for every milestone, even if you know that the dates may not exactly fit your action plan. You don't have to get it perfect. Over time, your selected action and the planned time line for implementation of that action will probably change. Life changes. Predict the future the best you can, then leave room for flexibility. Together, your action and your measurable milestones constitute an action plan. Here is a possible template to use in setting up a calendar for completion of your action.

WORLD PEACE BY 2014 ACTION PLAN

My ideal outcome on this day looks like_____

_____

_____

The name of my Peace Action Plan is _____

The action I will undertake is _____

I commit to completing this action by _____ (date)

Milestone: At February 14, 2014

The measurable results I will have created are:

1. _____

2. _____

3. _____

Milestone: At June 30, 2013

The measurable results I will have created are:

1. _____

2. _____

3. _____

Possible areas of contribution and projects_____

_____

_____

People and organizations to collaborate with_____

_____

_____

_____

You can use this template to create a full schedule of milestones for your action plan. Make entries for every three- to six-month period, depending on a reasonable schedule of accomplishments. If your action plan can be achieved before 2014, mark the time frame and set up your milestones according to your best estimates of what your progress will be. Having definite goals and measuring your progress will help you keep your commitment to your action plan and help us achieve world peace.

REPORT YOUR RESULTS AND CELEBRATE YOUR SUCCESS

When you reach a deadline in your action plan, it is vital that you report your results to the person who will hold you accountable for your actions. Accountability is about declaring a commitment you are passionate about, a standard you want to live by, to someone. When you talk to your accountability person, share what you did or did not do. Acknowledge yourself and what you've completed. If you did not complete your commitment, tell them what you noticed, learned, and what support would make a difference. This is still a success. This does not have to be a long conversation or process. Your accountability person is not your parent or therapist. During or after the conversation, write your new commitments in a place you will see them regularly. Celebrate your success.

Your commitment to world peace is not complete until you report the results of your actions to P5Y. This is a vital part of the program. If you do not report the results, others will not know what you have done and be able to build on it for world peace. First log onto www.P5Y.org and register. Then you will be able to see the specific needs for various projects that match your skills. You will be able to link up with other organizations and individuals who are working on similar projects. You can also see what other commitments people have made.

We will tabulate all of the information gathered from our peacemakers to create a monthly profile of world peace. Each individual record will be a vital part of this social action mosaic. Only with your data will we be able to measure the success or failure of P5Y. We will stand together to determine whether or not we created world peace in five years.

YOUR PERSONAL PEACE STATEMENT

You need to complete this section because it is a "cheat sheet" to capture all the value you have created for yourself so far. Keep it front and center in your life to stay oriented about what is most important to you. Filling this out and keeping it in front of you—on the bathroom mirror, as a screensaver, or taped to the dash-board of your car—to remind you will literally make you ten times more effective than if you don't do this.

Your personal peace statement is a summary of what you have created within this book so far. Fill out the following form and keep it with you to remind you of where you are and where you are going with peace.

THE TYPE OF PEACEMAKER I AM IS:

_____

MY HIGHEST OUTCOME ON FEBRUARY 14, 2014, LOOKS LIKE:

_____

MY PEACE BUDDY IS:

_____

THE ORGANIZATIONS AND GROUP PROJECTS I COLLABORATE WITH ARE:

_____

MY VISION OF GOVERNMENT AS SELF-EXPRESSION IS:

_____

I WILL ALIGN MYSELF WITH PEACE BY WORKING FROM THESE VALUES:

_____

MY MAIN OBSTACLE TO OVERCOME IS:

_____

MY ACTION PLAN FOR PEACE IS:

_____

THE PERSON TO WHOM I AM ACCOUNTABLE FOR THE ACTION PLAN IS:

_____

I REVIEW MY ACTION PLAN FOR PEACE EVERY:

_____

I TAKE CARE OF MY WELL-BEING BY:

_____

After a month of being dragged through your life, unless you have laminated your cheat sheet, it will be dirty and tattered, and it will be time for a new one. The only way to keep your commitment alive is to review the big picture regularly. We recommend at least once a month looking at the whole overview and making changes.

As you review your plan on a regular basis, make any necessary changes. You will most likely need to plan your most immediate actions more closely. This means that when you review your plan, you must specify the milestones on your calendar, plus write in any details you left hazy. World peace isn't penance. Please enjoy your life and integrate your lifestyle into your action plan.

PLAN YOUR ABUNDANT WELL-BEING

World peace is not about sacrificing your well-being; it is about increasing everybody's well-being. In following your action plan, it is important to maintain your well-being. How are you going to take care of your health during these next five years? You're going to be working hard, and if you don't take care of your body, you will get sick, and you'll be out of the game for awhile. The Internet and other media have given us the option of remaining busy and engaged at all times of the day and night. Sometimes it's difficult to unplug and let ourselves recharge, but this is vital if you're to remain physically, mentally, and spiritually healthy for the long haul. Take care of yourself. We all need you.

At a certain point over recent months of traveling we both realized that because of this enormous undertaking, we were not going to have our normal pace of life back anytime soon. Traveling has become the new normal. Life is now travel interspersed with time at home where we hang up clothes and wash dishes. For a while we fought it, saying things like, "When we get back to our normal routine . . ." and "When we finally get back home, I'm going to go to that favorite dance class . . ." Then it hit us one day: life wasn't going to go back to the way it had been. This is a good thing, but it's also jarring. Change is fundamentally unsettling, so it takes some getting used to. One of the biggest adjustments has been in taking care of our bodies and minds despite the rigors of travel.

Our work for peace has enabled us to make these adjustments much more quickly. The moment we moved from resentment to acceptance of our new way of life, we were able to look at things clearly and make choices. We saw that we did not need to eat as many big meals as we used to when we were home all the time—and with access to a gym. Just as important, we realized that we were going to spend a great deal of our time reading journals, reports, and history books, speaking to dignitaries and CEOs, and traipsing in and out of airports and taxis, with little personal time. We chose to divide duties where we could, delegate when we couldn't, and care for ourselves better on the road. It was going to become especially important for us to create space and time in our hectic lives for things that rejuvenate us.

Is there any area of your life that you've been pretending will change in order for you to take better care of your health? This could be the kids going back to school, a workload getting lighter, a new client, an old project, a better boss, another day. Well, news flash: It's probably not going to happen the way you imagine. Things are going to stay busy and crazy because that's the nature of life. Rather than fighting it, embrace it. You are a creative. Create a solution.

You are up to something that is going to affect people around you, so you'd better be accountable for how you will manage your energy and stamina. I recommend using P5Y as a motivational tool to create vitality for yourself. Write down what works for you to sustain your energy: exercise, nutrition, organic foods, lots of sleep, sports, travel, reading, you name it. Hit the Web, the library, or the natural foods store and get educated. Ask questions. Don't overextend yourself as part of your peace in five years practice and end up harming your health. If you're going to align your life and lead world peace, you're going to need vigor in your body, brain, and emotions. Your health is part of the health of this world, after all.

What will you do to keep yourself rejuvenated during your P5Y commitment? Write down ten things that regenerate you in life, then rate them from one to ten (ten being best) on how much you enjoy them and how available they are to you. For example, lighting a scented candle at home is very available, while a trip to an Asian health spa is probably something you can only do infrequently.

Rejuvenator	Enjoyment	Availability

This is your P5Y Rejuvenation Plan. Schedule at least one or two of these things a week. Your family, friends, coworkers, and peace buddy should know that you have to do at least one of them a day or else you will be fired from world peace. Actually, you'll quit.

This whole experience should be fun and energizing, not miserable. Our goal is for everyone to be transformed: you, your community, and the global civilization. But we have to work together and be responsible for replenishing our energy to make sure we have the stamina for the long term.

TAKING THE PLEDGE

Caution seldom goes far enough. It has been thought that the prudent citizen was the citizen who applied himself to solid gains, and did well for himself and for his family, and completed a lawful life without debt or crime . . . The prudence of the mere wealth and respectability of the most esteem'd life appears too faint for the eye to observe at all, when little and large alike drop quietly aside at the thought of the prudence suitable for immortality.

—Walt Whitman

THE PLEDGE IS a personal promise you make to yourself and the world to create peace by 2014. If you don't want to go through all the steps of articulating your passions and skills, figuring out your values, or aligning your life; if you want the super-efficient way through all of that, then the gesture that gets it all done in one fell swoop is to take the Pledge. This is pulling yourself through from the other side instead of pushing yourself from where you are now.

If you want to take your participation in P5Y to the next level, take the Pledge. All of what we have explored up until now about values, commitment, and measurement is very valuable, but there is a lot more available. Taking the

Pledge aligns your life with a "prudence suitable for immortality." This is like level twenty—the Ph.D. level of commitment, and also the Ph.D. level of value contribution. The difference between someone who has taken the Pledge, and someone who has not, is a matter of at least five times the contribution.

The Pledge, in itself, transforms. You are not the same person as you were before you took the Pledge. You are now firing on all cylinders. You are thinking of solutions and resources that you never thought possible. We are speaking from personal experience—the moment we took the Pledge, our lives took on a new meaning and shifted into high gear.

You are effortlessly coming up with ideas, making new connections, attracting resources, forwarding actions, collaborating, having new conversations. Your life naturally sorts itself out. You are no longer having pointless conversations, indulging habits that can hurt you, or wasting time on problems that are too small, because you are pledged to create a result that matters to you and those you love. All of your resources (once you have dealt with the ordinary prudence) are going toward that. It activates your intelligence. As our friend Raj Sundra, creator of World Peace Through Sports, said to us, "You become four times smarter when you take the Pledge."

If you are a person who would not normally be associated with world peace, or someone that the world does not yet listen to as a leader, then your taking the Pledge is ten times more powerful. Suddenly, your alert intelligence is activated toward a goal that is important to everyone on the planet.

WHAT IT MEANS TO TAKE THE PLEDGE

Up until now, you have focused on your relationship to peace as an individual. You have learned about the world's situation, the realities of war, and the possibilities for peace. You have traced the origins of P5Y and our campaign for peace, and you have studied our overall strategy for creating world peace in five years. Now the time has come to step outside of yourself and to start to consider your commitment beyond yourself. When you take the Pledge, you are making yourself *personally* accountable for peace in five years. You are acknowledging that you are dedicated to the goals of P5Y, a global movement that will incorporate millions of individuals. You are taking responsibility for all of our actions. You are taking yourself out of your own personal context and combining your spirit and your gifts with a vision that will reshape humanity.

To take the Pledge is to enter a new context for your life. It is to take personal responsibility for an area you do not have sole control over. You will become part of a global effort to create world peace. As we progress toward our goal, we will be traveling through new, unexplored political and emotional territory. We all have ideas about the way to create world peace, but none of us knows exactly how it will be done.

Thomas Edison didn't know how he was going to invent the lightbulb. Dr. Martin Luther King, Jr., did not know the final view of civil rights. Gandhi didn't know how England was going to leave India when he declared that he would lead India to independence. Badshah Khan didn't know that 100,000 Muslim Pathan tribesmen would join his nonviolent army in Afghanistan. Nelson Mandela didn't know how apartheid would end when he began his twenty-seven-year prison sentence. Sometimes all we need is to be certain of what a vision means and let the methods reveal themselves.

Taking the Pledge creates an umbrella of purpose over all of your actions. It envelops your actions in an emerging understanding and generosity that will energize your life. You will experience the raw thrill of living for something that is worthy of your attentions, toils, pressures, complaints, prayers, and celebrations. Now, you will be aware that everything you do matters to our entire planet. Your life is being lived *for* something. Whatever your concerns are, they consume your attention, energy, resources, and life. Upon taking the Pledge, your concerns must be turned toward peace.

PREPARING TO SIGN THE PLEDGE

This is an opportunity to take a risk, based on knowing your capacities and your intuitive faith. To take the Pledge is to take personal responsibility for causing world peace. This requires honest soul searching. We don't recommend this to anyone who isn't ready to make that promise. In fact, don't take the Pledge unless you know you will follow through. Only *you* know if you are ready to make that commitment. Taking the Pledge is an initiation that launches your life into a new level of being.

Before you take the Pledge, you may ask for help, collaboration, resources, ideas, or feedback from others, but once you take the Pledge, you are fully accountable. You are a resource. You are the key to creating world peace in five years.

After working through the book to this point, you may still feel that you are not ready to take the Pledge for peace. You have taken the time to discover what kind of peacemaker you are, and you understand how you wish to contribute to peace. You may have aligned yourself with peace. You realize that working for peace will tap into the fundamental energy spring of your life and allow you to participate fully in other areas of your existence. You have created an action plan and established a schedule for it. Still, you are hesitant to take the Pledge. This is understandable. Taking the Pledge is a major step in your life, the commitment to a five-year campaign that will have worldwide repercussions.

If you are unsure about your relationship to the Pledge, let's look a little closer. Are you unsure of the wording of the Pledge? The deadline? Maybe it seems too vague, big, or daunting? Maybe the Pledge feels hokey, or like you are being sold something? Your relationship to the Pledge is your own, both before and after you take it. If you take the Pledge, only you are responsible for what you do, say, or agree to in order to fulfill it.

Are you unsure of your capacity to affect world peace? Can you take action anyway, trusting the examples of the peacemakers who came before you, none of whom knew how they would succeed?

It is up to you to resolve any uncertainty or lack of clarity you may have in regard to the Pledge of world peace. No one gets the answers in advance, but as William Hutchinson Murray said, "Providence commits to great endeavors along with you."

As you consider whether or not to make this commitment, understand that there are some very good reasons *not* to take the Pledge. Do not take the Pledge

- because everyone is doing it.
- because you feel pressured by someone.
- because your favorite celebrity, political leader, or religious leader took it.
- because you want to look good.
- because it gives you permission to ignore important responsibilities (it doesn't).

If you feel pressured by any of these reasons or any reason other than your own internal certainty—your own moral compass—don't take the Pledge. The Pledge isn't something you take once and forget about. It is a continuous touch point for reflection, a constant part of your life, a tremendous responsibility to yourself and to the millions of others who will commit to creating world peace in five years.

TAKING THE PLEDGE

If you believe that you might take the Pledge, there are several things to consider. Think about what you will gain from taking the Pledge. Consider how you will feel about making a promise you do not yet know how to fulfill. How does making that kind of a promise change you? What happens when you throw your hat over the wall and declare that you will find a way? The Pledge represents a new orientation of your life until 2014, focused on your commitment to creating peace. Although the Pledge is a five-year commitment, we think it will change you for the rest of your life.

Take a moment to reflect on the Pledge itself. All we are saying is give peace a deadline. Imagine for a moment that you did take the Pledge. What is the first thing you would do? It is a wake-up call, an "oh, boy!" moment. Something will become immediately obvious as the next thing to do, that thing that will further your keeping your Pledge. Let go of your fear. Trust yourself.

If now is the time for you to take the Pledge, then write it out in your own handwriting and sign it:

_____

____ _____

By February 14, 2014, I will have created World Peace as measured by *The Economist* magazine.

_____   _____

        NAME   DATE

CONGRATULATIONS!

We recommend putting the signed Pledge in a place so that you will see it every day. We put it up as our computer screensaver. This is your vision, your statement, your Pledge. Together, all of us will create world peace by 2014.

FREQUENTLY ASKED QUESTIONS

HOW DO YOU DEFINE AND MEASURE *WORLD PEACE?*

Our working definition of *world peace* is "an end to politically organized deadly conflict." Said in another way, peace is an effective process among the family of nations to solve conflicts nonviolently and to adhere to practices of peaceful safety. Peace is constructive conflict.

HOW WILL ORGANIZATIONS THAT PROFIT FROM WAR EVER LET PEACE HAPPEN?

For us, there are no losers in world peace. It is important to include everyone in its success. This includes giving peace contracts to current weapons manufacturers and helping with education and job reallocation of that shifting industry.

Certain corporations or people may actively work against world peace. If there were not forces moving us toward war, we would not have it today. However, organizing and collaborating for peace will eventually win over these people. The practices of peace safety progressively reduce the sphere of influence of evil people to the point where they can no longer create war. Their actions to harm others then become a matter for the police.

WILL POLITICIANS WHO JUST WANT POWER EVER GIVE US PEACE?

This is a question loaded with assumptions. Politicians are individuals who want safety for themselves and their families as much as anyone. Politicians generally want to look good, stay in power, and serve their respective countries. Although there are many unfortunate exceptions to this, the practice of peace safety will include ways for easing leaders out of power that work for everyone.

WHAT IF 80 PERCENT OF CONFLICTS ARE SOLVED IN THE NEXT FIVE YEARS— IS THAT STILL FAILURE?

To us personally, yes. If in the United States slavery had ended in all but one state, would that be emancipation? Our goal is a fundamental shift and agreement in how we treat our conflicts among the family of nations. As of this writing there are seventeen politically organized deadly conflicts going on around the world. Our objective within five years is to have that number at zero and a standard process of peace-as-safety practices in place.

DON'T WE NEED TO SOLVE ALL BASIC NEEDS FIRST IN ORDER TO CREATE WORLD PEACE?

Great organizations are already working to provide the basic needs of humanity like food, shelter, healthcare, and education. Meeting basic needs is synergistic with practices of peace as safety. It will be easier to provide for these needs in a world where the family of nations has agreed to constructive conflict. As an organization we believe that we can have world peace even before basic needs are met.

DON'T PEOPLE NEED TO HAVE AN INNER SPIRITUAL TRANSFORMATION BEFORE THE WORLD CAN BE PEACEFUL?

We have had many years of millions of people working for their inner spiritual transformation. Different spiritual, consciousness, and self-development movements have been going on for decades. It is time to reap the fruits of all of this work. We do not believe that there is a further condition of spiritual transformation necessary to have world peace. What has all this transformation been for? If you look at it another way, where is the boundary between inside "peace" and outside "peace"? Can you really have peace inside knowing that the brutality of war is taking place now and the threat to you personally is increasing? In a world where the family of nations has agreed to prevent and solve conflicts through peace-as-safety practices, what would be available for your life? What could you no longer make an excuse about? Or complain about? It seems to us that the outer transformation of world peace also facilitates the transformation of inner peace. It is a lot easier to meditate or commune with the earth when you know you are not going to be raped or killed.

ISN'T WAR JUST HUMAN NATURE?

It was thought that the accepted institution of slavery was human nature. It had been going on since recorded history and was endorsed by every major religion. Yet slavery has been, if not completely eradicated, completely delegitimized. Likewise with war, education about human rights and the brutality of war has been emerging for generations: gaining momentum from the horrors of World War I that resulted in the Geneva Convention; outrage about the Holocaust that was an impetus for the United Nations Universal Declaration of Human Rights; subsequent and currently ongoing atrocities that continue to remind us of the cost of legitimate war on our planet. As humans we have differing views and will always have conflict, but the capacity to negotiate is more of an innate human trait than to kill. Some of the most optimistic people we have spoken to about creating peace in five years are survivors of war from Israel, Rwanda, Kenya, Palestine, Nigeria, and Lebanon. The same generation that endured brutal genocide in Rwanda created changes in their educational system to eliminate tribal rivalries, as well as to constitutionally guarantee women at least 30 percent of government offices. Everyday people in Lebanon who had lived through civil war spoke out to prevent it again in 2008. There is already momentum toward handling international conflicts through more efficient means than war. War is a cultural phenomenon that is politically organized violence; we can have peace in the same way, through a cultural phenomenon that is politically organized peace practices. The danger of war will always be a potential, just as we can imagine a return to institutional human sacrifice and slavery.

WHAT LEVEL ARE YOU WORKING AT—GRASSROOTS OR HEADS OF STATE?

We are working on all levels, from a committee of global leaders starting to create the Global Peace Treaty and standards of peace-as-safety practices to large networks of businesses and individuals contributing to plans within the P5Y model.

IS WORLD PEACE IN FIVE YEARS POSSIBLE?

Of course it is possible. People have been working on world peace for hundreds of years, and the current political trend is toward constructive conflict. P5Y is leveraging these serious efforts to speed up the process that is inevitably going to happen. Many other things that were once thought to be impossible have occurred in the world. If you doubt that, consider these five "impossible" changes that have occurred in the world: the fall of the Berlin Wall, the end of apartheid in South

Africa, women's rights in America, the computer revolution, and genetic engineering. Though five years may seem short, it is the culmination of hundreds of years of effort.

WHO IS GOING TO CREATE PEACE IN FIVE YEARS?

You are. We are. Every person who promises peace and takes on a peace project. The 1,000+ committed organizations, peace groups, and mediators who have already been working in this area, with added businesses and network resources. We have set up an organization to coordinate this effort, P5Y.

WHAT DOES THE ORGANIZATION P5Y ACTUALLY DO?

We provide infrastructure for the effective process of creating peace in five years: the process, the website, and coordination. We help you and millions of others answer the question: What is the most effective commitment I can make, and action I can take, to create world peace in five years? We do this with the website, this book, and media outlets. We do this by putting you in contact with other peacemakers, by using a team of experts in what is most effective, by focusing efforts, by honest communication, and by anything else we can think of.

- We accept your commitment, help hold you accountable, measure your results, and report on the aggregate of all the results.

- We provide you access to a personal practice of peace, planning materials, and a process that aligns your life with your highest values and frees your attention for the creation of world peace. We offer workshops in this process, if you have time for them within your commitments and our five-year deadline.

- We coordinate global and local action to allocate the resources that you and millions of other people provide so that our efforts succeed.

- We maintain a media and marketing presence to put our goal and deadline in the public eye of every country.

- We work behind-the-scenes with high-level government officials, diplomats, corporations, and individuals to increase our effectiveness. We work with media and ordinary citizens to educate, pressure, and change groups and government as necessary. Our goal is always to create effective collaboration for world peace by 2014.

- We identify and communicate the promise that each country holds for the world, and we help the citizens of that country deliver on their promise.

WHAT IS THE OVERALL STRATEGIC PLAN TO CREATE PEACE BY FEBRUARY 14, 2014?

The four strategic principles are: Make peace user-friendly; reposition world peace; invite and include everyone; and increase collaboration.

The six tactical modules are: a Global Peace Treaty, standards for peace safety, national plans for peace, implementation tools, grassroots action, and media services.

The procedural action plan is as follows:
Inspire➜ Discover➜ Commit➜ Collaborate➜ Measure➜ Communicate

We will inspire millions of people around the world with the message that peace in five years is possible. We will help people discover what kind of peacemaker they are and the most effective commitment to world peace they can make. We will commit ourselves to defined, measurable activities and help other individuals and other groups involved in P5Y commit themselves to and collaborate on measurable activities suitable for the kind of peacemaker they truly are. We will measure our progress toward peace, alter our activities and strategies in response to these measurements, and communicate our results to the world at large.

HOW CAN I CONTRIBUTE?

P5Y is for people contributing from their strengths aligned with their values. Look at what your life is already about and how it can be for peace in five years. Log onto www.P5Y.org to see how your skills and passions can contribute to current projects. Make a donation on P5Y.org, either to P5Y, or to an affiliated project.

I AM ALREADY INVOLVED IN WORTHY CAUSES AND/OR WORLD PEACE. DO I HAVE TO STOP SUPPORTING THEM IN ORDER TO DO P5Y?

There are no conditions of any kind attached to "doing P5Y." P5Y is about collaboration. Many causes and NGOs are already collaborating with P5Y. Where you put your efforts is entirely up to you. In order to achieve peace in five years, we need the expertise, commitment, and contributions of individuals as well as organizations. If your greater inspiration is to place the abundance of your resources in some cause other than P5Y, then go with your greatest inspiration. You may wish to turn your attention to P5Y for this period of five years, while the entire world is involved in working toward peace, then return to whatever cause most moves you, knowing you can contribute more effectively in a peaceful world. In other words, if you want world peace at all, the time is now.

IS MY CONTRIBUTION IMPORTANT?

Yes. P5Y needs all kinds of peacemakers. Acknowledgment, recognition, and appreciation are part of achieving any great goal, and certainly P5Y will recognize any contribution you make as part of the measurement on the website. But the ultimate importance of world peace in five years, and your relationship to it, rests with you as an individual.

HOW DO I GET INVOLVED?

If you are asking this question, then you are already inspired and ready for the next step in the P5Y process: discover what kind of peacemaker you are and what the most effective commitment you can make is. Our website at www.P5Y.org can guide you. There are people who have committed to accept phone calls to help you through the task; you can find their phone numbers on the website.

WHAT ABOUT ONGOING PEACE AFTER 2014?

Part of the P5Y plan is to create a Global Peace Treaty in which countries adhere to certain practices of ongoing peace safety. We assert that the process of creating peace in five years will remove the context of war as an acceptable course of action just as the legitimacy of slavery and human sacrifice has been removed. One of the core P5Y teams is looking at long-term global safety solutions.

HOW DO I TALK ABOUT PEACE?

Talk about peace from your own heart, and with specific numbers, dates, and what your accountability is. Help people who are inspired by you to continue with the process to discovery, commitment, collaboration, measurement, and communication.

HOW DO I FIND OR START A PEACE TEAM?

Reread the chapter on peace teams. Go to www.P5Y.org and click on the link to peace teams. You will find guides and a locator for peace circles that may already be in your area.

WHAT KIND OF PEACEMAKER AM I?

Reread chapter 12. The discovery phase of the process is to discover many things about peace in five years, including what kind of peacemaker you are, how your current circumstances and skills put you in a position to contribute, and what the most valuable and effective contribution is that you could make.

WHAT IS THE STATE OF PEACE AND WAR, AND WHERE DO I GO TO GET UPDATES?

There are many websites with information about the state of the world with regard to peace and many other issues. Our two favorites are www.sipri.org and www.icg.org.

WHAT IS A DHARMAMIX? WHERE CAN I GET FREE DHARMAMIX SONGS ABOUT P5Y?

Go to www.DharmaMix.com and click on the link for peace in five years. A DharmaMix is spoken words mixed over music for an inspirational and entertaining way to learn about peace in five years. Peace DharmaMixes are free; for a subscription fee you may have access to DharmaMixes in many other areas: relationships, finance, world leaders, politics, parenting, diet, and other personal and global areas of human life. DharmaMix LLC is a for-profit social venture business dedicated to peace in five years. It is owned by the authors of this book.

WHAT IS A "PEACE BUDDY"?

A "peace buddy" is a trusted friend with whom you can share and explore your deepening relationship to peace in five years.

WHAT IS "THE PLEDGE"? DO I HAVE TO TAKE IT?

The Pledge is the text of our original commitment to create peace in five years, made on February 10, 2008. We were in a strategic planning session for our transformational media company when we entered a conversation about world peace that resulted in the Pledge. The text reads: "By Feb 14th, 2014 I will have created world peace as measured by *The Economist* newspaper."
You do not have to take the Pledge. Your relationship to the Pledge is completely personal. We believe that the Pledge is a powerful tool to cement your commitment to world peace.

WHAT DO YOU MEAN BY "SELF-EXPRESSION"? AREN'T YOU ASKING ME TO DO SOMETHING FOR YOU?

What we mean by "self-expression" is that our wish for you is to discover your most aligned contribution that reflects your passions and strengths and to ally with P5Y from that place. We are asking you to do something for *you*, and for all of us on the planet, such that there are no losers. Václav Havel, the famous play-wright and founding president of the Czech Republic, describes in his book *The Power of the Powerless* (M. E. Sharpe, 1985) a politics derived from "living within truth." It is not a system of politics; it is an alignment with the truth of who you are and allowing your political expression to arise from that. This is the politics of the individual.

MY COMMUNITY HAS ALL KINDS OF PROBLEMS—SHOULDN'T I START THERE?

Your attention and passion have a natural range. Your most passionate commit-ment might be to your family, or your neighborhood, or your country, or the globe. World peace will be created through concentrated, cooperative, effec-tive, intelligent, coordinated action from inspired commitment. If you are most inspired by working within your community, find out how that work can spread to the whole globe to create benefits for all of humanity. Do what you do best for world peace.

I WANT WORLD PEACE, BUT I ALREADY FEEL OVERWHELMED WITH MY LIFE WITHOUT ADDING THE WORLD'S PROBLEMS. WHAT SHOULD I DO?

Align your life with your deepest purpose. If your life is habitually overwhelming, then you probably do not have excess resources to devote to creating peace in five years. Only make commitments that you can responsibly keep with a minimum of drama. It is best for you to put your life into order, to simplify and clarify it, so that you have room for world peace. However, there isn't a lot of time with our five-year deadline to work on your life, so if you want to contribute authentically to world peace, get your life in order now, to a point where *you* feel able to contribute.

Having said that, there is *nothing* that has to happen first in order for you to make a commitment to world peace in five years. Find your strengths, your best areas of contribution, and find a way to contribute.

DO I HAVE TO CHANGE MY WHOLE LIFE AROUND TO CREATE PEACE IN FIVE YEARS?

That depends on the commitment you make to create peace in five years. Five years in a human life is a long time, so it does not seem like a good idea to unbal-ance your life to make your peace commitment—that might be unsustainable. On the other hand, making a commitment to world peace with a deadline might be the inspiration you have been yearning for to make the bold changes in your life so that it feels *more* in balance. It's up to you.

IS P5Y IN MY INTERESTS?

Good question—what are your interests? Write out your interests and commitments and ask yourself whether they are affected by peace or war. For most humans, safety for themselves and their family is a primary concern.

DO I MAKE A DIFFERENCE AS TO WHETHER WE HAVE PEACE IN FIVE YEARS OR NOT?

We don't know if you make a difference or not. Because your commitments are measurable, you can measure the precise difference you make with your contribution.

If you make a monetary contribution, P5Y is structured so that you may make it to support someone with a specific commitment, so that your contribution then becomes tied to that person's or that organization's effectiveness in achieving their milestone. If your commitment is to make a general monetary contribution to P5Y, then the measurement of your making a difference is in whether we achieve peace in five years.

WHAT IS A "COMMITMENT" PRECISELY?

A "commitment" is a promise made to someone who will hold you accountable, with a deadline for accomplishment before 2014, and a measurable result completed when the result is reported back to P5Y on or before the deadline.

I'M A PERSON WITH SOME INFLUENCE—A MOVEMENT LEADER, CEO, POLITICIAN, AUTHOR, ACTOR, CELEBRITY, TEACHER, PHILANTHROPIST. WHAT CAN I DO THAT IS MOST EFFECTIVE AT CREATING PEACE IN FIVE YEARS?

If you are a prominent person, then your leadership is greatly needed to create world peace in five years. Please contact the P5Y office at vip@P5Y.org to arrange a phone call with the right person. We work with many prominent people, and we very much want your support. We welcome the conversation.

WHAT DO YOU MEAN BY "LEADERSHIP" AND "FOLLOWERSHIP"?

We are all leaders and followers. Be clear about what you lead—what you are accountable for is another way to put it—and what you follow. Only you can bestow your leadership and followership.

REFERENCES

Abraham Path. 2008. www.abrahampath.org.

Answers.com. 2008. Big Lie. http://www.answers.com/topic/big-lie.

Bartleby.com. 2008. *John F. Kennedy Inaugural Address, January 20, 1961.* http://www.bartleby.com/124/pres56.htm.

Bellis, M. 2008. The Inventions of Thomas Edison. http://inventors.about.com/library/inventors/bledison.htm.

Benjamin, D. 2005. *The Next Attack: The Failure of the War on Terror and a Strategy for Getting It Right.* New York: Times Books.

Blakeslee, S. 2006. *Cells That Read Minds.* New York: New York Times.

Bohm, D. 2002. *On Creativity.* New York: Routledge.

Bosmajian, H. 1984. Dehumanizing People and Euphemizing War. *The Christian Century.*

Breen, Bill, and Gary Hamel. 2007. *The Future of Management.* Boston: Harvard Business School Press.

Byron, K., and S. Mitchell. 2002. *Loving What Is.* New York: Three Rivers Press.

Carroll, B.A. 1970. War Termination and Conflict Theory: Value Premises, Theories, and Policies. *The Annals of the American Academy of Political and Social Science* 392 (1): 14–29.

Chopra, Deepak. 1994. *The Seven Spiritual Laws of Success: A Practical Guide to the Fulfillment of Your Dreams.* California: Amber-Allen Publishing.

Coles, C., and G. Kelling. 1998. *Fixing Broken Windows: Restoring Order and Reducing Crime in Our Communities.* New York: Touchstone.

Collier, Paul. 2008. *The Bottom Billion: Why the Poorest Countries Are Failing and What Can Be Done About It.* New York: Oxford University Press.

Collins, Jim. 2001. *From Good to Great: Why Some Companies Make the Leap . . . and Others Don't.* New York: HarperCollins.

Crutchfield, Leslie, and Heather McLeod Grant. 2007. *Forces for Good: The Six Practices of High-Impact Nonprofits.* San Francisco: John Wiley & Sons.

Damasio, Antonio. 2003. *Looking for Spinoza: Joy, Sorrow, and the Feeling Brain.* Orlando: Harcourt, Inc.

Deida, David. 1997. *Way of the Superior Man: A Spiritual Guide to Mastering the Challenges of Women, Work and Sexual Desire.* New Jersey: Plexus.

Dobson, James. 1970. *The New Dare to Discipline.* USA: Tyndale House.

Doidge, Norman. 2007. *The Brain That Changes Itself: Stories of Personal Triumph from the Frontiers of Brain Science.* New York: Penguin Books.

Dyer, Wayne. 1979. *Wisdom of the Ages.* USA: Vintage.

Elkington, John, Pamela Hartigan and Klaus Schwab. 2008. *The Power of Unreasonable People: How Social Entrepreneurs Create Markets That Change the World.* Boston: Harvard Business School Publishing.

Eswaran, Eknath. 1999. *The Non-Violent Soldier of Islam*. 2nd ed., California: Nilgiri Press.

Ferris, Timothy. 2007. *The Four-Hour Work Week: Escape 9-5, Live Anywhere, and Join the New Rich*. USA: Crown.

Foucault, Michel. 1970. *The Order of Things: An Archaeology of the Human Sciences*. New York: Random House.

Fradin, Dennis Brindell. 2007. *The Emancipation Proclamation*. New York: Marshall Cavendish, Inc.

Friedlander, J. Edward, J. Lee, and J.C. Merrill. 1997. *Modern Mass Media*. Boston: Allyn.

Friedman, Thomas L. 2005. *The World Is Flat: A Brief History of the 21st Century*. USA: Picador.

Fukuyama, Francis. 2004. *State-building: Governance and World Order in the 21st Century*. Ithaca, NY: Cornell University Press.

Gerzin, Mark. 2006. *Leading Through Conflict*. Boston: Harvard Business School Press.

Ghani, Ashraf, and Clare Lockhart. 2008. *Fixing Failed States: A Framework for Rebuilding a Fractured World*. New York: Oxford University Press.

Gladwell, Malcolm. 2000. *The Tipping Point: How Little Things Can Make a Big Difference*. New York: Little Brown.

Global Peace Index. 2008. http://www.visionofhumanity.org/.

Goldstone, J., and M. G. Marshall. 2007. *Global Report on Conflict, Governance, and State Fragility*. http://members.aol.com/CSPmgm/conflict.htm.

Grandin, T., and C. Johnson. 2006. *Animals in Translation: Using the Mysteries of Autism to Decode Animal Behavior*. New York: Scribner.

Grossman, Lt. Col. David. 1998. *On Killing: The Psychological Cost of Learning to Kill in War and Society*. Boston: Back Bay Books.

Harding, Douglas. 1952. *The Hierarchy of Heaven and Earth*. London: Faber & Faber.

Havel, Václav. 1985. *The Power of the Powerless: Citizens Against the State in Central-Eastern Europe*. Armonk, NY: M. E. Sharpe.

Haynes, S.R. 2007. *Noah's Curse: The Biblical Justification for Slavery*. New York: Oxford University Press.

Herman, Edward S. 1995. *Triumph of the Market*. Cambridge, MA: South End Press.

Hermelin, M. Paul. 2008. *World Wealth Report*. Paris: http://www.capgemini.com/industries/financial/solutions/wealth/hnwi-asset-allocation.

Howe, N., and W. Strauss. 1997. *The Fourth Turning*. New York: Broadway Books.

Huxley, Aldous. 1945. *The Perennial Philosophy*. New York: HarperCollins.

Hyde, Lewis. 2007. *The Gift: Creativity and the Artist in the Modern World*. 25th Anv. ed., New York: Vintage.

Iacoboni, Marco. 2008. *Mirroring People: The New Science of How We Connect with Others*. New York: Farrar, Straus and Giroux.

icasualities.org. 2008. Iraq Coalition Casualty Count. http://icasualties.org/oif/.

Katzenbach, Jon R., and Douglas K. Smith. 2003. *The Wisdom of Teams*. New York: HarperCollins.

Keesing. 2008. *Zimbabwe: Tension Over Election Results. Volume 54.* Cambridge: Keesing's World News Archive.

Killner, Pete. 2000. U.S. Academy: Military Leaders' Obligation to Justify Killing in War. Paper presented to The Joint Services Conference on Professional Ethics, Washington, D.C.

Kim, W. Chan, and Renee Mauborgne. 2005. *Blue Ocean Strategy.* Boston: Harvard Business School Press.

Landau, Elaine. 2008. The Declaration of Independence and the Constitution of the United States of America. Washington D.C.: Cato Institute.

Landmark Education. 2008. www.landmarkeducation.com.

Lewis, J. Johnson. 2008. Margaret Mead Quotes. http://womenshistory.about.com/cs/quotes/a/qu_margaretmead.htm.

LOPA Berlin. 2008. Mahatma Ghandi: 1869–1948. http://www.geocities.com/CapitolHill/Lobby/8522/gand_eng.html.

Mandela, Nelson. 1995. *Long Walk to Freedom.* New York: Little, Brown & Company.

McKenna, Jed. 2002. *Spiritual Enlightenment: The Damnedest Thing.* USA: Wisefool Press.

Melville, Herman. 1967. *Moby Dick.* New York: Bantam Books.

Mennonite Church. 1995. *Peace Evangelists Program.* http://peaceevangelists.mennonite.net/.

Merrell-Wolff, Franklin. 1983. *Philosophy of Consciousness Without an Object: Reflections on the Nature of Transcendental Consciousness.* New York: Three Rivers Press (the Crown Publishing Group).

Mokushane, T. 2003. http://www.doj.gov.za/trc/. South Africa: Truth and Reconciliation Commision official website.

ORB. 2007. Newsroom: More than 1,000,000 murdered. http://www.opinion.co.uk/Newsroom_details.aspx?NewsId=78.

Pachamama Alliance. 2008. http://www.pachamama.org/.

Pagan, Eben. *Get Altitude* DVD.

Parry, J. T. 2008. "The Shape of Modern Torture: Extraordinary Rendition and Ghost Detainees." http://mjil.law.unimelb.edu.au/issues/archive/2005(2)/11Parry.pdf.

Perkins, John. 2004. *Confessions of an Economic Hit Man.* San Francisco: Berrett-Koelher Publishers, Inc.

Pinker, Steve. 1995. *The Language Instinct: How the Mind Creates Language.* New York: HarperCollins.

Polya, Dr. Gideon. 2007. U.S.-Iraqi Holocaust and One Million Excess Deaths. http://www.countercurrents.org/iraq-polya070207.htm.

Powell, Jim. 2008. *Greatest Emancipations: How the West Abolished Slavery.* New York: Palgrave Macmillan.

Priest, D. 2005. CIA Holds Terror Suspects in Secret Prisons. Washington, D.C.: *Washington Post.*

Rehn, Elisabeth, and Ellen Johnson Sirleaf. 2003. *Women, War, Peace: The Independent Experts' Assessment on the Impact of Armed Conflict on Women and Women's Role in Peace-Building.* New York: Unifem.

Riva-Palacio, R. 2006. *Self-Censorship as a Reaction to Murders by Drug Cartels.* Massachusetts: Nieman Reports.

Robbins, Anthony. 1991. *Awaken the Giant Within.* New York: Free Press.

Rosenberg, Marshall. 2005. *Speak Peace in a World of Conflict: What You Say Next Will Change Your World.* California: Puddledancer Press.

Rwanda: Advancing Healing and Reconciliation. 2008. http://www.healreconcile-rwanda.org/.

Servilius, L. 2008. Ancient Worlds: The Roman World. http://www. ancientworlds. net/aw/Group/139585.

Singh, Lekha. 2008. *The Making of an Activist.* Altona, Canada: Free the Children.

Smith, Adam. 2007. *The Wealth of Nations.* Hampshire, England: Harriman House.

Society for Ancient Languages. 2008. Roman Oratory. http://www.uah. edu/student_life/organizations/SAL/texts/misc/romanora.html.

South Africa: Truth and Reconciliation Commission official website. 2003. http://www.doj.gov.za/trc/.

Tapscott, Don, and Anthony D. Williams. 2006. *Wikinomics.* USA: Penguin Group.

Theory.org. 2008. Media Effects UK. http://www.theory.org.uk/mediaeffects.htm.

Thurman, Robert. 2008. *Why the Dalai Lama Matters.* New York: Simon & Schuster.

Twain, Mark. "The War Prayer." http://classiclit.about.com/library/bl-etexts/mtwain/bl-mtwain-war.htm

UN Millenium Development Goals. 2007. http://www.un.org/millenniumgoals.

Ury, William. 2000. *The Third Side: Why We Fight and How We Can Stop.* New York: Viking Penguin.

Warren, Rick. 2002. *The Purpose-Driven Life: What on Earth Am I Here For?* Michigan: Zondervan.

Watts, Alan. 1966. *The Book: The Taboo Against Knowing Who You Are.* New York: Random House.

Whitman, Walt. 1959. *Leaves of Grass.* New York: Penguin.

Wilbur, Ken. 1979. *No Boundary: Eastern and Western Approaches to Personal Growth.* Boston: Shambhala Publications, Inc.

Yates, D. 2008. How to Master Fear Before It Becomes Your Master. http:// ezinearticles.com/?How-to-Master-Fear-Before-it-Becomes-Your-Master&id=1226160.

Zakaria, Fareed. 2008. *The Post-American World.* New York: W. W. Norton & Company, Inc.

ACKNOWLEDGMENTS

We would like to thank the following people, without whom this book would have been impossible: Amber's mother, Sally, her brother, Jaya, her father, Steve, for their unconditional support and encouragement. Nathan's former wife, Malak Otto, for masterfully, skillfully, and lovingly taking the lead role in caring for their four children, and his mother, Susan Gore, for her loving support. Our friends Lekha Singh, Ibrahim Alhusseini, and our entire social circle of Be Love or Bust (BLOB). We thank our social circles in New York, Boulder, Prague, Austin, Nebraska, Iowa, and Los Angeles. A special thanks to Patrick Grace and Caroline Stoessinger for their unflagging efforts at world peace and for P5Y.

We would like to thank our editors and collaborators at Greenleaf Book Group, and our editors Tim Vandehay and Ryan Smith. All of their professional and warmly offered services improved this book beyond measure.

We thank William Ury for his wisdom and encouragement, and for providing much of the material on the specific activities related to peace safety. We wish to thank Terry Kelly, CEO of W. L. Gore and Associates, for her time and contribution.

Many thanks to the many dignitaries who have helped and encouraged us: F. W. de Klerk, Václav Havel, Michel Rocard, Mike Moore, Elisabeth Rehn, Abdul-Kareem al-Eryani, Cassam Uteem, Madeleine Albright, Paul Wolfowitz, Saone Crocker, Kaspar Villiger, Sir Robin Christopher, Jean-Guillaume de Tocqueville d'Herouville, Jamil Mahuad, Garry Kasparov, Donna Hicks, Oldřich Černý, Jan Schneider, HH the Fourteenth Dalai Lama, Sadhguru Jaggi Vasudev, Petar Stoyanov, Prince Karl von Schwartzenberg, and many others.

A special thanks to our early supporters and friends Michael and Margie Loeb, Eva and Yoel Haller, Shelly and Don Rubin, Josh Mailman, Steve Killelea, Mark Gerzon, John Steiner, Paula Perlis, Tim McGovern, David Levy, and Ben Schick.

We want to thank Riaz Karmali and his associates at Sheppard Mullin for their generous pro-bono representation of P5Y.

We wish to thank our personal assistants Martha Maloney, Robin Howe, Alex Frost, and Yana Apostolopolous and everyone at DharmaMix—your support for peace in five years has been and continues to be phenomenal.

A very special thanks to Eben Pagan for his amazing friendship, outstanding brilliance, and marketing support.

We want to acknowledge every participant in the Power and Contribution gathering of 2008 who came from all over the world.

We would like to thank our teachers and influences: Gail Visentine, Brian Tracey, Tony Robbins, Maharishi Mahesh Yogi, David Deida, Landmark Education, Sofia Diaz, Marshall Rosenberg, The Integral Institute, and many, many others. We thank the great poets and philosophers that provided inspiration: Walt Whitman, Herman Melville, Henry David Thoreau, Franklin Merrell-Wolff, Spinoza, and others. We are grateful for the wisdom of the great traditions: Shankara, Gautama, Mohammed, Jesus of Nazareth, Shams of Tabriz, and all those who carry out those traditions with open hearts. We thank all of our teachers.

We wish to thank the tradition of personal development and modern spiritual thought leaders: Louise Hay, Shakti Gawain, Maryanne Williamson, Deepak Chopra, Jed McKenna, Tony Parsons, Joe, and all who are part of advancing human happiness and potential.

We wish to thank the entire conference of TED, for advancing humanity's evolution.

We send a special thanks to Nathan's children whose contributions, both directly and by their example, serve as a foundational inspiration for this book.

We would like to thank all of the people who participated in our first peace circles who offered authentic feedback, vision, and support.

If there is anyone who should be on this list whom we have left off—we love you and thank you for your dedicated support to this mission.

INDEX